THE
MAKING
OF A
MANAGER

Launch Your Management Career
on the Fast Track

Donald A. Wellman

**KOGAN
PAGE**

First published in 1993 by McGuinn & McGuire Publishing Inc, Post Office Box 20603, Bradenton, Florida 34203 USA

This edition published by Kogan Page in 1996

Kogan Page
120 Pentonville Road
London N1 9JN

British Library Cataloguing in Publication Data

A CIP record for this book is available from the British Library

ISBN 0 7494 1796 X

Printed in England by Clays Ltd, St Ives plc

CONTENTS

CONTENTS

ABOUT THIS BOOK

Industrial psychologists have said that only about three out of every one hundred people in the work force today have the attributes essential to become successful managers. In most developing countries, this would be an overstatement. The statistic is discouraging because nearly 15 to 20 percent of a work force is needed to fill roles in management. Some organizations conduct extensive searches for qualified managers. This usually is as futile as looking for a piece of meat in the soup after everyone else has already dipped from the pot. Some organizations simply fill managerial openings with favored individuals; still other organizations select those who are considered to be *born leaders*. The results are all too often disappointing, the simple truth has been overlooked: managers are made, not born.

There are dozens of top business schools that teach all there is to know about management – except how to do it. There are workers who never earned a BA or an MBA, and may never own a BMW, but, nevertheless, get thrust into management positions.

Graduate supervisors will gather their workers together and say, "You've probably heard, I'm the boss, now. So if you have any problems, bring 'em to me."

That's exactly what they do, and the boss spends more time stomping out brush fires than supervising.

A worker telephones his boss: "Hey, boss, I hate to tell you this, but the truck ran out of petrol and I don't have any money."

"Where are you? Stay there, I'm on my way," says the boss.

"What a swell boss," say the workers.

"What a swell boss," say the executives.

What someone should be asking is, "Why did the truck run out of petrol?"

Organizations do train their novice managers in policies, rules, regulations, and how to fill out forms. All too often, what is lacking are the personal systems and know-how essential to the effective, efficient reduction – and even prevention – of crisis management situations. This book fills that vacuum.

For managers at the entry level, the mid-level, and those who want to become managers, this book offers systems of personal management, as well as techniques for working successfully with and through people. This book, in part, is meant to provoke managers to help themselves learn what has to be learned, and master the skills to be mastered. The guidelines for doing these are all here.

The overall objective of this book is for line managers to work smarter instead of harder, in order to get out from between a rock and a hard place.

To know what a manager is, it is of primary importance to know what a manager does.

I
THE WORKINGS OF A MANAGER

While conducting a job interview, the general manager asked a young man, "What do you eventually want to be?"

The young man answered without hesitation. "I want to be a manager."

The general manager smiled. "And just what is manager?"

"I don't know – I just want to be one."

What Does a Manager Do?

A manager manages things, money, and people. Of the three, the management of people is the most difficult. To manage the other two – things and money – the manager must work with and through people. For this reason, the manager's job activities are, for the most part, concerned with the management of people.

All managers perform the same job activities. Rank makes no difference. The duties are the same for a high level executive as for an entry level supervisor. However, the time spent on each activity and the importance given to each will differ considerably. The following list of job activities will show how they relate to various managers.

1. Planning: Before any action is taken, a plan is made. Planning for a large production increase will take most of an executive's time. There will likely be many meetings and conferences to attend. The executive may sit at a desk for hours, thinking and doodling through myriad notes and figures.

At the same time, a shop manager may also be making plans. There will be space adjustments to be made; there will be additional employees and training schedules. Time, space, people, and production – these are the puzzle-pieces that must be fitted into the shop manager's plans. Some of the planning will take place while driving to and from work, or while taking a shower. The shop manager must, of course, get on with daily duties. This boss is not paid to sit in the office just to make great plans.

2. Analyzing: This activity is the examination and interpretation of various kinds of data. Some managers analyze a vast accumulation of records and reports that flow daily from various sections of the organization. A line supervisor may study only one daily report. One manager may spend several hours at analyzing data, while another manager may need to spend only a few moments   But in all instances, sharply focused concentration is required.

3. Reporting: Daily activities and their results must be reported. The reports are generally in writing. Oral reports are difficult to analyze and share with others, and are impossible to file. Some reports are of such a complex nature that they may take days to prepare. Simple printed forms are used for some reports. These require only that a manager fill in the blank spaces.

4. Staffing: An executive will determine the manpower needs of an organization. A personnel manager will recruit and play a major role in the hiring of qualified people to fill the job openings. A work group manager must occasionally shuffle employees around so as to better accomplish the work to be done. This, too, is staffing.

5. Training: It is unreasonable to expect employees to do their jobs well if they don't know how. Therefore, every manager throughout an organization is involved in some way with the process of training. Executives write policies and rules; other managers write methods and procedures; still other managers serve as instructors. Many managers believe that the training of employees is their most important, most challenging, and most rewarding work.

6. Direct Supervision: The results of the employees' efforts, over any recorded period of time, can be read from reports. Some managers rely on hoped for results to be favorable. All too frequently, a manager's hope turns to despair when results are reported as poor. Poor results cannot be reversed. It is too late. Good results are shaped by direct supervision, as the work progresses. A manager who supervises closely is in a position to see what is happening and to make corrections as needed.

7. Expediting: When all workers are adequately trained – when they are qualified, competent, and at their jobs – there should be no need for a manager to expedite work. Unfortunately, this is not always the case. Things do go wrong, and when they do, a manager has to make a choice: do nothing and let the work pile up, or expedite? Expediting is the giving of assistance so as to speed up a work process, or finish some task.

Expediting, by name, is generally not written as one of a manager's duties. Nevertheless, when employees are incapable of completing a job on time, a manager is expected to give assistance willingly. However, if a manager finds that expediting occurs too frequently, there may be a different and even greater problem. The problem may be in the manner by which the manager manages other activities.

8. Personal Production: Some managers think that they should not have any personal production. Some managers make this a fact – they don't do anything. The true fact is, every manager has something to do that no one else can or should do. One manager's personal production may be approving bills, signing checks, and making final decisions. Another manager may be responsible for personally taking critical measurements, making complicated repairs, or processing special accounts. Whatever it is, a manager's personal production is not to be given away to anyone else without the approval of a higher authority.

Sometimes, a manager – by choice, more than by necessity – will prefer to spend more time at one or two of the eight functions than on any of the others. One manager may enjoy analyzing data and making plans, when the job actually calls for spending most of the time at training and supervision. Another manager may prefer to be out in the shop tinkering with the machinery, when what really needs to be done back in the office is writing a month-end report.

Managers must avoid the costly mistake of letting personal likes and dislikes influence the time to be spent on any of these eight managerial activities. A manager must understand the priorities of the job's various areas of responsibility and direct all work actions accordingly.

Who Is a Leader?

An effective manager is a leader. The definition of a leader is easy to remember: A leader is one who has followers.

Leading is not simply giving orders. Giving orders is much like shoving. That's not leading. And employees don't like to be shoved. A manager who leads has little need to give orders – to push employees. Employees will follow because of what a manager is, rather than who he is. There are three ways for a person to become a leader: through knowledge, through charisma, and through delegated authority.

Knowledge: In an office, shop, or out in the field, wherever people work, workers frequently will go to a particular employee with a question about their work or about the organization. It is interesting to note that workers do not always go to their manager first. The workers quite naturally feel more comfortable with a fellow employee. They know that they will not be embarrassed or criticized. This one employee, as all the workers know, has considerable knowledge of the organization and of all the work that is done by the group. And this employee is always available. The person with knowledge is often looked to as a leader.

Charisma: At a party that seems dull and lifeless, a person enters the room. Through this person's presence, the party suddenly comes alive. Everyone begins to talk, laugh, and have a good time. The new-comer doesn't say anything about taking charge of the party. It just happens. Without plan or purpose, this person becomes a leader. Such a person is said to have *charisma*. Charisma is a natural ability of a person which allows him to gain a following of a large number of people.

Delegated Authority: A person can become a leader through delegation. A person receives the duties, responsibilities, and rank of a leader from a source of authority. To an appointed leader, the authority must also hand over some power. Employees will generally follow a person who has power, if for no other reason than fear. But a leader with only power, without knowledge or charisma, is likely to fail.

Although there will be individual differences in managers, effective leaders will have a blend of all three qualities.

As a manager, look in the mirror once in a while and ask, "Mirror, mirror on the wall, who is one of the greatest managers of all?" The mirror should answer, "If you manage, if you lead, then you are truly one of the greatest."

*Without obstacles
there would be no opportunities.*

2

HOW TO EXPLODE YOUR PERSONAL OBSTACLES

Are obstacles keeping you from getting ahead in the world? Do you feel that all those people you read about – the ones who have attained success after overcoming impressive obstacles – are super stars? Or that, perhaps, they are the ones who get all the lucky breaks?

The truth is, the people who have evolved from have-nots to over-comers to achievers are people who simply have learned to overcome personal obstacles. They are people quite like you: talented, normally intelligent, wanting something, but otherwise, nothing special. They have had no special breaks that couldn't be called logical consequences. These winners did have something, however, that made those logical conse-quences happen. They had a method for exploding the obstacles which stood in the way of their goals: a Go-For-It Bomb.

The outstanding benefit of the Go-For-It Bomb is that it doesn't destroy lives, it improves them. There are big Go-For-It Bombs and little Go-For-It Bombs, for long-range or short-range goals. And anybody can make one.

Here's How to Make a Go-For-It Bomb

The Casing

The Go-For-It Bomb begins with a hard casing. Within the casing shell are your goals, ambitions, needs, dreams, wants, and desires. Each *bomb-maker* should describe these, specifically, in writing. The casing can do nothing by itself. It can only sit there on a table, on a shelf, or in your mind – quite worthless.

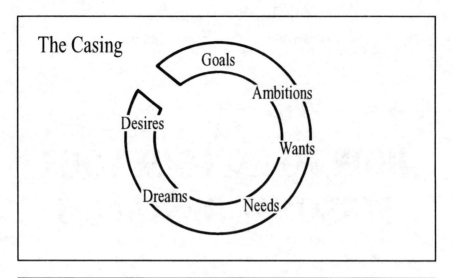

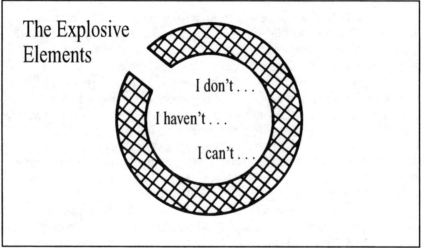

The Explosive Elements

Your obstacles – the reasons and excuses that stand in the way of your wants – must be exploded. Here are a few of the more frequently heard obstacles that others might have put in your mind:

"You don't have the patience."

"You don't have enough education."

"You don't talk well enough. You don't write well, either."

"You gotta have a lot of money."

"You don't have enough experience."

"Who will give you a chance?"

"You can't do it at your age."
"Your sex is against you."
"You're just a minority to them."
"What about your physical handicap?"
"But you don't know the right people."
"You just don't have the right attitude."

As a bomb-maker, you must list your own personal obstacles. Then pack them into the bomb.

The Go-For-It Bomb thrives on obstacles. This bomb considers all obstacles to be fuel for its ultimate explosion. When the obstacles are exploded, the casing will burst, and your goals, dreams, and ambitions will be released to fly into reality.

For the moment, the explosive elements – the obstacles – remain unthreatened. They won't go off without your help.

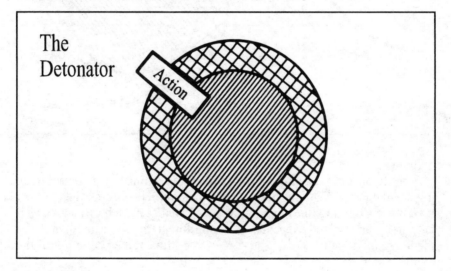

The Detonator

The Go-For-It Bomb needs a *detonator* – a small device that goes off and causes a larger explosion within the casing. In the bomb, the detonator is made of *action*. This is where the explosion begins. Amazingly, when you take action – do something – all the seemingly insurmountable obstacles begin to vaporize. You are propelled toward your goal.

An action is a step taken toward a goal. A person's first action may be to read a book that will expand knowledge, to enroll in a school for a course that will be of value, to learn the mechanics and operation of an unfamiliar piece of equipment, or to cultivate a friendship. You must take some action toward your goal you wish to accomplish, whether you are ready or not.

Make a written, detailed list of all the actions you can take now, today, this week, this month.

Unfortunately, a detonator will not act on its own. Actions, too often, are put off until tomorrow . . . or the next day . . . or the next week. And so, the bomb, even with a detonator, cannot explode.

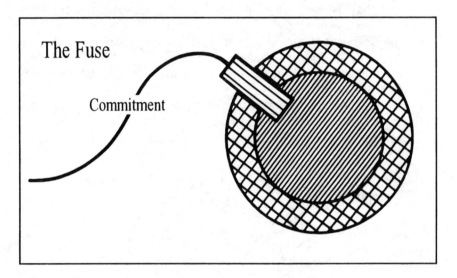

The Fuse

Commitment

The Fuse

A detonator must have a *fuse* – something to transmit a current or an impact of energy. Without a fuse – no explosion. The fuse for the Go-For-It Bomb is a burning line of commitment. The fuse must burn as long as it takes for your goal to be reached. A commitment, then, is a bomb maker's pledge or promise to take action – and to continue taking action until the bomb explodes.

Some people, unfortunately, have had long histories of broken promises and forgotten commitments. What happened? Why did the fuse go out before their actions were completed? The answer is that somehow, their ignition systems failed. In many instances, people have simply failed to light the fuse in the first place.

The Igniter

Your fuse must be ignited. It must be set off with a spark, a flame, or something hot. The Go-For-It Bomb's igniter is called emotion. The bomb makers who have exploded their bombs have learned from experience that it is essential to keep the ignition hot, the emotion high. The ignition must be continually applied to the fuse; the emotion must continually fuel the commitment.

Emotion is any strong feeling – joy, sorrow, faith, fear, love, hate. Each successful bomb maker will be motivated by a personal, main emotion – perhaps some secondary emotions, too.

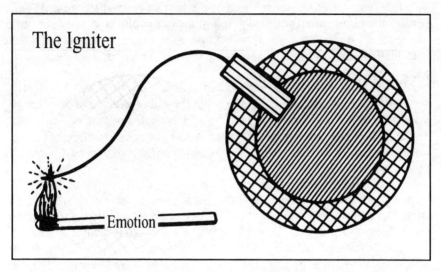

A successful business executive kept a picture on his desk of a small, unpainted, dilapidated farm house situated on a few acres of barren land. At the bottom of the picture was a tiny piece of paper with a single typed word, "Move!"

When visitors asked about the picture, the executive would explain, "That farm is where I was born and raised. The poor, hard soil could barely yield enough crops for our family to survive. I swore that someday I would be in a position where no one in my family, nor any person employed by me, would ever live like that. How I hated that place!"

Think of the emotions that influence you – emotions that you can use to fire your personal commitment. Write them down, then choose the one emotion that will influence you the most.

Keep Your Emotional Spark Alive

One way to strengthen your primary emotion is to get close to the work you want to do. Meet with the people who do that work. In many instances, they will give you sound advice, valuable information, and perhaps even assistance of some sort. If you want to be transferred to more administrative responsibilities, talk with key people in administration. If you want to be a leader among the technical people, seek them out. Make friends. Read. Look interested, act interested, and people will take you to be interested. And they will help you to keep your flame of ambition burning.

There is one final piece of advice. Other than the people with whom you live, and the carefully selected few who can really help you, do not speak of your dreams, ambitions, and goals to anyone else, whether they are relatives or friends. Speak to no one who does not understand your true feelings and the intensity of your desire. There are two reasons to support this advise.

First, friends and relatives may mean well, but they will frequently see only the dark side. With all sincerity, they may attempt to discourage your actions with the very obstacles you have already stuffed into your bomb. They may encourage you to abandon your cherished dream – for your own good – for a more easily attainable goal, a goal they believe to be more "sensible."

Second, the mind plays tricks. When you tell people of the great things you expect to accomplish, the mind derives some sort of satisfaction. Once the news is spilled, the mind doesn't seem to find the goal quite so important anymore. A kept secret, on the other hand, is like an explosion waiting to happen. The emotion wants to get out. If you don't talk about your goal, the emotion must find another way to escape. Let the impatient emotion express itself in action. Whether you dare to dream, and even more important, dare to act, take comfort in this thought: You may not climb as high as you had wished, but, when you are there, you will find yourself higher up the mountain of success than you have ever been before.

*For those who are prepared, getting ahead
comes in unexpected ways, at unexpected times.*

3
UP THE CAREER LADDER

For employees who are trying to get both feet on that first rung of the management career ladder, and for the present ladder climbers who are seeking to go higher, some thought should be given to the career ladders that are leaning up against various organizational towers.

Where Your Opportunities Are

Most organizations prefer to promote from within – to select managers from their own pools of employees. There are good reasons for this policy: more is known about the present employees; an experienced employee will have knowledge and understanding of the organization, its policies, and its people; and morale is improved when workers know that there are opportunities for advancement.

Some organizations carry their management search to the outside. These organizations generally are looking for special skills and talents that cannot be found locally. A few organizations believe that continually promoting from within breeds a sameness – the same ways of doing things, the same plodding pace, the same stale thoughts. An organization may want new ideas, new skills, new energies, and new blood.

Family-owned organizations may select only relatives or close family friends for important positions. One reason for this is family loyalty. Also, family structured organizations may believe, whether right or wrong, that relatives and trusted friends will be' more honest, dedicated, dependable, and that they will take the interests of the organization to heart. For the ambitious promotion seeker, there may be few advantages for remaining with a family controlled organization for very long.

In some geographical areas, there may be no need to make a choice between working for a large organization or for a small one. There may be no large organizations. Nevertheless, some considerations of the two should be of interest.

There are advantages to working for a large organization. Wages are generally better than those offered in small organizations. There are more avenues for advancement. Large organizations are more likely to have modern equipment, advanced methods of operation, and structured training programmes.

On the other hand, ambitious employees may feel that large organizations might regard them as statistics rather than as individuals. There may be a fear that they will become overly specialized and locked into specific jobs. They may become discouraged by the number of other ambitious employees standing ahead of them. In a large, complex organization, promotion seekers may be at a loss to know which doors will lead to where they want to go. None of these expressed disadvantages are as serious as they might seem. Most progressive organizations will seek, encourage, and assist the ambitious employees who have the potential for management advancement.

There are also advantages to working for a small organization. Employees are close to the people at the top. A small organization is more like a close knit family. Workers and managers generally know one another on a first name basis. Everybody is friendlier and better informed – for everyone knows what is going on at all times. It may by easier in a small organization for employees to learn a variety of job skills in different operations. Ambitious promotion seekers may encounter little competition; often there is none. A newly appointed manager becomes a *big frog in a small pond*.

Remember, however, that should a supervisor or manager of a small organization move to a large one, the *big frog* is likely to be regarded as only a *tadpole in a big pond*. It is unlikely that the previous manager of a small automotive repair shop, for instance, will be qualified to manage a large organizations's shop for heavy duty equipment repair.

A thorough understanding of the various organizations that are available to you as sources of opportunities is essential to your career planning. Before approaching any organization, it is advisable to learn as much as you can of its structure, policies, rules, key people, the employees, their internal politics, methods of operation, and stability. The more you know about an organization, the better prepared you will be when you open its doors.

How Will an Organization Measure You?

Within an organization, the responsibility of selecting a manager may fall on the shoulders of one person, or it may be shared by two or more. In some organizations, an applicant for management will appear before a group of interviewers. A candidate may be called back for additional interviews. Later, these people will meet to make their final selection.

Whatever the methods of recruiting, interviewing, and selecting, you should know what an organization looks for in a manager. Give some thought and attention to the measurements that may be discussed when you are being considered for hire or for promotion.

Age: Regardless of the legal view forbidding discrimination, the organization may have age boundaries and even private attitudes regarding age.

Health: Specifically, are there any limiting health problems?

Family Situation: Is there any situation at home that might affect your performance?

Personal Character: Have you ever been known to lie, cheat, or steal?

Personal Projection: Are you clean, neatly dressed; do you move briskly, sit up straight, look the interviewer in the eye, listen attentively, speak clearly and decisively?

Internal Motivation: Do you have the willingness to take difficult assignments? Do you have confidence in your abilities? Are you a self starter; do you jump into your work without being told to do so? Do you finish what you start?

Knowledge: What are your levels of formal and informal education? What is your know-how of the work you are seeking?

Experience: How long have you worked at your trade or profession? What have you learned from your experience?

Intelligence: What is your quickness and ability to learn, your ability to reason and to cope with circumstances?

Behavior: The interviewer will be looking ahead at your predictable behavior: how you might respond, comply, act, conduct yourself in various situations.

Values: What is it that you really want in life – money, power, security, social involvement?

Technical Skills: What are your skills? Just how good are you? How much additional training will you need?

Hobbies And Outside Activities: Are any of these of value to the organization?

Problem Solving Ability: How much of this ability is required by the job? What problem solving experience have you had? Will you be part of the solution or part of the problem?

Attention To Details: Are you accurate? Will you check the accuracy of others? Might you catch mistakes before the organization catches them for you?

Sense Of Urgency: Do you understand the organization's sense of urgency? Can you match it?

Qualities Of Leadership: What indications are there that you can lead people?

Ability To Express Yourself: Can you write a business letter, or a report? Can you speak well before a group?

Ability To Get Along With People: As a managers, how well will you get along with employees, other managers, executives, and the public?

Personal Contacts: Who do you know? Are they inside or outside the organization? Are they of any importance to the organization?

Other Possible Considerations: Proficiency in a specific second language may be a requirement. Your willingness and availability to travel extensively may be an important factor. Professional licenses may be required. You might have to accept flexible hours and certain manners of compensation that are not certain at all.

If the job opportunity exits where you are now employed, the interviewer will likely gather much information about you from your personnel records – your original application, the training record, performance evaluations, incident reports, any record of previous jobs held within the organization, and the duties performed.

You can bet that the person or persons making the selection will dig deeply into your past.

What You Have, Use; What You Don't Have, Get!

Now that you know of the factors that are most likely to be examined by a selection person or committee, you can begin your preparations to be considered in the most favorable light.

1. Learn everything you can about the job. When a job vacancy is posted or advertised, the job description is generally shown in its entirety. If the advertisement appears sketchy, visit the personnel office and ask for the job description. If none is available, ask questions. Try to talk with someone who has intimate knowledge of that job. Perhaps you can talk with the manager who is in charge of the job or an employee who knows the job well. Take notes so you can review the information later when you are alone.

Job Descriptions are nearly always written in a standard format, with only slight modifications.

First, there is the job title. The title should describe the nature of the job accurately. The title *Office Manager*, for example, implies that the job requires a person who is proficient in office procedures and the use of office equipment.

Next, a full paragraph should explain the duties and responsibilities of the job.

Following, a paragraph should outline the minimum requirements – education, work experience, certification, or whatever else is essential – for the job.

The final paragraph should the compensation package – the pay range and benefits. In a job opening advertisement, there will be a statement as to how, where, and when an application is to be submitted.

2. Practice writing a resumé. A resumé, or curriculum vitae (CV), is not difficult to construct. You'll find books on this subject at the public library and in book stores. You should be able to tell your story, in outline form, in one or two pages. The following should serve as an outline.

YOUR FULL NAME

Present Address:

Telephone Number:

Professional or Work Experience: (This is the heart of your resumé. The period of time employed at a particular position; the job title; name of the organization; description of your duties and responsibilities. Stress what you accomplished. Expand and stress those experiences that relate to the job you seek.)

Licenses and Certifications: (If any.)

Education: (Highest level of schooling attained; years completed and/or diplomas and degrees earned. It might be a positive contribution to describe any courses of study, workshops, or seminars that pertain to the job you seek.)

Additional Activities and Interests: (State the outside organizations you have belonged to, positions you have held, activities you have been engaged in.)

Personal Data: (Optional. You may wish to describe yourself as to age, height, weight, health, etc.)

Military: (Some organizations give veterans preference.)

Other: (You may wish to add something, such as your extensive travels, or anything else you feel might be a contribution.)

References: Available upon request.

Your Signature:

A resumé is your story, your personal history. Express it in the strongest terms. Do not apologize for any of the information you present. Do not say such things as, "I did that sort of work for only a few months." Or, "I was not very good at that subject in school." Leave it to the interviewer to determine the importance and value of your information.

3. Examine your personal strengths and limitations with a critical eye. Your intelligence is inherited, there is nothing you can do about it. But you can improve your knowledge. You cannot make yourself older, but you can become a more mature person. You cannot become younger, but you can keep yourself in good physical condition and remain mentally active. Most health problems can be cured, others can be compensated for. New values can be formed, attitudes can be changed. Skills can be practiced – so can most everything else on the list.

4. Develop and expand your personal contacts. Do not depress yourself with the expression, "It is not what you know, but who you know." It is not a matter of one over the other. You need both. You need to know what, and you need to know who. The action you must take is obvious. Get to know someone – someone who is in a position to advance your career. Since you don't always know who this person might be, project the person you want to be at all times. Begin with experienced co-workers and your immediate supervisor. Ask questions about work related things – procedures, systems, controls, equipment. Ask to be shown how to perform some task, or how to improve a skill. Let people know that you want to learn new things and gain new experiences. When there is a work overload and your own work is light, volunteer to help out. You will be surprised at how most managers and skilled workers enjoy explaining their duties and responsibilities, how much they enjoy teaching someone to master a skill, and how greatly they appreciate knowing of people they can depend on.

Your objective is to cultivate influential people. But don't become labeled as a *teacher's pet*, or worse. Be sure you are good at your own job. When you have your own work to do, get it done without fanfare and without drawing attention to it. Let the results speak for themselves. Don't cause waves. Don't wave flags. Be tactful, be patient, and be yourself.

5. Get the experience you need. Understand that gaining experience is by continually acquiring both knowledge and skill. Years spent on a job without improvement is not experience, but merely longevity.

6. Take your share of the risks. Don't be afraid to gamble on yourself. Some employees are unwilling to gamble on a chance for success. They are unwilling to pay the price of preparing themselves before an opportunity arises. They may say, "Give me a job in management, teach me what to do, pay me well, and I'll be a great manager." When these employees are passed over, their words are heard: "No one will give me a chance." No organization would.

It is not uncommon for ambitious employees to invest their own time and efforts in preparing for promotions and then seeking opportunities to prove themselves.

Plans, preparations, self improvements – these are some of the things you must do. And when you do these, there is no guarantee that you will advance. Should you be passed by on the first try, take another chance at the next opportunity. For each person, the circumstances of employment will vary. Circumstances that may stand in the way of your goal are to be acknowledged, but not bowed down to. An inspired, creative, ambitious employee will push through adverse circumstances, or will go around them. Preparations and self improvements are never made in vain. A person becomes better for them. And there will always be an organization, somewhere, that is looking for a better person.

Plug into Success through Networking

Networking, as a concept, is simple. You meet people, you share information, and you help yourself advance in your career.

But, in practice, networking can be difficult.

– Networking, done well, can be extremely time consuming.

– For some people, meeting and mingling with others is awkward and stressful.

– Networking is more than just seeking out people who can do something for you; networking is also seeking out people for whom you can do something. It's a two way street.

So why would a person want to spend time and emotional energy in networking? Think about it for a moment.

– Outside sales people learn and earn through systems of networking.

– Recruiters have *pick of the crop* applicants for their respective organizations through networking.

– Secretaries, supervisors, managers, executives, and small business owners all share information pertinent to their respective fields of interest, and thereby broaden their personal knowledge base through various webs of networks.

– Expanding and developing personal contacts within one's place of employment leads to career advancement.

– Helping a person get a *leg up* in life is personally satisfying. And what goes around, comes around.

– For those who have had the financial rug pulled out from under them, job hunting becomes a smoother road for individuals who have developed a vast resource of concerned people. 85% of all jobs are found through networking.

When should a person begin networking?

Ideally, somewhere between primary school and the end of university. During those years, you met, you shared, you learned, you traded support . . . but you probably didn't keep track of your classmates. Have you ever wondered about some of the kids you knew in school? How richer your life would be today if you had maintained contact. The same can be said of those you met in the armed forces, or at previous jobs, or in previous neighborhoods. Contacts, yes, but contacts lost.

If you haven't already developed a system for the preservation of contacts – some, just plain good friends; some, influential – it's not too late to begin.

– Buy a large address book. Write in everyone you now know – names, addresses, phone numbers – and what they do for a living, or other areas of expertise.

– While networking, continue to add to your book those with whom you feel it advisable to maintain contact.

– Include the names of people not yet on top, but seemingly destined to get there on the fast track. When you learn of an acquaintance's promotion or receipt of some honor, send a congratulatory note.

– Should the news be of a personal tragedy, let that person know you are there to help.

– During the December holidays, personalize your cards with handwritten messages. Perhaps you have noted birth dates and wedding anniversaries in your book. All the more excuses to stay in touch.

Where does a person go to network?

Begin networking with family and friends. These people may be of no help at the moment, but they do have your interests at heart. And should a family member be in need of information or assistance, your involvement will tighten the family ties.

If you now have a job, networking with co-workers, supervisors, even top executives, will serve to increase your knowledge, improve your skills, demonstrate your expertise, spread the word of your ambitions, and also provide the opportunity for you to leave indelible footprints.

Should your job be eliminated through cut-backs, your highlighted in-house reputation will certainly earn favorable support in forms of leads to other companies still seeking people of your caliber, letters of recommendation, personal phone calls, or other means of leverage.

Membership in civic, professional, and other organizations also offers fertile fields for networking. These are organizations and associations where the members have similar interests, do similar work, and understand the needs, wants, and workings of one another's profession or trade.

Civic organizations give you the opportunity to learn management by heading committees and serving the community.

Professional organizations let members know what is going on within the profession – such as opportunities – and provide current information on technological advancements. Should you be promoted to a new or somewhat unfamiliar position, you will do well to seek the counsel of a welll experienced person, in a similar role, who will gladly replace that flush of success feeling with sobering, practical advice and know-how.

One membership may not be sufficient for your present career needs. For example, if you are in the service business – say landscaping, commercial laundry, pest control, home repair and remodeling – you might find it advantageous to have lunch with people representing estate agents, hospitals, home builders and others. Not only are there businesses and professional associations that appeal to a wide variety of individual interests, there are memberships that address political, social, environmental, and other interests, as well.

Subscriptions to trade magazines might also be considered a door to networking. Certainly a trade journal does disseminate current information of the trade, industry, or profession. Generally, in the classified section of the magazine, advertisements of opportunities are featured.

"But I don't have the time . . . and I don't like to meet and mingle."

Welcome to the club. Most ambitious people frequently feel they don't have time for all the social and commercial demands. But most will make time to expand and exploit their network resources, and to advise and help others. Others might join organizations and never go to meetings, but they do get a lot of mail concerning what is going on.

Don't beat your breasts with remorse if you haven't the time to become totally involved in networking. Simply be aware that you continually need to become more visible so as to receive information and support, and to be available to do likewise for others. The priorities will take care of themselves on a need-to-do basis.

As for not liking to meet and mingle, simply keep in mind the following:

1. Do it. Each morning when you get up, brush your teeth, comb your hair, smile at yourself in the mirror and say aloud, "Look out world, here I come!"

2. Do believe that successful networking is continually pulling assorted threads. With luck, at the end of the thread there may be a string to pull. At the end of the string, a rope. At the end of the rope, a precious bit of information, or perhaps a better job offer. The message here is to treat every piece of information with respect, and follow it through to the end, even if the information is of little interest to you at the moment. Nothing will turn off a source of information more than not showing gratitude through interest and action. After you have followed through on pertinent information, report back to the provider and share your experience.

3. Do keep the faith. While your efforts may sometimes seem futile, networking can't hurt you.

4. Do nurture your self-esteem. Don't be intimidated by powerful figures at professional, public, and social gatherings. If you have recently lost your job, in what was thought to be your chosen, permanent career field, it can rightly be considered a traumatic experience. But reject all thoughts of personal failure. Look at the big picture, the competition, the economy, changes in technology. Affirm that you are a more experienced and qualified person, now, than when you began your employment. Approach these impressive, influential people to tell of your availability.

5. Do recognize that while you are networking, you'll undoubtedly have good days and bad days. If you wake up some morning not feeling

good about yourself, don't go out to make contacts. Your momentary lack of self worth will show. Believe it. Find a nice quiet spot of nature. Relax. Think of all the fine things you have done, your achievements in school, on the job, in the community, and within your family.

6. Do understand that, when networking in job searching situations, it is natural for people to ask what you do, and even what you want to be. A focused answer is fine. "I am a fire fighter, and I want to be a fire chief." If the inquirer just says, "Oh," and drops the subject, you won't know whether or not that person had another line of interest in mind. It would be better to reply with broad brush strokes, reminding your contact of your field of training and experience – sales, administration, mechanics, construction, education, medical, or whatever. Then add that you would like to stay in that particular line of work, or that you would like to try something else. You might also ask the person, "Do you have anything in mind?" Or say, "I'm open to suggestions."

7. Do believe that door to door networking can be an effective means of penetrating an organization and building your image. Job seekers and sales people do it all the time. But know the organizations you are calling on.

Before starting out for a day of cold calling, check yourself out. Are you well dressed and well groomed? Can you field such questions as "What can you do for us?" Or, "Why do you want to work for this organization?"

Do you have several, eye-catching resumés or proposals? Job seekers generally head directly for the office of Human Resources. There, a personnel clerk will likely say, "We're not hiring, today," or, "Please fill out this application." If the company is hiring, expect to find a crowded waiting room.

For the daring, there is another approach toward an opportunity to promote yourself or a cause. This is the approach fund raisers, many sales people, and some job seekers take. Get through the door to the head of the organization. If you make it that far, the top executive will likely be impressed by your approach. People in command generally admire people who can cut through the fat and get results. When an executive finds a person worth having on the team, the people in personnel will certainly be motivated to find a slot in the organization.

Getting to the head of an organization takes some doing. Don't go in as a job seeker. Think of yourself as a salesperson with an exclusive service to sell.

The first hurdle may be a receptionist. Don't ask to see the head of the organization. Ask to see the head person's secretary. Ask the receptionist for the secretary's name, also the chief executive's name, if you don't already have it.

The secretary will ask if you have an appointment and the nature of your business. Explain that you are contacting several organizations in town, and if the head person – by name and title – cannot see you now, you would like to make an appointment. As for the nature of your business, you have an exclusive service that you think her boss will like to consider. No guarantees on this approach, but what do you have to lose?

8. Do depart with style. When you have had an opportunity to talk with the head of an organization or the executive secretary, but they have nothing at the moment to offer you, thank the person for the time allowed, shake hands, and say something like, "Oh, by the way, can you suggest anyone whom I might see?" It's also a good idea to write short notes of appreciation to those with whom you have had an interview. Again, this includes secretaries.

9. Do go to all the private and public gatherings you can get invited to. Most of time, you'll see more strangers there than people you know. That's good. The people you know already know of your status. The people you want to meet are the strangers. Chances are, those strangers are standing around in small groups, chatting. They know each other. It would be tacky to just invade their circle. Be patient. There will come a time when you'll be one-on-one. It might be in the restroom, at the refreshment table, outdoors during a break – it'll happen. The meeting usually begins with "Hi," followed by small talk about the gathering. It may sound forward, but someone has to ask, "So, what do you do?" Now the two of you are on your way to becoming acquainted. But don't hang on to this new acquaintance throughout the day or evening. Ten minutes should be sufficient. If the two of you desire more time, suggest another meeting for coffee, lunch, or at one's office. Keep circulating. You just might walk away from that gathering with a fistful of threads to pull, tomorrow or in days following.

10. Do be curious of other career fields. If you are seeking a job, call the Chamber of Commerce or the local newspaper and ask if there are any job fairs to be held soon. Community colleges often sponsor job fairs. These are ideal environments in which to learn of various career fields. Visit all the booths and talk with all the representatives. Maybe you don't want a particular job the representative is pitching, but learn about the organization anyway. There may be some other position within the organization that may be of interest to you. There is no harm in asking.

11. Do leave a tangible reminder. There are times, at meetings and job fairs, when business cards are exchanged. A networker might feel a flush of embarrassment when a business card is received and there is no business card to give in return. Business cards are inexpensive in shops where cards are gang printed. But what should the card say? In only a few lines, a business card should state your name, address, phone number, and something that speaks of your expertise and availability.

One young man, starting out in business, did not give out business cards. When someone asked about his line of work, he whipped out a service contract which said it all. You might take a lesson from this story and prepare an abbreviated resumé and sales pitch – perhaps an oversized card, or a two-fold, 8½ by 11 inch page, with an attention-getting headline on the fold-over. Your handout might well be more impressive and longer lasting than a traditional business card.

12. Do remember that networking is a numbers game. The more contacts you make, the better your odds are for improving your knowledge, advancing your career, and serving others. Networking is not a science, it is an art form – and art is self expression. By doing, you learn what works and what doesn't work. Master the art of networking, and doors of opportunity will continually open for you.

Only those people with the ability to keep themselves intact can manage to keep their worlds from falling apart.

4

HOW TO GET ORGANIZED AND STAY ORGANIZED

Who in your work organization is your most important person? Whom must you manage and supervise more closely than anyone else? The answer, of course, is you. You are the most important person; you need the most management and closest supervision. Your first managerial task, then, should be to learn and practice the systems and methods by which you can manage yourself. When you have done this, you will be in a better position to manage others.

Mastering the techniques of personal organization and personal management requires discipline, patience, persistence, and a gram or two of God-given creativity. Once the mastery is attained, the following benefits will be yours:

– You will work smarter, not harder.
– You will prevent problems from overwhelming you.
– You will be more relaxed and confident.
– You will be seen as a reliable, efficient achiever.
– You will be considered as a candidate for promotion.

The Place that Serves as Your Office

A manager must have a place to work. A manager might work out of a briefcase, an automobile, or the cab of a pickup truck. But most managers are likely to have an office.

If you work out of a briefcase, have it well organized. Use small containers for paper clips, pencils, pens, and other materials. Use file folders for various classifications of papers. Use rubber bands for brochures and other loose items.

If you work out of an automobile or a truck, organize the driver's compartment. Use boxes to store items. Put these on the floor or the seat on the passenger's side. Consider attaching one or more clamps to the dash board to hold work orders or other papers that must be accessible quickly.

Offices come in various sizes and degrees of comfort. A comfortable office, where one can work efficiently, will give a manager a sense of pride, and mastery over all that is managed.

Generally, the size and luxury of an office is determined by a manager's rank. Rank, however, is determined by the functions of management that are given the most importance. Functions of management also determine the amount of time a manager must spend in an office. A manager might spend considerable time analyzing, planning, developing comprehensive reports, hosting meetings with other ranking managers, and making big decisions. Such a manager will have a large, well appointed office, as well as a private secretary. On the other end of the the managerial spectrum is a manager whose time is mostly spent at training, supervising, expediting, and personal production, with few reports to analyze and fewer to write. Planning will be done while on the move. There will seldom be more than one visitor at a time in the office. This manager is not likely to require much space or posh surroundings.

Your Desk

A manager's desk usually has three or more small drawers, plus a deep drawer, and perhaps a thin center drawer. What goes into and on top of your desk is of the utmost importance.

A management consultant was permitted to inspect an organization's office desks. The consultant's objective was not to find fault and blame individuals, but to show reason for setting up a training programme in personal organization. Here is what the consultant reported:

> What I found in the desk drawers amazed me. I found stacks of papers whose purposes and values, I am certain, have long been forgotten. I found blood-warming magazines and novels; scattered business cards; scattered paper clips, pencils and pens; a bottle of hardened correction fluid; spare and broken indistinguishable parts; important *one of a kind* business documents that should, long ago, have been returned to their proper files. There were also pieces of food, mostly half eaten; half-filled coffee cups; soft drink cans; and even a half-full pint of booze.

If you have become a bit sloppy in maintaining a neat desk, now is a good time to do something about it. Take everything out of your desk – everything. Consider for a moment what you need to work with. If you need letterhead paper and envelopes, put them in one of the drawers. Preferably put blank notebook paper and scratch pads in a separate drawer.

What more do you need? If you require such things as a straight edge ruler, a compass, a divider, or other drawing tools, try to keep them all together in a container. The same applies to pencils, pens, erasers, an extra typewriter ribbon, a paper hole punch, a stapler, and other such items. If possible, these are most convenient when kept in the center drawer located above the knee-hole opening of your desk. If not there, place them in one of the side drawers.

Some drawers are divided into sections. Use these separations wisely. Containers, ideal for your purposes, can be found in the house-wares section of hardware and department stores. What you don't need in your desk, leave out.

Don't store junk in the deep file drawer. This is a storage drawer, but only for important records, reports, correspondence, and other papers that you will want to get your hands on from time to time.

On top of the desk you may wish to keep some frequently used work items, such as pencils and pens. These can be handily kept in a container – an unused coffee cup or a clean tin can, for instance. You may want to keep a few personal items on the desk top, such as a picture of children, a spouse, or a sweetheart. You may also wish to keep a small vase with one or two flowers. These few items will pose no problems to your work. Your main objective is to maintain a desk-top that offers the maximum work space.

Your Telephone

Where the telephone is located requires no discussion. If you have a telephone, it will most likely be located near where it was originally installed. Hopefully, your telephone will be sitting within arms reach.

Filing Cabinets

If you are responsible for the care of records, reports, correspon-dence, and other important papers to be saved over long periods of time, then you need a filing cabinet. If you don't have one and can't get one, find one or more boxes of a size that will comfortably hold file folders. Be sure to label each box so that they won't be thrown out with the trash. When anyone should ask to see a current report, you will probably find it in the deep file drawer of your desk. If someone asks for an ancient record, it will be filed in your filing cabinet or in your box.

Bookcases

When you keep books and manuals in your office, it is advisable to have a bookcase, or at least some book shelves. If you do not have a bookcase and the organization will not provide one, make your own. It doesn't have to be fancy, it just has to hold books without falling down. If you don't feel handy with a saw, a hammer, and a screw driver, consider getting some large cinder or concrete building blocks, or some similar, hard, flat objects. Blocks and boards, about three shelves high, will give you plenty of book space. If lack of space in your office is the problem, consider mounting shelf brackets to the wall, at a reachable height, and place boards across these.

Tables

Computer print-outs, large ledger books, blueprints, or similar large and bulky objects can be somewhat of a problem when they must be kept in your office. To keep such items from winding up on your desk, you may find a table to be quite useful. A table is also a good place to stack technical and business magazines if your bookcase is crowded.

If your work leans more toward mechanical things rather than paper items, it should be of no surprise to have people dragging in pieces and parts of mechanical objects to show you. These things, if you really want them around for a while, can be neatly displayed on a table. Neatly, is the key word. Don't allow your table to become a junk pile or a trash dump. Keep the items well arranged. When something fails to serve its purpose, get rid of it. It will only take a few seconds to observe your table, become aware of its contents and arrangements, and take any corrective measures that might be necessary.

Storage Cabinets

When the number of parts, supplies, and other valuables are few, there is no need for a storage room. Instead, a storage cabinet will meet your needs.

Perhaps you are responsible for storing and issuing inventories of parts and supplies that are used only by your work section. You may have numbered keys to a fleet of vehicles. When you accept the responsibility for the safekeeping of valuable items, you have the right to insist on having a storage cabinet with a good lock. Do not keep valuables in a filing cabinet. A filing cabinet is for paper files, nothing more. Locking the office when you are away is no solution, either. There are managers, executives, and key employees who may have a need, and will undoubtedly have a right, to enter your office.

Some managers have one storage cabinet to safeguard valuable items and another to keep things that would otherwise be kept on a table. With a cabinet, a table may not be necessary.

Everything in its place, all your work in order.

Your bookcase, your table, your filing and storage cabinets – all these will serve you more effectively if you keep everything orderly. In addition, your office will be a nicer and more attractive place to work and to receive visitors. Let the people who clean offices do just that – clean. But let no one else arrange your things without being trained by you to do so.

– Always keep everything in the same place, where you can always find it.

– Do not store things on the floor. A manager may ask, "If not on the floor, where then?" Utilize your storage facilities – a cabinet, shelves, table – but not the floor. Things that remain on the floor are unsightly and hazardous. They tend to get dirty, stepped on, tripped over, or thrown out.

– After you have used something, put it back.

– Always put things away before you leave the office.

If your office facilities are not adequate for items stored in your office, make arrangements to have them stored somewhere else. Get out and observe, then apply the decision making process.

At least once a year, go through everything in your office. Pay particular attention to the deep file desk drawer. Keep only those files that pertain to the past twelve months. Anything that is older than one year and is to be retained should go into the filing cabinet. You will find it appropriate to throw some things away.

A good rule to remember: If it has value to someone, keep it; if it has no value to anyone, toss it out.

If you are unsure of something's value, ask questions in the right places. There are some items that, by law, must be retained for specified periods of time. Know these.

With a little effort on your part, the office and everything in it should be organized to serve you. Now it's time to look at some personal systems of control by which you can more effectively serve the organization and the people with whom you work.

Stack Trays and Control Towers

By whatever name, stack trays, baskets, or boxes serve as a control tower for paperwork that moves, or that sits and waits for orders to move.

Almost everyone who has a desk has an IN basket and an OUT basket. But what happens to all the papers between the IN and the OUT?

What happens between the time papers arrive and the time they leave? So as to know what paperwork must be done, where the papers are located, and how the work has progressed, a system of four or five tier stack trays is one possible control.

Some managers think it logical to have the IN tray at the top of the stack. The problem with this is that the incoming pile will frequently grow too high, causing papers to spill onto the floor. This can't happen when the IN tray is located at the bottom. If you leave this slot unattended and it begins to resemble a garbage compactor, surplus papers will spill out onto your desk reminding you to do something. From this bottom slot, all the paperwork will bubble upward and eventually out.

Every employee who has reason to bring paper work to your desk must be instructed to place papers in the bottom tray. This will pose no problem once you have labeled the trays.

Below, the name of each tray describes its purpose. On the opposite side is shown how the labels might be abbreviated.

Distribute and/or File	DISTRIB/FILE
Immediate Action	IMMED. ACT.
Hold Action	HOLD
Hold for Discussion	DISCUSS
Incoming / To Read	IN/READ

Label the work trays so that they can be read from either end – the end facing you and the end facing whoever comes into the office.

Never work the bottom slot.

When you are ready to work the IN/READ tray, take out each paper and read it – memo, letter, invoice, statement, report, record, whatever – then determine where it should be filed in your control tower. Here are some examples:

1. While you were away from the office, a telephone message was noted and forwarded to your desk. You are asked to telephone a senior officer of the organization immediately. Do not reach for the telephone. Place the note where it should go – up in the slot marked IMMED. ACT.

2. A letter requests some information. You don't have all the facts, so you cannot answer until you have a meeting with the managers of the service and sales departments. Which slot? The one marked DISCUSS.

3. An employee has brought in a form with the required social security number. There is nothing more for you to do except see that it

goes where it belongs. Toss the personnel form into the top slot DIS-TRIB./FILE.

4. Next is information for you to read, initial, and pass on to the next person listed. Watch out! Is there anything you are supposed to do with the information – post a notice, hold a meeting? Do you need to discuss the information with anyone else? Is there a need for urgency? The answers will determine the slot you will use. Practice will teach you to make correct choices quickly.

5. An invoice comes in. You know that a statement will soon follow. The accounting department demands that the shipping notice, the invoice, and the statement be forwarded together. You reach for the HOLD slot. The shipping notice is there. Clip the two papers together and place them back in HOLD to await the statement.

6. There is a trade publication in the bottom tray. It has a couple of articles you want to read. If you are going to read the magazine at work, leave it where it is, under IN/READ. If you want to take the magazine home, put it in the top slot, DISTRIB./FILE.

The bottom IN tray is now empty. It has taken only two or three minutes to read all the papers and slot them. Now you are ready to tackle the work. The logical place to start is with IMMED. ACT. Now you can make that important phone call, then you can perform any other task that demands your immediate attention. All the items in the IMMED. ACT. may not be completed daily, but the system will continue to remind you of what you have not done. That in itself is important for the control of unfinished tasks.

Check the other trays, in turn. As the day goes on, you may complete some items of business, others may be moved to different slots. For instance, you may get the information you needed from the managers of service and sales, but now your boss says to put a hold on the task. The boss wants to think of how the information can be presented best. So the original request for information, plus the inputs of the service and sales managers, come out of the DISCUSS slot and go into HOLD. Add a notation and date of the instructions to await the boss's ideas on the subject. When the boss informs you as to how the information is to be presented, and asks you to send it without further delay, then this becomes IMMED. ACT.

The statement you have been expecting arrives in the mail. You match it with the shipping notice and the invoice that have been parked in your HOLD slot. With your initialed approval, the three papers go directly into DISTRIB./FILE, and on to the accounting office.

At the end of your working day, two trays will be empty. Everything in the top tray should have been mailed, distributed to other people, or filed. There should be nothing in the bottom tray except, perhaps, the magazine which you didn't have time to read. If you don't want to take it home, it can stay in the IN/READ slot. No other IN items should remain there. The other trays, even IMMED. ACT., will most likely have some remaining business to attend to. But you can go home without worry or concern. Your mind should be free. You can look forward to enjoying a pleasant evening. Tomorrow, those pieces of unfinished business will be right where you left them.

Never leave unfinished work on your desk if it can be avoided. A desk that is left cluttered does not look professional. The cluttered desk can tempt curious hands to paw into your business.

The next day, when you arrive at your desk, you can quickly determine what kind of a day you are going to have. Until the mail arrives and people begin bringing paperwork to your desk, the top and bottom slots – IN/READ and DISTRIB./FILE – remain empty. But you have other trays to look into.

Begin with IMMED. ACT., then HOLD, then DISCUSS. You may find that there is nothing in IMMED. ACT., or at least nothing that is really urgent, but the DISCUSS tray may be loaded. This, then, may be the day for you to whittle down the items that need to be discussed and resolved.

Under HOLD, you may find an invoice that you have been holding for a long time. Your immediate action may be to place a phone call or write a letter to inquire as to why you have not yet received a statement. Note and date the action you take. Jot it down on the paper with which you are working, such as the invoice. Return it to its proper place – HOLD – until you eventually have reason to move it out.

Throughout the day, mail and other paperwork will be shoved into your IN/READ tray. This will occur whether you are at your desk or not. When it is convenient, repeat the process of assigning papers to their proper slots.

Your control tower of stack trays may function in a similar manner, but it may be labeled to suit different purposes. For instance, if you have few occasions to place papers in the DISCUSS slot, put these in HOLD, instead, and do away with the DISCUSS slot. Perhaps you have work that is on-going, a project that requires attention over a long period of time: an annual report or some other manuscript; a long range plan; a statistical analysis; the planning of an awards presentation, or a Christmas party. It might be advantageous to convert the DISCUSS slot to WORK IN

PROGRESS. You might want a slot labeled TO READ, just for all the magazines and brochures that come your way.

It may be that you can only afford to have shoe boxes lined in a row and labeled to suit your paper flow needs. That's fine. Any system that gives adequate control over the flow or your work is a good one. But don't close your mind to change. Periodically, appraise your work and your controls. If a slightly different system will give you better awareness and control over your work, use your ingenuity and initiate an improvement.

A Calendar Is Watching After You

A calendar can be a manager's good friend. It can do more than mark the passing of days, weeks, months, and years. The calendar, as a management tool, can be used to ensure the completion of work in accordance with specified deadlines. It can relieve the busy, tired brain of remembering appointments – and sometimes it can gloatingly and critically remind the overly busy (or lazy) manager of what did not get done as scheduled.

Some managers prefer a desk calendar. It has sufficient space for writing abbreviated notes. Others prefer a wall calendar. It has less space for notes, but it has the advantage of quick reference, forward and backward in time. Some managers want both – a desk calendar and a wall calendar. So that a manager will not have to search through the pages of a desk calendar frantically, the manager will write appointments on a wall calendar. Notes of things to do on a daily basis will be written on a desk calendar.

What reminders go on a calendar? Anything that is to be done on a specified day – meetings, tasks, projects . . . even remembering a special birthday or anniversary.

Before writing a reminder on your calendar, always ask these questions: Who? What? When? How? Why? Choose only those questions that must be answered in a concise manner so as to trigger your memory for the details. On a given day a week from now, someone's desk calendar may have the notations:

1. Staff meeting, 9 am.
2. Lunch with Jones.
3. Smith re: purch., 2 pm.

It is not necessary that all of the questions be answered. For instance, you will know where the staff meeting is always held. The second memo tells you what, when, who, why, where. And you will undoubtedly know the what and why and through whom when you discuss purchasing with Smith, at 2 o'clock.

A final tip: Do not scribble a single message across an entire page. Do not use your calendar for a scratch pad by jotting down meaningless notes and figures. Treat your *friend*, with respect. Your calendar can keep you out of trouble; it can do much for your success as a manager.

The Endless Task and Project List

Managers are generally successful when dealing with day to day routine happenings and the occasional problems that rise up and bite them. But some managers are less successful when juggling unexpected, untimely, or out of the ordinary tasks and projects.

Tasks and projects, simply stated, are things to do. Some people call them that – Things To Do. A task is not difficult to accomplish, and it usually doesn't require much time. A task, in most instances, can be completed during a single undertaking. A task might be making a non-scheduled, surprise inspection; or it might be getting a haircut. A task is something done just once.

A project, on the other hand, has several parts. Planning is required. There are several areas to explore and sources to tap. There may be decisions to make. A project might be setting up a new training programme or planning a party for your employees and their families. A project cannot be completed all at once.

The biggest problem with tasks and projects is that they all don't seem to fit into the scheme of things. Some can't, at the moment, be written on a calendar because they are things to do – not now, but sometime. The first step is not deciding when; the first step is deciding what. Then the where will be decided: where the list of things to do will be kept. Then comes the when. And finally, the how: how the system will be worked.

Task and project lists involve several steps taken over a period of time. You most likely have some ideas of things you need or want to do during the days, weeks, or months ahead. The first step is to write down those ideas. If you don't have too many tasks and projects, a single list may be sufficient. Then again, you might want two lists: one for tasks and one for projects. The reason for separating the two is that tasks turn over rapidly. Things get done, and other things to do are quickly thought of or assigned to you. Projects may stay on your list for a month or more while you work on getting the bits and pieces to fall into place.

After you have written down your tasks and projects on a single sheet of paper or in a notebook, where will you keep the list? A list of things to do needs a place of its own. You can keep it in the HOLD slot of your desk trays, or you might want to keep the list in a drawer. Choose one that you get into frequently – a place where the list will practically jump out at you. Your briefcase may be the right place for you. Check the task and project list as frequently as you think necessary, but certainly not less than once a week. There is an old saying, "Out of sight, out of mind." These important things to do must not be allowed to slip your mind.

Your best bet is to plan a time each week to review your tasks and projects. It will make you feel good to see the ones you have drawn lines through as they were completed. You may frown when you see those old familiar ones, but they will also cause you to make new decisions regarding their priorities.

Some managers can determine the importance and urgency of a task or project simply by looking at it. Others may need to devise some simple method of showing the degree of priority for each item. The date of each entry can be noted. This will tell you at a glance how long a task or project has been on the list, and will give you some idea as to its urgency. But age does not necessarily match the importance of something you must do. It may be helpful to jot down a priority code before each item. This system is easy as ABC. In fact, that's all you have to do. Read down your list of tasks and projects and give each item a mark of A, B, or C. "A" is for a high priority, "C" is a low priority. Remember, as you review your things to do, priorities may have changed. A reason may come up to delay an action. It's not dead, but the need to attend to that particular item is certainly less urgent at the moment. So you change the code symbol. You will find that the longer an item remains on your list the more important it will become. Last week's thought of getting a haircut may now be today's most urgent matter, especially if you are scheduled to attend an important function.

When your daily routine is running smoothly, you should easily find times during the days ahead when you can concentrate on knocking out some of those nagging tasks and projects. When you think you have some available time, note on your calendar the task or project you want or need to do. By scheduling that thing to do, you have given it a high priority. All you have to do is do it.

Some things to do will evolve to another form. Calling your boss, for example, to discuss that raise you want, may get you an appointment. You can even schedule that meeting on your calendar. But the boss may have asked you to put together some information before the meeting. So now you have a new task pertaining to an old subject.

You can be assured of stress-free management of tasks and projects when you remember to do three things:
– Account for the things you have to do.

– Know their priorities.
– Order yourself to get things done according to their importance.

I forgot.
                            - Famous last words.

5

HOW TO MAKE THE MOST OF YOUR MEMORY

As a manager, you cannot afford to forget. Many people are counting on you to act upon an endless list of questions and tasks. Your personal organization will depend, in part, upon your memory. If your memory is sometimes similar to that of a sieve, letting ideas and thoughts sift into a fine nothingness, you will need systematic ways to remember the numerous things that managers are asked to do. See what you can do with the following lessons, so as to tie your thoughts outside of the office to your systems inside of the office.

A Pocket Full of Remembrances

In the office, a manager is not likely to forget messages, general paper work, tasks, or projects. All the pieces of information are where they should be, where hands and eyes can quickly get to them. But the manager's systems of personal organization must frequently extend beyond the office. While away from the office, a manager must remember where to go, what is to be done, what happens, what is said, and what there is to do upon returning to the office.

Without needing to rely heavily on memory, you can plan and conduct your outside activities with confidence. All you need is a small notebook and a pen or pencil to carry with you. This traveling notebook will be used to tie together your outside activities and your personal, in office, control systems.

Each morning at your desk, check your calendar notes, the task and project list, and your stack trays. In your notebook, write down one or more tasks to do, a project to set in motion, some immediate action to pursue, a subject to discuss with someone, or the name of an employee who has an anniversary that day.

Away from your office, as you attend to your list of duties, you will likely have occasions to jot down additional notes. If, for example, an employee asks a question that you are not prepared to answer at the moment, write it down. The employee will notice your action and will feel assured that you will not forget to provide the requested information. In another instance, you might give instructions to an employee and then jot down a note to serve as your reminder to follow-up on the results. Writing down the reminder will impress upon the employee that you will do just that.

Back at the office, check your notebook. The things you had written down to do and have now completed can be crossed off from the source record – the calendar, the task and project list, the stack trays on your desk. Transfer the new entries you jotted down while away from your desk onto the appropriate places of record. Any of the planned activities that were not completed will remain as unfinished business. You can take care of these at another time.

Notebook Housekeeping Rules

1. The day's date should be entered at the top of each page.

2. Number each entry. Notes should be written down the page, on the lines, rather than scrawled at random over various pages.

3. Check off or draw a line through each activity as it is completed. Carry forward items to the next day if they were not completed.

4. At the end of the day, when you have reconciled old and new notes with appropriate, in-office source records, write a large X over the day's page. Every page in your notebook that shows an X can be ignored.

5. Do not write notes on scraps of paper and stuff them into any pocket that is handy. Notes get misplaced, lost, or sometimes washed with the laundry. Whatever the reason, precious notes can quickly be forgotten. Use your notebook.

6. Do not write or read notes while driving. Such a habit can be dangerous.

During busy times, a manager may feel it is unnecessary or too time consuming to write down the things that must be remembered. But the time it takes to write a note is nothing compared to the time that must be spent taking care of a problem caused from something forgotten. And the disappointment and inconvenience that other people experience because of a manager's forgetfulness can never be fully repaired.

All successful managers, while on the move, have systems for keeping track of ideas, inspirations, and things to do. These people are successful because they treat their own personal systems with respect and with a discipline to make them work successfully. You can do the same.

A Perfect Memory in Thirty Minutes

Personal organization and systems are the manager's tangible tools of control over a variety of things to do. But the intangible key to a manager's success is the basic reliable memory.

Even when surrounded by a well organized desk, stack trays, calendar notes, a task and project list, and a personal notebook, a reminder will not be noted and retained unless a manager remembers to do so.

There are times when a manager may find it impossible, or at least inconvenient, to jot down thoughts that were so important to remember, such as: those ideas that flowed so freely while driving a car, then became lost in the usual traffic snarl; the midnight inspiration that is forgotten by morning; the boss's instructions that were blurred as his voice droned on; the employee who caught you away from your office without pen or pad and asked a question that you were momentarily unprepared to answer.

Whatever the excuse for not writing down something important, it is not enough to say, "Sorry, I forgot." That comes across as, "You are not important." An apology will not erase the disappointment totally, nor will it relieve the stress of the situation.

Fortunately, a person does not have to be a genius to have a reliable memory. In just thirty minutes, with a little practice, you can learn to recall a list of ten instructions – things you might be asked to do – with confidence . It will not be necessary to memorize these instructions. You will simply learn them, in seconds.

Hang the thoughts in your mind.

Here is the way the memory system works. You will be given a thought to remember. This thought will be assigned a number – any number, one through ten. The number will immediately make you think of a *thought hanger*. On it will hang a *fantasy*. That imaginative story will then bring to mind your important *thought*.

This memory system begins with your learning the ten thought hangers. Because of their imaginary relationships with the ten numbers, you will find it easy to learn the thought hangers quickly. Once learned, the thought hangers will be fixed in your mind. You will never forget them. You can make up your own hangers – or you can try using the following:

Number 1 is a *spear*. It can be as tall as a tree or as small as a toothpick.

Number 2 is a *pair of pants*. Long, short, old, new, dress, work - pants have two legs.

Number 3 is *tongs*. When the jaws are open, tongs look something like a number 3.

Number 4 is a *table*. All kinds of tables have four legs.

Number 5 is a *sickle*. You'll be a real cut-up with this.

Number 6 is a *golf club*. Putt, chip, or drive your thought. The club looks like a 6.

Number 7 is a *police officer*. Standing at attention, arm outstretched stopping traffic, the officer looks like a number 7. But in your fantasy the officer can do anything.

Number 8 is a set of *revolving doors*. When looking at them from the top, the double revolving doors look like the figure 8.

Number 9 is a *rural mail box on a post*. Everything you want to do or get can be handled through that mail box that stands there like a number 9.

Number 10 is a *prison cell*. There are ten heavy steel bars on the cell door. It's easy to put a thought in jail.

Test yourself. Take a piece of paper and write the numbers one through ten, down the page. Then, in any order, write down the correct thought hanger for each number. Take number six. If you are thinking of a golf club, you have the right idea. Try the others. Skip around. The order in which you call off the numbers and hangers is unimportant. If you miss any, try again. One more time through and you'll know them all.

You now have ten unforgettable thought hangers, and you are ready for step two.

Thoughts and Fantasies

Have someone tell you ten thoughts to remember. Or make up your own list. In any order, assign each one a number. Pick a number. This will make you think of a thought hanger. To hang your thought on a hanger, make up a highly imaginative story using both the hanger and the thought to be remembered. Make your fantasy as ridiculous and as exaggerated as possible. If your story seems too logical, you may be apt to forget it.

Here are a few examples:

Let's say someone asks you to take home a dozen eggs. The thought is arbitrarily assigned to number 8. A colorful fantasy quickly comes to mind. You buy a huge box of ostrich eggs. To leave the store you must pass through revolving doors which are revolving at a high speed. You lose control of your large box of giant eggs, and the revolving doors take on the appearance of twin blenders whipping up an omelet. Number 8 –

revolving doors – a dozen eggs splattered all over everything. You won't forget to take home a dozen eggs.

An employee wants a day off to attend an important family function. You must remember to rearrange the work schedule so that the employee's job is covered. You decide that this task will be number 4 on the list. In a moment your mind envisions the employee at a large gathering of people. The employee is dancing wildly on a table, kicking over glasses and stepping into the punch bowl. Number 4 – a table – employee dancing on a table during a day off from work. You won't forget to rearrange the work schedule.

This thought will be number 10. You are told to see the boss at three o'clock. For some reason, the boss has been hauled off to jail. The big clock at the court house bongs three as you peer through the ten bars of the jail cell and ask the boss why you were summoned. Number 10 – ten jail bars – the boss, of all people, in jail, as the court house clock strikes three. You won't forget to see your boss at 3 P.M.

A few pointers may help you make your memory system more meaningful and effective. If you continue to have trouble locking thoughts into your mind, determine whether you are comfortable with the thought hangers. If not, think of some new ones and try them. If you are satisfied with the hangers you have, you likely just need practice in creating dramatic or humorous, indelible stories.

You will seldom have ten thoughts to remember at one time. A more reasonable estimate is three or four items. On some days, you may have no thoughts to remember.

If you are interested in remembering more than ten items, experiment with putting together combinations of numbers and thought hangers. Then, make up a fantasy to fit the dual thought hangers. Number fifteen, for instance, is a combination of one and five. See if you can take a thought and tie it to a spear and a sickle.

Many managers frequently forget to use their memory systems. Strong habits are formed with continual practice. Several times a day, wherever you are, check the numbers of your memory system. See if any thoughts are on the hangers. When something needs to be remembered place it on a hanger, even though it may already be written down.

Don't trust your memory system completely. It can fail you. Hold on to a thought long enough to write it down. Once written and in its proper place, a thought is safe. Also, if something takes you away from your work for an extended period of time, your written thought remains for others to see and, if necessary, to act upon.

Only the last impression placed on a numbered thought hanger will remain in your mind. When you wish to erase that impression, you need only to think it gone – and it will be. Also, a new thought will automatically erase any former impression.

Memory improvement can be demonstrated in just thirty minutes. The heightened assurance that comes with successfully remembering and carrying out many, varied, impromptu tasks may take a bit longer.

How to Remember Those Special Occasions

Ask a group of employees their dates of employment. Chances are that everyone of them will know it, right down to the day. And to many employees, their birthdays are equally important occasions.

Some organizations give recognition to employees for their years of service. Employment anniversaries are generally featured in the organization's newspaper. Handsome pins are awarded to employees who have worked for a specified number of years. In some organizations, an employee's birthday is honored by giving a day off with pay. As generous as all this may seem, it is not enough.

People find a personal touch to be more meaningful. The memory of receiving a formal award for excellence or achievement may become blurred in time. But you clearly remember the occasion when a teacher, coach, parent, or friend gave you an affectionate pat on the back and said, "Way to go!"

Some managers are sensitive to the importance employees place on personal, special occasions; some are not. In either case, there is a practical reason why a manager should remember, respect, and acknowledge such important dates as birthdays, employment anniversaries, and, perhaps, wedding anniversaries. The practical reason is this: to get the most from employees, a manager must be a leader. To be a leader, a manager must have followers. To earn followers, a manager must serve the employees' interests, as well as those of the organization. Employees are impressed with a manager's ability to remember birthdays and anniversaries. They respect a manager whom they regard as thoughtful and considerate. From their respect comes loyalty, and loyalty is the stuff that followers are made of.

Watch the wide grin, the startled look, or the shy, embarrassed smile spread across an employee's face when you, in passing, offer your congratulations on this special, personal occasion. Just a few timely, appropriate words can put you close to your employees – but without the problems of being overly intimate or involved.

Remembering all the special occasions your employees may have might seem to be a tall order. It's not. No particular talent is required, just a simple system and a small amount of initial effort.

Accounting for those occasional occasions.

If you were to account for hundreds of employees and all their special days, you would need a computer, or at least a Rolodex™ file. A line manager, however, should need only a single sheet of paper to track all the dates to be remembered.

List the names of your employees down the page. Opposite each name, jot down date of birth (D.O.B.) and date of employment (D.O.E.). You may also want to add wedding anniversaries. Enter these as dates of marriage (D.O.M.).

Take another sheet of paper. This is for the monthly record. The first heading is January. Look at your work sheet. For any dates that fall in January, write the employee's name, the abbreviated event, and the day, month, and year. Repeat the process for the other months.

Understandably, an employee may appear under three different months: one for date of employment, one for a birthday, and one for a wedding anniversary. Your form could look something like this:

Special Dates

January
      Joe – D.O.E.: 17 Jan. '80
      Linda – D.O.B.: 21 Jan. '63

February
      Linda – D.O.E.: 3 Feb. '83
      Joe – D.O.B.: 8 Feb. '52;   D.O.M.: 23 Feb. '75

March
      Linda – D.O.M.: 15 Mar. '83

This record can be kept in the deep file drawer of your desk.

Remembering those special days.

On the last day of each month, pull your record sheet from its file and study the list of special occasions for the coming month. Until you are able to pull this record routinely, remind yourself with a note on your calendar. Transfer the information to the appropriate days on your desk or wall calendar.

When that special day arrives, you will be ready to express your sincerest best wishes to an employee who will be made to feel very special.

The success of your programme for remembering employee's special occasions will likely remain unmentioned, but you can bet that, in your employee's mind, he will be thinking, "You remembered."

We know, what we know.
What we don't know, we can learn.

6

HOW TO IMPROVE YOUR POWERS OF OBSERVATION AND AWARENESS

Within any organization, it is readily apparent that much of a manager's success is born of observation and awareness.

A manager with keen powers of observation and awareness is the envy of less perceptive managers. Unpleasant occurrences seldom come as a surprise to him. The observant and aware manager generally prevents them from happening in the first place. This type of manager looks after his employees and provides them with the tools and materials that are essential to their work. In return, the workers give that manager their loyalty and productivity. Success, then, is a reasonable expectation for any manager who sharpens these skills.

A frog would not make a good manager.

Some years ago, an experiment was conducted in the interest of behavioral science. Psychologists placed a young, healthy frog in a man-made pond, complete with water, plants, and smooth, submerged stones. Each day, humans in long white coats brought the frog flies and other good things that frogs like to eat. Mindlessly, the frog croaked happily. This was the good life. The frog, not a prisoner, could jump out of the unfenced pond at any time. But why would any frog in its right mind want to do that?

Unknown to the frog, those people in the long white coats – the ones who brought the frog food every day – were also heating the water in the pond. The temperature was increased just a fraction of a degree at a time. The frog took no notice of the increasing water temperature. After all, it really didn't seem any hotter than it had been just a little while ago. And so, after a time, the frog died – in its own stew, so to speak.

Today, psychologists are not so interested in frogs. They are more interested in managers. Now, the pond has become an office. The smooth rocks are now a desk and a chair. Instead of flies, there are paychecks. But, much like the frog, a manager may not notice the ever increasing temperature, the stress of the work environment.

Is it possible that humans might be as unobservant and unaware as frogs? As much as people might dislike being compared to frogs, the answer is, "yes."

People's observations and awarenesses are determined by their habits, customs, attitudes, and mental sets. People sometimes see only what they expect to see; hear only what they want to hear. People are frequently so preoccupied with their own thoughts that they are unobservant of the world around them.

Few of us take close notice of our surroundings during a routine drive home from work, over a familiar route. Many of us have experienced a misunderstanding because we failed to listen closely and understand what was said. Some of us have failed to see something on a shelf because it had been moved slightly away from where it normally would be. And most of us have been unaware of closing darkness while reading, until someone comes into the room and switches on a light.

Still, there are managers who will insist that they *always* pay attention to *everything*. Try teasing them with a few test questions.

Ask, "How many months of the year have 28 days?"
Will they say, "One, February."? Or will they say, "Twelve, they all have 28 days."?

Ask, "Does England have a fourth of July?"
Will they say, "No, of course not."? Or will they say, "Sure, it falls between the third and the fifth."?

Trick questions? Maybe. But they demonstrate how readily our minds become pre-set to reflex responses.

Here's another. How many squares are there in the illustration at the top of page 49?

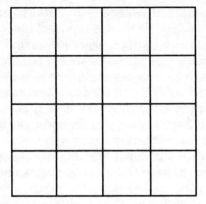

Now that you are aware of the game-playing, you will likely be careful to count *all* the squares, and you'll come up with thirty.

Games Managers Play

There are real-life games of a more practical nature that can help a manager improve the abilities to observe and to become more keenly aware. These games can be played in stores, restaurants, offices, repair shops, a bank, a hospital – any place where business is conducted.

The first part of the game is *observation*. What do you like or dislike about the manner in which an organization functions? What of it products, services, facilities, employees?

The second part is *awareness*. Why do you like or dislike whatever you observed? In other words, if an organization is not running smoothly, why not? If it is running well, why? What might be some consequences for an organization that functions poorly? In some situations, do you suspect a disaster is waiting to happen?

The third part of the game is *management*. Pretend that you are the manager of the organization under observation. If you observe an operational situation that you don't like, if you are aware of possible destructive consequences, what will you do about it? If you are impressed with an organization's operation, what lessons can you learn? How can these lessons be applied to your own sphere of management?

Seven Ways to Sharpen Your Seven Senses

1. Prepare yourself. Once again, study the rules, policies, and objectives of your organization. These are important standards. It is your job to see that the employees – their behavior and productivity – measure up to these standards.

2. Study the jobs that are under your direct supervision. You must have a thorough knowledge of the functions and tasks of every job if you are to recognize and solve small problems before they become big ones.

3. Observe with the five senses – seeing, hearing, smelling, tasting, and touching – plus your sixth sense and your common sense. Wherever you are, practice concentrating on the sensations around you. You may notice a worker using a knife where the light is poor, or the sound of a truck laboring up a hill in the wrong gear, or the smell of something burning, or the taste of poorly prepared food.

Test your sixth sense. Upon walking into the work place, experienced managers seem to have an awareness of how things are humming – the workers' moods and their productivity.

Sharpen your common sense by asking questions of others; "What would you do?" "What do you think?" Get a consensus. Compare what you hear with what you feel and what you think.

4. Be alert to details. Details provide key measurements of general conditions. Details frequently provide warnings of impending troubles. How do you feel about the dirty coffee cups sitting in an office; the flag that isn't flying from its mast because someone forgot to put it up; an important document that sits out in the open overnight on someone's desk? What might these incidents of neglect indicate?

5. Ask questions about things you do not understand. Your boss is one source of information. Other experienced managers may also have many of the answers to your questions. Don't overlook your employees; they often may know more than you.

6. Stand back and look at the total situation. View all the conditions. People sometimes stand so close to the trees that they can't see the forest. A situation you do understand may be affected by circumstances of which you are not yet aware. Strikes or layoffs, certain changes in ordinances and laws, a winter flu epidemic, an employee with a serious personal problem – any of these, and more, could sooner or later affect your job.

7. From what you observe, become aware of the situation, not only as it is, but also as what it may develop to be. Tools and supplies left unattended or unsecured sometimes seem to just *walk away*. That forgotten flag raising might indicate other forgotten tasks. A supplier with labor problems or equipment failure might cause a breakdown of your services or production. An employees's problems, health or otherwise, could soon be seen as absenteeism or termination.

With practiced and keenly honed powers of observation and awareness, you will be better prepared to make correct decisions and take decisive, effective actions. The combination of these are the stuff of which successful managers are made.

The fountain of knowledge does not spring accidentally.
It is dug through layers of ignorance by educators who seek ways to
quench mankind's thirst for knowledge.

7

HOW TO DEVELOP YOUR OWN TRAINING PROGRAMME

When work turns sour, some managers blame people or circumstances; some managers bang their fists on their desks, tear at their hair, and yell; and some managers simply shrug their shoulders and mutter, "That's the way it goes. It's just one of those days."

No matter how managers react, when projected expectations are not met, top executives – and perhaps even the general public – will be apt to point fingers of accusation at supervisors and middle-managers and say, "It's all their fault; their workers should be better trained."

More training, better training – managers and employees, too, do not argue the need. They want it, they ask for it. Certainly there are many people who do think that supervisors, middle-managers, and workers are getting the training they need. However, it just may be that the meanings of *more* and *better* are not fully understood.

More training describes quantity; better training describes quality. More training can be a partial solution to little or no training. Better training is a solution for poorly constructed training programmes, and/or incompetent trainers.

A delicate blend and balance of the two is necessary for the successful development of workers and the improvement of a work unit's performance.

There are five good reasons for you to have your own training programme:

1. Training is one of the eight functions of management; training employees is part of your job.

2. Thoroughly trained people have more self confidence; they take more pride in their work, their organization, and their leader.

3. Thoroughly trained workers are easier to lead; when promoted, they become good leaders.

4. Training others to become trainers extends your own capabilities.

5. Your own training programme will catch and correct any misunderstandings that employees might have formed elsewhere.

Training begins at the moment of hiring; it continues until employment is terminated. The training process takes place in offices, shops, the field, meeting rooms, and classrooms. Generally, most training is done on the job.

Many large organizations employ training specialists. Specialists have some important advantages. As instructors, they know what they are doing. They have a variety of detailed courses, and they know how and where to tap outside resources to support their training programmes. In-house training specialists have the training resources: books, handout materials, and audio-visual aids. They carefully maintain training records on all employees.

Small organizations cannot be expected to afford the services of a full-time training specialist. In this situation, bosses do the training themselves, or they assign their most experienced workers to train others. There is nothing wrong with bosses and experienced workers doing the training. The advantages have already been mentioned. The key is in how well bosses and experienced workers can train. It is all too easy for a supervisor or middle-manager to take for granted that employees who have been trained by others know all the answers and have the required skills. The person who is really in the best position to polish the training programme is the immediate supervisor – you. You are closest to the kinds of work being done and you are directly responsible for the results. You therefore, should be the person most interested in the thoroughness and effectiveness in your employees' training. You are the one who should know best how, what, where, and when to train.

The Consistent and Inheritable Training Programme

On the job, it may seem impossible to bring the same quantity and quality of training to each employee. On some days, you may have all the time in the world to do a thorough job of training. On busy, stressful days, you may be forced to cut down on the time spent training. Important information may be skimmed over; some material may be omitted. Such short cuts can lead to even more stressful and busier days later on. Then, when something goes wrong, an employee might offer the defense, ''No one ever told me that.'' And you might not know whether you did or didn't. To avoid such a scene, it is essential that training be of the same quality and quantity for all employees who are engaged in similar kinds of work, regardless of job pressures.

To be inheritable, a training programme must be in a form that can be easily handed on and used by others. In its proper form and usage, the training programme will remain consistent. Trainers whom you recruit will know exactly what they are to teach. All you need do is train your trainers to teach as if you were doing it yourself.

Setting up a training programme is no particular problem when you are already personally organized. There are only three steps of preparation:
– Have the necessary training resources and materials.
– Prepare a training outline/record.
– Be proficient in teaching, using the simple method of instruction.

Training Resources and Materials

In the deep file drawer of your desk, you should keep a folder labeled, *Training Resources And Materials*. Here, you might keep advertisements for training literature to send for; you might collect pertinent magazine articles. You may also include a list of places where you can borrow or rent training materials and equipment, and a list of specialists who can assist you with training. These bits and pieces of training information should be easily accessible.

On your bookshelf, you should keep books that can be used to make employees more successful at their jobs. These reference books may range from a dictionary to technical operations manuals. A loose-leaf binder of training notes might also be included.

Don't expect employees to flock to your library. They won't. Don't expect to memorize all the contents of your books. You won't. Do expect employees to come to you with questions. They will. And, do expect to look up information frequently. You'll need to know.

Your most important training resources are the tools, machines, supplies, and other items that are used on the job.

A Training Outline and Training Record

If your organization has a method of maintaining training records, it is essential that you comply with it. However, there is nothing wrong with having your own system of keeping training outlines and records that can better serve you.

A training outline is absolutely necessary for a consistent training programme.

– The outline will assure that every employee receives the same points of instruction.

– Subjects need not be taught or presented in a specific order. The outline accounts for all subjects regardless of the order in which they are presented. Thus, a trainer can teach only the material that is important and timely for the moment.

– An instructor can tell at a glance the subjects yet to be offered.

– Only those subjects that have been taught and learned will be dated and initialed.

An instructor should not hastily sign off the subjects as they are taught. Nor should an employee be allowed to initial the form too quickly. It has been said, "If the student has not learned, the teacher has not taught." Be certain of what the employee has learned.

Creating the training outline/record.

The training outline/record is easy to use. Creating it will take a bit of thought, experimentation, practice, and patience. The down-the-road results will be worth your efforts.

Take a job with which you are thoroughly familiar. Begin writing down all the details of the organization, your department, and the job – all the information that you will want an employee to know. Don't worry about the order in which you write your list. The subjects can be rearranged later to suit your purpose. There are some general classifications that will help you to organize your material.

Orientation
1. Review of job description
2. History and organization of the work place
3. Walk-through of pertinent work areas
4. Introduction to personnel
5. The communication of personal problems and grievances

The walk-through of work areas is important. You will want your employees to have a sense of belonging, not only within your work unit, but to the whole organization, as well. In your work area, show where everything is located, including the places where people eat and take their breaks. Don't embarrass a new employee by making him ask where the toilets are located. Show where they are.

Introductions are also important. You want your new employees to know who the other workers are and what they do. A new employee will not remember the names of all these people, but the newcomer will at least be able to associate faces with jobs. Introductions will also serve to let your experienced workers know that there is a new worker on board.

While making your list of things for the training outline, keep in mind how bewildered and nervous you felt during your first day or two on a new job. What were some of the questions you would have liked answered? A thorough orientation will make it easier for a new employee to become better adjusted to the new job.

On-The-Job Training

Begin this section with another review of the job description. If you have not personally performed this work, talk with other workers who have held and who now hold this job. Get the specifics. To demonstrate the details that should go into training a new employee, below is a training outline/record written for a young woman on an island in the South Pacific as she began the very first job she had ever held.

TRAINING OUTLINE/RECORD

Employee: _____
Job Title: _____ Office Manager _____ Date of Hire: _____

Orientation	Date	Instr.	Empl.
1. Job Description			
a. Duties and Responsibilities			
b. Qualifications			
c. Wages/Benefits			
2. History, Organization, Objectives			
a. Internat'l Red Cross			
b. National Red Cross			
c. Constitution / Goals			
3. Walk-through of Office			
Desks, office equipment, files, cabinets; medical storage, misc. storage; conference area, library; bulletin boards; kitchen, restroom.			
4. Introduction to Red Cross Personnel			
a. Office personnel			
b. Executive members			
c. Volunteers			
5. Communication of personal problems and grievances			
a. By the employee			

	Date	Instr.	Empl.

b. By the senior field officer re. tardiness, absenteeism, character, behavior, conduct.

B. On-The-Job Training
  1. Telephone / Visitors
    a. Greeting: Voice projection, taking messages, giving information, general attitude and helpfulness
    b. Responding to emergencies
      – disaster relief
      – blood donors
      – tracing service
    c. Outgoing Calls
      – list of available names and numbers
      – directory assistance
      – overseas calls
  2. Typing
    a. Correspondence format
    b. Stencils
    c. Records, reports, minutes
  3. Copy Machine
    a. Operation
    b. Maintenance
  4. Filing
    a. Field Officer files
    b. National Secretary files
    c. Disaster Relief files
    d. Treasurer's records
  5. Handling of Money
    a. Petty Cash
    b. Hospital Store On Wheels
    c. First Aid Supplies
    d. Fund Raising
    e. Memberships
    f. Receipts and Records for the above
  6. Medical Supplies
    a. Storage
    b. Sales
    c. Receipts
    d. Stock Record

	Date	Instr.	Empl.
7. Library			
a. Organization			
b. Book maintenance and repair			
c. Checking In/Out			
8. Housekeeping			
a. Conference area, office, kitchen, toilet, windows, floors			
b. Cleaning equipment and materials			
c. Trash			
d. General organization and neatness			
e. Opening and closing office			
9. Personal Organization			
a. Desk, priorities, time control			
b. First Aid Certification			

It should be apparent that a specifically detailed training outline will serve you well in locking a new employee into the duties and responsibilities of a job.

Such a training outline will serve you further in another way. Experienced workers can be readily taught to become effective trainers. This will allow you more time to pursue other managerial tasks and projects – and that's a valuable asset.

Here are some other occasions when a training outline/record will be useful:

1. When you delegate training to one of your employees, you will want to check the progress of the training programme. The outline/record will show you what subjects have been covered by the instructor, and what the employee has agreed to as having been learned.

2. If an employee makes a work related mistake and argues that instructions were never given, you will have the record of what was taught, when, by whom, and the worker's agreement that the lesson was understood. Don't rub the employee's nose in it. Give room for doubt. Say something like, "Hey, I'm sorry if we missed that during training. Let's take a look at the record and see what happened." With that argument out of the way, you can spend your time determining what really went wrong and why.

3. You will find it advisable to review training records when preparing performance evaluations.

4. You will also find it advisable to review the training record of an employee being brought up for disciplinary action.

5. When one of your employees is selected for transfer to another

department, or is being considered for promotion, you will likely be asked about the person's qualifications. You will be asked for facts, not vague opinions. The training outline, along with other records, will provide the essential information needed for a sensible decision.

6. You will need training outline/records when you embark upon a program of cross-training your employees.

The mere fact that you possess the necessary training tools and the training outline/records does not guarantee success. It is like owning an airplane without knowing how to fly. To get your own training programme off the ground, you must be certain that you know how to teach.

Knowledge – what we know – means little
unless intelligently applied to the service of others.

8
HOW TO BECOME AN EFFECTIVE TRAINER

Productive workers are made when training is made to stick. A newly made productive worker then becomes an economical asset to the organization. Now, the worker can share the work load and be considered as an equal by other employees. A manager who develops productive workers is highly regarded by top management. But before jumping into the business of training, be sure that you understand the answers to this question: What is a productive worker?

A productive worker is one who creates value by producing goods and/or services. You will likely have opinions and standards as to what values of production are expected for each job. Your opinions and standards should be the same as those set forth by the organization you serve.

Three Areas Essential to Complete Training

1. Train For Knowledge

Putting forth knowledge is the easiest form of training. For instance, in a very short time, someone could teach you everything you would need to know about selling pots and pans door to door. You could quickly acquire the knowledge of what pots and pans are made of, how a non-stick coating permits cooking without oil and ease of cleaning, and how each pot and pan has its own particular use. You could learn these things, but you might not sell many pots and pans, even when your price was cheaper than the price at the stores. Something would be missing.

2. Train For Skill

Selling requires more than just knowledge. A person needs to learn particular skills of a trade. If a sales manager were to go with you during your first few outings, skills would be demonstrated. Your efforts would be observed and developed as you practiced making the opening approach, making the presentation, handling objections, and closing the sale. This area of training would take longer than the time spent acquiring essential knowledge. Even then you might not yet be productive as a pots and pans sales person. Something still could be missing.

3. Train for Attitude

What good are knowledge and skill if you don't like what you are doing? Certain people may not like working alone. Others may not like working in large groups. Some may not like working outside or inside an office, or being paid a straight commission, or paid for piece work, or paid only by the hour. There are people who think certain kinds of work are demeaning. As people think about their work, so shall they perform at their jobs.

It is difficult to change someone's attitude. In fact, it is impossible. You cannot change an employee's attitude. If a person's attitude is to change, it must be changed from within. This does not mean that training for attitude is non-existent. It merely means you cannot stuff attitude into an employee as you would stuff dressing into a turkey before you roast it.

There are three things you can do:

– You can show the overall importance of an employee's work.

– You can provide attitude learning experiences, pride of accomplishments, enjoyment of working on a winning team, and recognition.

– You can control behavior as long as the employee wishes to remain with the organization.

Only in time, through the influences of leadership skills, can changes be brought about in an employee's attitude. There will generally be no sudden, outward change, no admissions of previous wrong-doings, and no apology. The only detectable sign – and the only one you should be concerned with – will be improved performance. You will now have your productive worker.

While most of your people will have healthy attitudes toward their jobs, the development of desirable work related attitudes is a continual process. The need for special attitude training may arise at anytime during an employee's employment. Continually observe the work related behaviors of your employees. Have awareness of workers' attitudes that spawn damaging behaviors on the job, such as:

– A worker knows what to do, how to do it, and when a task should be completed. But, still, the job doesn't get done.

– A visitor asks a worker for directions to a certain office. The worker shrugs and says, "Don't ask me, I'm just the custodian here – you know, a janitor."

– A caller asks to speak to the manager. An employee answers with, "The boss isn't here." The caller asks when the boss will be available. "I don't know," comes the answer, "No one ever tells me anything."

There are no short-cuts to being a good trainer.

A trainer's first job is to introduce the job, the training materials, and the training process in such a manner that selected trainees will want to learn. Then, when students begin to participate, the training process becomes a learning process. Sounds easy enough. So easy, in fact, that most supervisors and managers believe they already know how to teach, and that they are good instructors.

To illustrate a point – that most managers only think they know how to teach – an attention-getting demonstration was employed during a workshop for bosses.

The ten supervisors at the workshop counted off in pairs. Those with number one would be trainers. Those with number two would be new employees – trainees.

In a manner so that the trainees could not see, the workshop leader carefully gave each trainer a different screw. The appointed trainers were instructed to stand back to back with the students and tell everything there was to know about the object concealed in their hands. A trainer could describe the object and could even tell of its purpose and use, but the object could not be shown or referred to by name.

In less than a minute, each student held up a hand to signify that the object had been identified. The workshop leader collected the objects from the trainers, still being careful not to reveal their identities. The trainees were called to the head table where the objects were then placed in front of them.

"Listen, now," the leader said, "I want each of you to pick up the particular screw that was described to you."

The trainers grinned with embarrassment as their students moved awkwardly from one foot to the other while studying the ten screws on the table. No two were alike. Some were long, some were short. Some had flat heads, some had round heads. Some were stainless steel, some were bronze. Some were wood screws, some were metal screws. Hesitantly, one participant reached for a screw.

"Hold it," the workshop leader interrupted, "I want to know the exact screw that was described to you." The hand was withdrawn.

The workshop leader told of another demonstration – that is no longer used – where a manager was asked to teach the leader how to smoke. The training process turned into a humorous disaster as the leader tore the pack to pieces when told to tear off the top. The cigarette was stuffed into the mouth when the trainer said, "Put this in your mouth." The box of matches was opened upside down and the contents spilled on the floor. A shaken trainer finally held a lighted match to the cigarette hanging from the leader's mouth, there was no attempt to inhale. The volunteer trainer lost what little patience remained, "Inhale, damnit, inhale!"

These play-action demonstrations are easier to deal with than the real, on-the-job situations where unwanted problems occur because of improper training.

Consider the impatient heavy equipment foreman who is expediting an emergency repair. The foreman yells for a newly hired helper to go to the tool shed and check out a wrench and to do it in a hurry, on the double. The inexperienced worker, wanting to please the boss, runs the length of the repair yard, bursts through the door, and tells the tool shed foreman that the repair boss needs a wrench, right away. The tool boss smiles and says, "Sure, they're right over there." There are big ones, tiny ones, and all sizes in between; closed face, open face; a wrench of every design and for every purpose. Will the foreman be angry when the new helper returns empty-handed, or with the wrong wrench? Will the new employee be embarrassed? Will valuable time have been wasted? Would it have helped the new employee to have been told to bring back a four-inch pipe wrench?

In the classroom or on the job, project your thoughts and instructions carefully and thoroughly. Employ the simple training method as your guide.

A Simple Training Method

The simple training method is not new. It is as old as the wheel, and just as simple. As a matter of fact, it is a wheel.

The training wheel – this method of training – has four spokes, plus the orientation to give it a shove and get it rolling.

Orientation

Do not take orientation lightly. Give it thoughtful attention. Respect its power of influence. Attitude training begins here.

The orientation is a one-time push of the wheel that starts the training programme rolling along the right track. Sometimes this vital step is called by another name – a briefing, a familiarization, a pep talk – every language in the world will have a name for it. By any name, orientation precedes almost all new undertakings. Orientation is a process that defines the

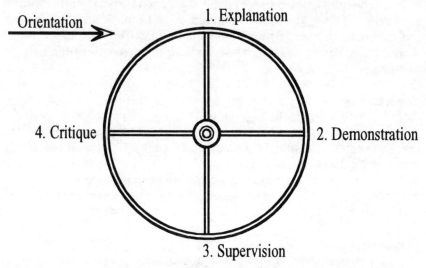

Orientation →

1. Explanation

4. Critique

2. Demonstration

3. Supervision

direction a course will take, and the explains the exceptions and adjustments that can be expected. A well thought out orientation can exert powerful influences on employees who are starting a new job. It is a time when leaders take command and followers become dedicated; when leaders begin preventing tomorrow's problems; and when employees begin forming positive attitudes.

The orientation is usually presented in two parts:

1. The presentation will embrace the entire purpose of an employee's labor, not just the end results. The employee will be told how the work will contribute to other people in the organization, and how the fruits of such labor will benefit the general public served by the organization. It may not seem like much of a job – emptying ash trays and trash baskets, sweeping and mopping floors, and cleaning toilets – until a talented manager spins some magic into the orientation.

The orientation may begin with a tour of the facilities; then meeting with the heads of each department, even with the top boss of the organization. In each case, the newly hired custodian is warmly greeted. The new custodian has been led to know the importance of the work and the true status of the role. The job will have been given a higher purpose. The custodian will now feel that when things are made sparkling bright, clean, and fresh, the efforts will be appreciated by employees, visitors, and customers. There is a feeling that people not only appreciate the work, but also depend upon the custodian to continue the work. Certainly not a janitor, the custodian might even be considered as a sanitation engineer. Orientation can and should be such an inspiration.

2. The orientation will also cover the various aspects of the tasks to be learned. This will include the introduction to machinery, equipment, and materials, followed by the observation of how the work is performed by other employees. This is where the four main spokes of the training wheel come into play.

Explanation

An explanation is the beginning of the teaching process. If the job is a simple one, like running a copy machine or nailing boards together, the entire job can be explained at one time. If the job is complicated, it will probably be necessary to break it down into step by step operations or tasks. Everything must be explained; nothing can be assumed. For each operation, treated as a separate subject, continue to explain the steps until both you and the trainee are satisfied that all is understood.

Demonstration

A demonstration is sometimes conducted simultaneously with an explanation. This is time saving, but it tends to divide the trainee's interest. If there is a particular fascination for what the instructor is doing, the student may fail to listen to the explanation of how and why something works. Demonstration should be a step of its own. Talking should be restricted only to the action that is being performed by the trainer.

Supervision

The greatest amount of learning comes by doing. Some instructors don't like to have trainees touch their precious equipment and machinery. But doing is an important link between knowledge and skill. Supervision forges that link. Supervision is the role of a trainer while the student performs the operation that has been well explained and demonstrated.

Mistakes, more than anything else, will reinforce the learning. It is difficult to forget a mistake. Expect mistakes to happen. Let them. The exception, of course, would be when a mistake could cause personal bodily harm, or break or destroy expensive property. When it is nothing more than jamming a copy machine, or bouncing an airplane on a bad landing, no real harm is done, and the lesson is well worth it.

Critique

The critique is the time of debriefing. Now the instructor praises the student's first-time efforts and accomplishments, and points out the few small errors. The critique should be offered not so much as criticism, but more toward constructive improvement and confidence building.

Teaching a worker to perform new tasks is much like teaching a child to eat new foods.

– Make the foods-for-thought appetizing and interesting.
– Offer small, bite-size potions.
– Repeat the servings over and over again until the taste is acquired.
– Then leave the person alone to feed until the habit is formed.

And, like a child eating, the learning process can be messy in the beginning. Like a parent, the trainer must show considerable patience while teaching the process, and while drilling good habits and proper manners into each part.

Keep in mind that people differ in levels of intelligence, education, experience, and anxiety. These will have an affect on the rate of learning. However, unless there are extremely serious physical or mental health problems, everyone can learn most things eventually.

Don't be fooled by a ready smile and a quick nod. These manifestations do not necessarily mean that the trainee understands. Also, do not be dismayed if a trainee appears bored or disinterested. Perhaps the student does know all about what you are explaining. Maybe this person likes to act as if learning is no big deal.

Ask questions periodically. Don't just ask, "Do you understand?" Ask for specific responses, or ask to be shown. Be prepared to adjust your teaching to the levels of understanding and the attitudes of your students. Get feedback.

Remember that manual proficiency, alone, is not enough. A worker must understand not only what is happening, but the how and why as well. It is one thing to be capable of driving a truck, yet another to understand that a truck requires fuel in the tank, water in the radiator, oil in the crankcase, grease on the moving parts, air in the tires, distilled water in the battery, and routine maintenance. Without these, the truck won't work, nor will the driver.

When more than one student is being taught at the same time, the general practice is to keep the teaching speed down to the learning speed of the slowest student. However, when a slower pace makes the majority of students restless, it would be wise to hold the slower member aside and provide special instruction, later. This is extra work, but an instructor's job is to get people prepared for their jobs, however long it takes.

Once you have gone through the first turn of the training wheel, you will know your student better. As it is not expected that a trainee will understand and master everything the first time, roll the wheel around again. Do not eliminate any of the steps. The second time, while you are giving the explanations, give special emphasis to the weaknesses of the trainee's first performance. Supervise the second effort. During the second critique, again praise the successes and point out the errors. Turn the wheel again. Continue to direct your explanations and demonstrations toward the student's few remaining omissions and mistakes. As long as a trainee remains less that perfect in the understanding and execution of the lesson, repeat the entire process as many times as necessary.

Each time you take a student through the four training steps, the wheel will turn faster. Things won't take as long to explain; the demonstrations will be done more quickly; the trainee will perform the tasks more smoothly and with greater confidence; and the critiques will be shorter. When a student finally does a sequence perfectly, you might say something like, "Good! Now, one more time,"

When a newly trained employee is turned loose on the job, observe the work closely for the first few days. It is not unusual for a newly trained worker to suffer a memory lapse under the stress of trying to keep pace with other workers. Too, some unforeseen occurrence might require the help of an experienced person, before a situation becomes serious.

It takes time to lead a few good employees through a training programme, but the time you spend is a good investment. By reducing employees' mistakes and improving their pride and productivity, you will save far more time than you invested.

Blessed are those who can teach teachers to teach.

9
HOW TO BUILD A TEAM OF TRAINERS

Although training is one of your eight managerial functions, you cannot spend all your time as a trainer. To increase the number of productive workers rapidly, you must work with and through people.

Well-trained trainers from within the work force may be ideally suited to give other employees the best on-the-job knowledge and skills. Furthermore, a worker is generally more at ease when learning from a fellow employee, rather than from a boss.

It is reasonable to expect that, at some time, most managers will ask experienced workers to help with the training of inexperienced employees. Managers can rightfully delegate this responsibility of producing productive workers, but they cannot delegate the accountability that goes with it. Whatever the outcome, the manager will be accountable for the results of training.

Perhaps you have heard an appointed trainer say, "I don't know why that guy fouls up all the time. I taught him everything I know." Such a remark is a *red flag*. Perhaps the manager hasn't done an adequate job of developing a trainer.

Building a team of trainers starts with the answers to a couple of questions: (1) How should a trainer be selected? (2) How should a trainer be trained?

The Selection of a Trainer

As you begin recruiting for someone to assist in the training of other employees, consider these qualifications:

Attitude

Think over what values of conduct and production are expected for each job. Whoever you select to assist you with training chores must share these same values with the same intensity. In other words, to meet your training objectives, an appointed trainer must treat such values – urgency for completion, attention to details and quality, consideration of economy and safety, personal relationships with other employees and/or customers – with a sense of importance equal to yours.

Once appointed, a trainer may develop an unacceptable attitude, not easily observed. For instance, because of work pressures, or so as to look good by completing the worker's training quickly, a trainer may talk an employee into signing off one or more of the subjects on the training outline by taking a shortcut. "You should know these things," a trainer may explain. "If you have any questions, come see me."

A trainer must get along smoothly with co-workers, employees in supportive positions, and all supervisors and managers with whom there is contact.

Knowledge

A trainer must know the work involved, the work flow, the interactions between departments and their employees, and the ultimate objectives of the organization.

When you consider employees who supposedly have had long-time experience, be certain that *experience* includes recent knowledge. Some *old timers* remember and practice old procedures, but not new ones.

Skill

A trainer should have better than average job skills. Good skills, when properly demonstrated, will give an inexperienced worker a skill level to shoot for. A typist who is teaching the format of report writing will be setting a standard by clicking off 80 words a minute or more. Pecking out a report at 50-55 words per minute will only teach a new office employee how to make a manager froth at the mouth when a special report is urgently needed.

Charisma

A trainer must be a leader, one who has followers. A charismatic personality gives a substantial edge to the trainer who already has attitude, knowledge, and skill.

Humor

A trainer should take the work seriously, but not himself. During training, mistakes are common. A little tolerance, spiced with humor, will do wonders to ease the tensions of student and trainer alike.

Patience

Much learning is done through repetition. A trainer may need to repeat instructions several times; and it is essential that the trainer remains calm throughout each performance, and covers pertinent material as slowly and as carefully as was originally presented. This is no job for the impatient or the hot-headed.

Take your time while considering the candidates. The person you select as a trainer will be representing you and your organization. The right person will help you develop a crew of productive workers while freeing you to concentrate on other functions of management.

The Training of a Trainer

Once the right person has been selected to assist in one or more phases of training, you need only to teach the steps that you learned while becoming an effective trainer.

1. Review the training resources your trainee trainer will need: reference aids and training aids.

2. Introduce your appointed trainer to the particular job outline/ record form to be followed.

3. Drill the trainer in the workings of the simple training method:
   – Orientation
   – Explanation
   – Demonstration - Supervision
   – Critique

Remember, your task will be to develop a trainer having knowledge, skills, and attitudes equal to yours, as they apply to this particular job.

How to Reward Your Trainers

Training is a part of your job. Not quite so for your employees who, aside from training others, have their own jobs to fulfill. How, then, shall they be rewarded? Or should they be?

Many workers are paid a set salary or hourly wage, without being tied directly to levels of production. Their pay will most likely increase in relationship to acquired job knowledge, job skills, job performance, and years of employment. It is not necessary to give extra pay to these people for helping other employees to learn their jobs.

Employees whose pay is based on personal production do not earn money while they are serving as trainers. They should be compensated for lost income. How much these commissioned or piece-rate workers should be paid must be approved by top management. You, as a manager, may wish to forward your idea as to how your part-time trainers should be rewarded. Consider these factors:

– The number of students assigned to a trainer.

– The amount of time spent as a trainer.

– The complexities and difficulties of the job for which the trainee is being trained.

– The trainers' average hourly earnings, as computed by dividing past monthly earnings, through personal production, by the number of hours worked.

In general, trainers, whose pay is based on production, should receive no less than what is equivalent to hourly pay rates, and their pay should also reflect the number of students they teach and the degrees of knowledge and skills required. Some organizations, after taking all factors into consideration, pay a flat bonus to their instructors for each worker proven to be trained effectively.

Not to be overlooked or discounted, an appointed trainer will receive what is commonly referred to as psychic income. These intangible rewards may include the worker's pride of status – increased recognition, attention, respect; the feeling of importance, power and responsibility. To many trainers, feelings are worth as much as, or even more than, money.

An employee who instructs will generally recognize that the door to advancement has opened a bit, and that a better job will mean more money.

Additional recognition and show of appreciation by the organization will further enhance an instructor's sense of pride. Here are ways this can be accomplished:

1. At an assembly of employees, someone from top management can introduce the instructors and expresses appreciation for their services.

2. Certificates can be easily designed and inexpensively printed. The certificate can serve as a *license* to teach specified subjects, or it can be given as a certificate of merit. A reputable printer can offer suggestions as to paper stock, layout and design, and may show you certificates printed for other organizations. Based upon your selection, the cost can be accurately estimated.

3. A trainer's badge can be simple and inexpensive, or it can be jewelry of quality and very expensive.

4. Distinctive shirts are sometimes given to line instructors. Issuing two shirts allows for one to be washed and one to be worn. Find out how

much it would cost for a tailor or seamstress to embroider the word *Instructor* or *Trainer* over the left shirt pocket. T-shirts are a good choice for working conditions where it is quite warm. Check the cost of having silk screen printing done on the shirts.

5. Where employees are in uniform, some organizations buy shirt sleeve patches for their trainers. A local uniform supply company may be able to provide these at a small cost.

What else can you think of that will improve the image and pride of the trainers you have selected and trained? Use your imagination. Be creative. The benefits you get back from identifying and honoring your instructors will be far greater than the small cost and time involved.

When workers have questions about work they are doing, and you are not around, your appointed trainer will be there. The workers will get correct answers immediately, and you will be spared the problem.

When you are not on the scene, some workers may not feel like working. But they will know better than to goof-off because the trainer who trained them to produce will be watching them.

A stone of multi-facets is a gem.

10
HOW TO USE CROSS TRAINING EFFECTIVELY

Except for the few managers in businesses of high employee turn-over, most managers are not likely to hire employees frequently. Thus, they may rarely need to train new workers. It is more probable that there will be an immediate need for a programme designed to cross train those who are already employed.

Four reasons for cross training.
Cross training means teaching employees to do jobs other than their own. Here are four reasons why employees should be cross trained:
1. Many employees feel that they are getting stale at the same old grind, doing the same thing over and over again. Then, there are some employees who prefer the secure, familiar routine of their never-changing jobs. Both kinds of employees need some form of stimulation to keep them alert and productive. Cross training offers this stimulation.
2. For many managers, a worker's sudden absence is a time for frustration and stress. Such managers might be at a loss as to how to staff the temporarily vacated job that only the absent worker can perform. These managers may see only two alternatives: Expedite – jump in and do the job themselves, which will keep the manager from doing his own work. Or they can allow the work to pile up, offering some kind of a story to their bosses as to why the work isn't getting done. Cross training provides a better solution.
3. When top managers are looking for promotable people, they will ask, "What can these workers do?"
The same is true when managers are being considered for promotion, but with one difference. The question will be asked, "Which manager can

develop people?'' The evidence of cross training, as it appears on the training records, will answer both questions.

4. An employee who is the only one who can do a critical type of work, and knows it, may, at a most crucial time, make demands upon the manager. The demands may be for additional money or for special privileges. For such cases of potential threats, cross training offers a solution.

A Cross Training Programme in Five Easy Steps

Cross training – teaching employees to perform other jobs – must start somewhere and then follow a plan. The starting points and plans must be worked out by individual managers to suit particular situations.

There are, however, some basic steps to follow.

1. Select one job for which you most want to have another person trained. Begin by examining the training outline for each job within your work group. These outlines will remind you of what people do. Concentrate first on jobs that require specialized knowledge or skills. These are the most difficult jobs to fill in an emergency and are where you will want substitutes ready to step in. The worker in the job you choose for cross training will most likely be the instructor.

2. Choose an employee who has the aptitude and interest for learning new knowledge and skills in the line of work that the job represents. This means that a person who is experienced in some form of simple bookkeeping will be a better choice to learn the payroll clerk's job than someone who is qualified only for typing and filing. An electrician would not be a wise choice to train as a repairman of vehicle transmissions. Employees should advance gradually through jobs of increasing difficulty. They should not leap from jobs they know something about to kinds of work where they know nothing.

Although most employees prefer to learn and advance within kinds of work with which they have some liking and familiarity, there are exceptions. Occasionally you will find a person who has an insatiable interest in new knowledge and experiences. This may be a person who also learns and masters new challenges quickly. Should such a person seek a totally new and different job classification, it might be wise to give the employee a chance. If not given the opportunity to try new experiences while trying to find an interesting and fulfilling career field, a bright, ambitious employee may seek opportunities elsewhere.

3. Inform all employees of what you are doing. So as not to jump to false conclusions, employees need to be assured that nobody's job is being threatened and that cross training is beneficial to the smooth operation of the work unit. Let them know that others will also have the opportunity to

be cross trained, so as to experience a relief from boredom and greater work satisfaction. The employees need to know that their support and help will be needed while one member of the group is being called away from regular duties for a short time.

4. If you choose to have a regular worker do the training, be certain that this person knows how to use the training outline/record and how to follow the four simple steps of training. Brief the trainer as to who and when various job functions are to be presented. These will generally fall into a natural order as job functions occur throughout each working day, week, or month. Think about interruptions that might arise during the training sessions. As much as possible, both the trainee and the trainer must be spared from bothersome telephone calls, visitors, and small routine tasks. This is where other employees will be asked to help out. As the manager, you can help the instructor set priorities so as to attain the right balance between essential, on-going work duties and the desirable teaching objectives. The routine work of your organization must get done.

5. Supervise the training programme as it progresses. Ask the trainer about schedules and time arrangements. Ask for opinions as to the quality and quantity of the training thus far. Ask if there are any problems with personal communications, work pressures, or the cooperation of other workers. Ask the student, alone, these same questions. Check the training record frequently. Check to see that normal work duties and responsibilities of the trainer and trainee are being carried out.

Let On-the-Job Training Occur Naturally

As your cross training programme continues, and workers begin to learn different jobs, you will likely be aware of the smoothness by which trainers, trainees, and other employees pull together and support one another. You might hear such comments as, "At the end of the week, I'm going to do the inventory. Get as much of your work done as possible before Thursday, and try to get someone to cover for you on Friday, so you can learn how to do this." Or, "Put that exhaust and silencer down and come over here. This job just came in, so now I can show you how to do a wheel alignment."

It will become obvious that some jobs involve several staggered and strung out processes. These, too, are best taught as they occur. Here is an example of instructions given in sequence:

"Do you have a moment? I'm going to write a voucher
for a purchase out of petty cash. I'd like for you to watch."

A few days later: "When you are finished with what you
are doing, come to my desk and I'll teach you to reconcile
petty cash."

A few days later: "Let me know when you have time for me to show you how to prepare a request for petty cash. I should turn it in tomorrow afternoon. See, it's always marked right here on the calendar."

Then, the next week: "The office manager needs some office supplies to be paid for from petty cash. Why don't you write the voucher this time. I'll watch."

There is a saying, "Necessity is the mother of invention." This goes for training programmes too. Some managers begin cross training their employees without an outlined plan. They simply start when the need arises.

On a small island in the South Pacific, the working supervisor of a maintenance crew at the marine repair dock was driven to a plan of cross training by frustration and anger. This supervisor was the only trained heavy equipment mechanic available. He had to do the most difficult repair jobs, and, in his opinion, all the jobs were too difficult for his men. From time to time, he wondered how he would ever get the other workers to help with the more technical repair work.

One day, while the supervisor was making a critical repair lying on his back beneath a piece of heavy equipment, he saw a half dozen pairs of bare feet walking past where he was working. They belonged to his so-called mechanics who were taking an unauthorized break from work. The boss mechanic was angry and decided to do something about it.

The next time he went out on a difficult job, he took one of his mechanics with him. The supervisor went through the four training steps until the novice mechanic could do that one job. The next day, the young boss took another crew member. After a few months, each mechanic had learned one or more mechanical skills. The boss had more time to watch over their work and add a little more to their knowledge. After a few more months had passed, the supervisor noticed that the mechanics were bragging to each other about what they knew and could do, and they began to help one another.

What to Do When Cross Training Hits a Snag

Some workers may resist your attempts to cross train them into other types of work. There are several possible reasons:

– They may feel comfortable with their own routine and don't want interruptions.

– They may feel *professional* at what they do. Any other job would make them feel less so.

– Having to learn a different job may bring about mistakes and embarrassment.

– Certain workers simply may not want to cooperate with you.

It is equally possible that some workers may resist your efforts to have them train other employees for their jobs.

– They may believe that they are too busy and that the job is too important to spend time showing someone else how things are done.

– They may feel that their job is threatened by having someone else know how to do it.

– They may think that no one else is smart enough to do what they do.

– They may have an attitude that, "Why should I train someone? No one ever trained me."

– And, again, some workers may not want to cooperate with you.

Should you have an employee who is posing some sort of hindrance to your cross training programme, ask yourself these questions:

– Why won't this person participate in the cross training? Perhaps the reason given is not the real reason. What, then, is the true reason?

– How can this person best be reached: through direct confrontation on a take it or leave it basis; more and more explanation and reason; more time for the person to observe the actions of other workers and to see the results; or indirect methods?

– How important is this person to the organization?

Keep in mind that any snag in a plan of cross training instigated by the organization must be gone around, gone over, pushed aside, or removed. As a boss, there are many ways and means for you to accomplish your purpose. These may require talented applications of patience, diplomacy, accounting, and communication; but nothing more than one would expect from a leader.

Here are some ideas to think about when presented with a difficult team member:

1. Consider a one-on-one private conference in your office. Some people just want an opportunity to express their views. Some just like the special attention.

2. If you are dealing with a person who doesn't want to train another employee, find someone else to provide the training.

3. When the difficult person is absent – on sick leave or on vacation – use this time and the worker's job to cross train another employee.

4. You may be fortunate enough to have a key employee who is well

respected by all other workers and may be sufficiently influential in getting your obstinate worker to go along with the group effort.

5. Perhaps you can get the support of higher management in the form of a written directive saying that cross training will take place throughout your department within a given span of time.

6. If you feel the worker's resistance is seriously detrimental to the effectiveness of the unit, write an incident report. Write other incident reports if warranted.

7. Use the performance review as another occasion to communicate with the uncooperative, as well as with higher management.

8. You might have an employee whom you would just as soon get rid of. Don't use this person to train others. Find someone else who knows the work to do the training. Training may have to be done after regular working hours.

Whatever the snag, deal with it. Be inventive. Effective cross training of your people will do wonders for your personal effectiveness and the effectiveness of your work unit.

Has Anyone Been Cross Trained for Your Job?

Some supervisors and managers like to think that their jobs are exempt from cross training. Such thinking is erroneous, for there are many benefits to be derived from teaching employees to perform at least some of your job duties.

To begin with, a truly successful manager is one whose absence can be covered by a well-qualified subordinate. Top management knows that a manager who can delegate some work to other employees, and still get the desired results, is ready for promotion. The organization seeks managers who can develop people. The managers who rush around doing most of the work themselves and coping with preventable problems, or problems that should easily be dealt with by others, do not impress the executives. Such managers are considered to be loyal and hard working, but hardly promotable.

When you have motivated and trained employees properly, you can develop extra hands to do parts of your work, extra feet to run your errands, extra ears and eyes to learn what is going on, and other minds to understand your objectives and problems, think, reason, and render sound second opinions. You will be more free to attend to other business matters, to work on high-image projects, to counsel employees, or to acquire new knowledge and skills for your own personal development.

When you have personally developed one or more employees to provide support, you can be called away from the work group knowing that a delegated person can be left in charge. When key employees are invited to participate in some of your management activities, morale and motivation improve. These people form a fuller understanding and a better attitude about what you do and why. These selected employees feel freer to make suggestions, because they know you respect them and you listen.

It is harder for executives to get into the cross training mode than it is for line managers and supervisors. For one reason, executives are generally caught up in heavy responsibilities and results-oriented pressures. Such a boss is likely to feel that anyone who enters the executive hierarchy had better come prepared with adequate credentials, knowledge, and experience. Another possible reason is that executives have secretaries. Secretaries are closer to the executive's work than any other person. Secretaries frequently execute the executives orders and wishes. One executive said that the only difference between an executive and a secretary is that a secretary doesn't get to make the big decisions and doesn't earn as much money.

How to Spread the Managerial Load

1. If you have not already done so, write a training outline for *your* job. Think about the eight functions you perform, then list all the detailed tasks and projects that are involved.

2. Find the right people to be developed by you. Start with the employees you trained to be trainers. Review the considerations for their selection. It may be advantageous to select more than one person for management training. But watch out for petty politics and jealousies. If you cannot select a capable person, don't bother to go on at this time. Do not try to develop a person who does not have the essential qualifications. You will only damage that person's career, as well as your own.

3. Do not give titles, such as *assistant manager*. You have no authority to create such a job slot and this could lead to sticky morale problems. The exception is when a qualified person has been selected to be prepared for promotion, as approved by top management.

4. Be sure that your trainee has slack or discretionary time before calling him away from regular duties. If you are teaching more than one employee, call them in one at a time. Give individual attention.

5. As you share one of your duties with a trainee, present a sound orientation, followed by the four simple steps of the training wheel. Check the work carefully. When you are satisfied that a task can be performed to your standard, record, date, and initial it in the training outline.

6. Continue to move your trainee though the training outline, not simply by taking items in order, but rather by taking the simplest tasks

first, then progressing to work that requires more knowledge and initiative.

7. Don't keep a trainee too long at a time. The employee's job must remain the highest priority. A worker who feels personal job pressures mounting while spending time in your office may be reluctant to spend more time learning to do parts of your work.

One or more employees who can help occasionally to reduce some of your work load and represent you well when you are away will prove to be a most important asset. It is essential, however, to bear in mind that, while you can delegate responsibilities, you cannot delegate accountability.

Workers are different; jobs are different.
As soon as we come to know them, they change.

11
HOW TO BUILD JOBS THAT BUILD PEOPLE

Some managers frequently become discouraged with the seemingly endless task of finding and correcting employees' mistakes. "How," some managers may wonder, "can workers fail at the simplest assignments?" It is likely that these managers simply are unaware of exactly what workers do.

A manager's first task is to learn what the jobs really consist of and then find out what the workers do. The needed correction should then become obvious. Managers fortunately have three methods by which to diagnose and prescribe:

> Job Descriptions
> Job Analyses
> Job Outlines.

The Purpose of a Job Description

Applicants are introduced to new jobs through job descriptions. They are the basis for writing job training outlines. When performance reviews are scheduled, the job descriptions provide standards against which employee performance is measured. In these ways, job descriptions are of help to the employees as well as to the managers.

Job descriptions help employees to understand their jobs. They might be more familiar with their job descriptions than are the managers. It is essential that a manager be thoroughly versed in the wording and meaning of workers' job descriptions so as to prevent such misunderstandings as: "I don't have to do that. It's not on my job description."

Be certain that job descriptions cannot be misunderstood. Read them carefully. Ask workers just how they interpret the wording of various job descriptions. It is general practice for every job description to conclude with a statement similar to:

> The job incumbent will be required to perform any additional duties as requested or ordered by the immediate supervisor.

During an applicant's interview and during a new employee's orientation, this final statement of duties should be stressed by every manager, and the worker must acknowledge acceptance of the statement. From time to time, some employees may need to be reminded, so as to head off misunderstandings.

Job Analyses Solve Many Mysteries

It is often difficult for managers to watch employees and know whether or not they are working. Some employees can appear to be working when, in fact, they are not. Some people can look busy while tossing straw up in the air, or leaning up against a building.

The manager's measuring stick is the production record. When the work is not getting done, even when a worker appears busy, the manager is going to ask, "Why?" Is the employee incapable or just working below capability? When productivity lags, some managers ask permission to hire more workers.

Before adding to the labor cost, a manager should thoroughly understand the work load and demands of each job, also the duties, responsibilities, and capabilities of each employee. If the truth were known, it might not be necessary to hire more help. To find the truth, a job analysis is often used to probe behind work appearances.

There are four ways by which a manager can analyze a job.

Do the job yourself.

An office worker was not compiling essential reports required by the home office before the noon deadline. The office manager was being criticized by superiors. What was the problem? Was the job too difficult for one person? Was the worker insufficiently trained for the task?

The office manager decided to expedite – to jump in and do the job personally. The employee was given the day off with pay. The office manager had not performed this routine in a long time, yet the work was completed by eleven o'clock. The manager now knew that the task was a reasonable one. One question remained: Could the clerk do the job?

The next morning, the office manager went through the entire process with the employee. The report was ready by ten-thirty. For the next few days, the office worker finished the compilation before the critical noon deadline. Extra training, it seemed, had been the answer to the problem. But it wasn't. The employee returned to old habits of making excuses for unforgivable delays. A replacement quickly and enthusiastically learned to put out the work, and always before ten o'clock.

The office manager had successfully analyzed the job and found it blameless. The problem was through no fault or lack of training. The employee, it was found, had been beyond help.

Let someone else do the job.

More than a few managers have had little or no practical, hands-on experience in the various jobs they supervise. It would be impractical to insist that all managers prove mastery of each job skill. But a manager can analyze a job by comparing the performances of workers who do similar work. If each of four workers can change a tire in a given period of time, but a fifth worker takes twice the time, the manager, who may have never in his lifetime changed a tire, can rightly suspect that the problem is with the employee, not the job.

Occasionally, in some organizations, regular workers will agree amongst themselves to set a work pace slower than normal. A manager who is suspicious of such conduct may arrange for one worker to be absent for a day and then bring in a trusted, experienced worker to do the work and help analyze the problem. At the end of the shift, the trusted substitute may report, "That job is really tough. I'm glad I don't have to do it all the time." This is a warning to the manager that the job may be a *people eater*. The manager will likely ask the substitute to explain each function and task using the job outline as a basis for discussion. The experienced worker will be asked to identify critical problems, point out possible causes, and offer recommendations for a workable solution.

Production slow-downs may be through no fault of the regular workers. The work area may lack proper lighting or ventilation, or may be improperly arranged for efficient work flow. There may be a shortage of needed tools or materials. An experienced substitute worker might be aware of what a manager, and even regular employees, cannot see.

On the other hand, a substitute worker may report, "The work was really easy. I hardly had a thing to do." This may be just what the manager suspected. On a job that is too easy, a worker becomes bored and unmotivated. Also, when one worker has little to do, it is unfair to the employees who do more. Drawing from the analysis given by a substitute worker, a manager can distribute work more fairly.

It is important that you know your substitute workers well. Some employees may tell you the difficulties of jobs so as to impress you with how hard they work. Other employees may show off with a short-time burst of productivity causing the job to appear easy.

Learn from the job's history.

A service dispatcher handled all customer calls – those for new services and those for service problems. Service personnel were instructed to call the dispatcher throughout the day. The dispatcher also processed all service production daily reports. The office manager was worried because the work wasn't getting done. Too many customers were not being responded to quickly enough. Paperwork was lagging. There were other problems. The dispatcher was arriving to work early and leaving late, amounting to unauthorized overtime. Furthermore, the dispatcher was not taking break periods. Lunch was being taken at the dispatcher's desk.

Although the office manager was impressed with the dispatcher's knowledge, skill, and attitude, it was thought, perhaps, that once again someone else should be hired to fill this critical position. The manager had also been impressed with the three previous dispatchers. Two had been fired, the other one had quit.

The manager began thinking of the job's history. Ten years ago the department had ten service people. Now there were thirty. Today there were three times more telephone calls from service workers and three times more calls from customers. There were three times more outgoing calls. There was now three times more paperwork to process. The job description had never changed, but the job had obviously grown far beyond the capabilities of one dispatcher.

The manager analyzed all jobs throughout the office. Some tasks were reassigned, new job descriptions were written, and new training programmes were put into practice. One new office employee was hired. The dispatcher's job became workable within lunch hours, and no longer needed the overtime to complete the work of dispatching service personnel.

Make a time and task study.

When analyzing a job, a manager must sometimes learn how much time an employee spends at each task. This is particularly true of jobs that have been recently reorganized or newly created.

Imagine that the manufacturing company where you work has given you a new job with the title of Wind Generator Assembler, your own shop, new equipment, two weeks of intensive training, and . . . oh, yes, a raise in pay. Imagine further that after a month on your own, you cannot keep up with production demands. You may be discouraged, and rightly so. You may be wanting to hire a worker to help you assemble wind generators. Your boss decides that the first step is to make a time and task analysis.

To begin a time and task study, you and your manager would sit down together and record everything you do during a work day. This would give you an opportunity to explain how the telephone rings all the time with calls from people asking questions about the wind generator. The same is true with visitors – distributors, sales people, people from the advertising department, and a bunch of curious employees from throughout the company. Then there are all the meetings you must attend, records to be kept, and reports to be written. You would explain that it takes time just to set up the machinery for assembly, to say nothing of the time it takes to operate the equipment. You would welcome this opportunity to impress the boss with how hard you are working.

After determining which tasks are included in your job function, you and the boss would make out a time and task work sheet (figure 10-1) and agree on the following guidelines:

1. Record your times once every hour. Don't record the times while doing tasks as this is a waste of time.

2. If you have difficulty remembering what you have done during a period of one hour, you can rewrite the form with half-hour intervals. This is the maximum number of entries that should be made. If you can remember what you have done over a two hour interval, you can write the form with two-hour periods. For accuracy, this is the minimum number of entries permitted.

3. Account for time to the closest five minutes. For instance, if you spend 27 minutes at a meeting, record 30 minutes.

4. Average the time spent on tasks. If you receive five telephone calls, you may estimate that they averaged out at three minutes each. Put down 15 minutes total.

5. At the end of each day, total the columns. Add the column totals to arrive at a total for the day. Don't expect the day's total to equal eight hours. Some of your estimates will be inaccurate and there may be some breaks and interruptions that are unaccountable. Just be as accurate as you can.

6. At the end of the week, total all the daily totals for a one week summary. Discuss these records with the manager.

At your regular Monday morning meeting, you and your boss talk of how the different functions absorbed your time during the past week. Just as you said, your worksheet shows that too little time was spent on actual production work; too much time was spent talking with visitors, entertain-

Figure 10-1 – A sample Time and Task Worksheet.

TIME AND TASK JOB ANALYSIS

JOB: Wind Generator Assembler   DAY/DATE: _____

Time	Phone	Visitors	Meetings	Records	Reports	Production	Remarks
7-8							
8-9							
9-10							
10-11							
11-12							
12-1							
1-2							
2-3							
3-4							
Totals							

Day's Total: _____   Employee Signature: _____

ing visitors, and going to meetings. Your manager thinks that people will soon begin to leave you alone once they have learned what they need to know. The curious will have been satisfied. More time will be available for the production of wind generators. It is agreed that the time and task analysis should continue for another three weeks.

At the end of three more weeks, it becomes apparent that production has, indeed, increased. The manager has noted that demand for wind generators is on the rise. Armed with his analysis, the manager approaches the organization's decision makers and receives approval to hire a person to work in your office to take care of telephone calls, respond to the growing pile of correspondence, and maintain all the records and reports. You concentrate on the production of wind generators, knowing that high level approval has also been given for hiring and training another assembly specialist.

The disciplined use of a time and task studies can be an extremely useful tool in determining the facts of a job at the moment and in helping to prescribe cures for apparent problems, resulting in improved performance and better employee morale. It is essential, however, for a manager to pay close attention to the entries on the daily worksheets. A worker may not want to admit to the excessive time spent talking on the telephone and chatting with visitors. A worker may skimp on the actual time spent at these two tasks and pad the time spent on production. An observant manager will know what is happening. If the employee is spending so much time at work, where are the results?

Conversely, a worker may attempt to cover up low production by blaming the interruptions of telephone calls, visitors, and meetings. In this instance, the truth will be tougher to uncover. A supervisor or manager will need to ask for specifics regarding the interruptions. Who? When? Where? How many? Why? There should be some evidence to back up an employee's explanation.

Distribute work fairly.
The fair distribution of work is one of the purposes of doing job analyses.

There are a few employees who will argue against this purpose. Some workers who have little to do will not want more work. They are likely to enjoy doing as little as possible. Nevertheless, what is fair for most should be accepted as being fair for all.

Then, there are some managers who will reason that there are employees who cannot do as much as others. So they load up the motivated, productive workers by taking work away from those employees whose work performance is marginal or less. The reasoning is not entirely without merit, but there are other considerations. What will happen, for instance, if the overloaded, high producer becomes sick, goes on vacation, or is promoted? Who will or can fill the job? How do hard working, high performance workers feel about those who have easier jobs? Do they feel that they are being used? Do they suspect favoritism? What about performance reviews?

One employee puts out 100 units of work per day. Another worker can produce only 50 units, which is all that is expected. Does the 50 unit worker deserve the same mark of excellence as the 100 unit-a-day worker?

The commonly accepted management practice, then, is to distribute work fairly. When eager producers finish their work quickly, use them to help slower workers. Use them on challenging, satisfying tasks or projects. Use them to train other employees. Recognize and reward their excellence.

Job Outlines Build Strong Work Habits

The one unwritten, unspoken function of a manager is to make employees successful using every means possible. No matter how carefully new employees are selected and trained, they are, for a time, far from being successful. New employees fail, not for lack of knowledge or skills, but because their work habits are not yet fully developed. As you have found, habits can be learned. Workers, like managers, need their own special systems of personal organization. Job outlines satisfy this need.

The recently promoted supervisor of a rapidly expanding service department had hired three new employees. The supervisor had been impressed with their quickness to acquire technical knowledge and skills. Furthermore, they had initially shown considerable enthusiasm for the work. But after two weeks of working on their own routes, the three service workers had proven to be disappointments to the supervisor.

The supervisor told his manager of the pending termination of the three employees and the reasons. Although technically qualified and exceptionally skilled, the workers made a variety of mistakes, costly in time and money. The supervisor explained how the new service employees repeatedly forgot to stock up with the tools and materials needed for the day's jobs and how they would make extra trips just to get what was needed. Sometimes the three workers forgot to put petrol in their trucks before leaving the car park. The service employees frequently forgot to pick up their work assignments from the office. At the end of the day, they forgot to lock the trucks, their tool boxes were left open, and they seldom remembered to turn in their daily production reports. The supervisor was tired of yelling, pleading, scolding and threatening these three.

The manager told the supervisor to think of how the employees were feeling. Every afternoon they went home after being scolded and criticized. How would this affect a worker's family members? In what mood would an employee return to work the next morning? The manager reasoned that turning intelligent, talented, yet forgetful, employees into efficient, enthusiastic service workers would touch many lives.

This able manager suggested that a simple checklist of routine tasks might save the organization's substantial investment in this trio. Customers, too, would benefit. The manager told the supervisor to write out a job outline – a checklist. That same afternoon, the supervisor returned to the manager's office with three copies of the service job outline.

Service Job Outline

1. Check at the office, each morning, for work assignments.
2. Check out equipment, supplies, and materials needed for jobs.
3. Check vehicle – fuel, tires, tools, general condition.
4. Approximately 10 A.M. – call office for messages.
5. Noon hour - call office for messages.
6. Approximately 3 P.M. – call office for messages.
7. End of day – return all issued items.
8. Park vehicle properly; lock windows, doors, tool box.
9. Report any vehicle problems to repair shop.
10. Complete daily production report; turn in to office.
11. Check office for messages.
12. Report any service problems to supervisor.

The service workers did use their job outlines. They made no more mistakes. They were once again enthusiastic, as was the supervisor.

Should you find an occasion to develop a job outline for one or more of your employees, you might find it worthwhile to review these tips:

1. Don't confuse the job outline with the job description. They are different in both purpose and use. The job outline, or checklist, is to include every routine task that the employee must do in a day's work.

2. Don't give job outlines to all employees. Experienced, reliable workers might resent them. Give the job outlines only to those needing to develop sound work habits.

3. Don't yell or nag. It won't do any good. People who are unhappy at work will be unhappy when they go home. This is no way for employees to represent their organization. Let the forgetful workers know that you understand how difficult it is to keep track of the seemingly countless tasks and duties they must do. That is why you want to help with the use of a job checklist.

4. Tell your workers that they need not turn in the outlines when they finish work. It is *their* daily checklist to make their work easier. Point out that you, yourself, use systems to remember tasks to be done. Through the disciplined use of checklists, pilots, too, save themselves from the embarrassment of crashing airplanes. If a forgetful worker fails to use the job outline and continues to make mistakes, you may find it advisable to ask that the employee turn in a signed outline at the end of each work day.

5. Assure your workers that when habits have been learned, the job outlines can be thrown away. Surprisingly, many workers continue to keep their job outlines handy.

Work Management Means Economic Survival

Some jobs are like hollow logs. Every day, workers come to work only to thump those hollow logs. Some organizations would rather ignore useless jobs than analyze them. They believe they are doing their country a service by providing jobs for people. But too often they do not go about it in the right way. What happens to people who don't exercise? They get fat. Soon they don't even want to exercise. What happens to race horses that don't run races? Soon the horses don't have the muscles, stamina, or the attitude to run. So it is with workers who have little or no work to do. Jobs of small purpose do not serve the best interests of the people, the organization, or the country. Fat people, idle horses, and over-staffed organizations die young.

Dissenters will exclaim that jobs mean greater incomes and purchasing power. Many organizations throughout the world believe this. In those organizations, where workers are under-productive, more of the same must be hired to keep the wheels turning. When excessive labor costs cause prices to skyrocket, what happens to purchasing power? In the end, consumers of goods and services must pay the bill. Excessive labor and inefficient productivity in the public sector spell higher taxes. Taxes provide necessary services for the county, still, they don't exactly raise personal levels of purchasing power.

Over-staffed organizations are not as prevalent in the free enterprise sector. Most organizations in the private sector struggle continuously to keep expenses low and prices competitive. Competitive businesses stay lean so as to earn profits. Profits encourage new investors. Investments bring about research, inventions, innovations, new machines, new jobs, and higher employment. All these bring about growth. Profitable growth brings a combination of higher wages and lower prices. To attain profitable growth, managers at every level must see that their departments live within carefully projected budgets.

There are other immediate and practical reasons for keeping your work force trimmed for maximum effectiveness. Employees who have worthwhile assignments have pride in themselves and loyalty to their organizations.

At a meeting of managers, one manager told of an excessive labor cost and how work had been progressing slowly. This manager decided to take drastic measures. Over a period of several months, the manager reduced his group from 35 employees to 19. New job descriptions were written, new training programmes were initiated, and performance evaluations were given frequently. The manager passed out praise and recognition freely to deserving workers. The manager proudly ticked off the results:

– Employees now did more work in less time.
– The smaller work group was easier to manage.
– Morale was considerably higher.
– Absenteeism had practically disappeared.
– As production increased, labor cost percentage decreased.
– Workers' pay went up.

It is no shame to feel a reluctance to lay off workers. Just remember that when you analyze the jobs within your control periodically, you are preparing to make staffing recommendations to top management. Should layoff orders come down from the top, you will be ready to recommend those who should be let go and to defend the workers who should stay. Conversely, an efficiently run organization will grow, allowing more workers to be hired.

Regardless of rank or influence, you are important to the survival and prosperity of your organization. Keeping a trim, efficient work organization is the best way you can help your deserving employees.

From books, we glimpse the wisdom of others,
and we inherit their knowledge.

12
AN OPERATIONS-TRAINING MANUAL IN EVERY MANAGER'S BOOKCASE

It would be unfortunate if all the efforts that went into the development of a training programme were wasted and the lessons were forgotten. But situations do change within an organization: managers, trainers, and workers come and go; methods and procedures change. When changes occur, training outlines do not offer sufficiently detailed instructions. This is where an operations-training manual becomes an invaluable tool.

Within the manual, current instructional information is collected and stored continually, and obsolete information is purged. Thus, the operations manual survives all changes. Training remains as fresh as the data.

There are many reasons for keeping an operations-training manual:

– When a new manager takes charge of a work unit, the unit's operation manual, with its job descriptions and the training outline/records, tells of who does what. It indicates when employees need further training. Although the manager may know little about some jobs within the unit, the manual describes all that is necessary to train a qualified person for a given task.

– When a former trainer is promoted out of your department and an employee is asked to become a trainer, an operations/training manual provides the manager with the assurance that the new instructor will teach in the same manner and with the same thoroughness as before.

– When an administrative transaction, one that has rarely been processed through a particular office in the past, is suddenly required, the manager can rely on the operations-training manual to provide the details of the procedure.

– When the organization passes down a change in procedure, the new method will replace the present method beginning on the first day of the following month. The manager passes the information to the appropriate trainer with instructions to begin training all employees whose jobs will be affected by the change. In the operations-training manual, the manager replaces the old procedure with the new instructions.

How to Develop a Manual to Suit Your Needs

The development of an operations-training manual begins with planning. Consider dividing the manual into sections. You may want to number these sections by the hundreds – 100 series, 200 series, 300 series, and so on. This will allow you plenty of room for the many individual items that will go into the manual. For instance, you may want to break the sections down into types of work, such as the 100 section for office, the 200 section for sales, the 300 section for service, or in any other similar manner. You may want sections for job descriptions and training outlines.

Don't delay the project with too much planning. The best way for a plan to be born is to get the project started with what you have and make adjustments as you learn of your needs.

Begin gathering what you do have. Read the training outlines. Each item of these outlines will need to be explained and supported with facts, examples, and instructions. When practical, collect pictures, sketches, and sample copies of forms that demonstrate an item or process.

Remember that the first item on a training outline is orientation. You are the one who is most qualified to put together the first part of an introduction to a job. This will be general organizational information you can get from the office of human resources. Put together information you want to get across to workers, such as your expectations of them in the areas of conduct, cooperation, and performance. Include information regarding their rights and privileges, too.

Your on-the-job trainers can best write the second part of the orientation. This is the technical part of a job that precedes the four training steps.

Ask each trainer, or job incumbent, to write a description of the steps that are performed in each specialized task. If an employee lacks writing talent, arrange a time and place to meet. Let the worker or trainer describe the actions, and you write them down in a logical sequence.

It may be advantageous for you to observe the task as it is being performed. It will be as if you are the student and the worker is the instructor. Keep detailed notes. Ask questions about any point a student might not understand. After you finish writing descriptions of task actions, ask the worker to approve or correct your notes.

The easy method of training – the orientation and four simple steps – should be included in your manual. The description of this training method will serve as a short refresher course for anyone who has not instructed recently, and for newly appointed instructors.

An operations-training manual is not a difficult project, but it will take time to put it together. The more employees you can get to outline their job tasks conscientiously and accurately, the faster the project will go. Be patient. Let employees, and yourself, learn about writing bulletins for a manual as you go along. Don't write too much detail. For instance, it is not necessary to describe the specific steps in overhauling an engine. What a new mechanic might need to know is how work orders are made out and processed, where and how tools and parts are checked out, and how production and pay records are filled out and filed.

As you learn the errors and omissions, see that they are corrected and filed in the manual. If employees complain that descriptions and instructions outlined in the manual are not easily understood, have them rewritten. Pull out the old and update with the new. Any new piece of information that comes from you or from top management, to be included in the operations-training manual, should be assigned a bulletin number and dated. If the information replaces an old bulletin, the number remains the same. The new date should be preceded with the word "Revised."

It is better to begin developing an operations-training manual before a crisis forces you into action, as occurred in the following example.

One morning when the boss arrived at the restaurant, the two cooks were standing idly near the stoves . Out front, a few patrons were drinking coffee and munching on donuts and rolls.

"Why aren't you cooking breakfast?" asked the bewildered boss.

"The stoves went out and neither of us know how to re-light them," explained one of the cooks.

The boss re-lit the stoves, then went to his office where he wrote down the procedure for operating the stoves. The boss was still furious, so he wrote other operational bulletins for the emptying, cleaning, and filling the dish washer; and for the operation and care of the meat slicer, the fire extinguisher, and other pieces of restaurant equipment. Numbers were assigned and added to an index. The manager wrote a memo to discuss these bulletins at the next meeting with the employees.

A Training Programme Is What You Make It

Have you completed the following projects, or at least noted them on your task and project list?

– Develop a file of training information.

– Prepare training outline/record for each job.

– Write job outlines (checklists), when necessary, to build strong work habits.

– Perform a job analysis for any job that is not running smoothly.

– Train employees to be trainers.

– Cross train workers to perform other jobs.

– Teach key, reliable, capable employees to do some of your work.

– Develop an operations-training manual.

If you can answer yes for all of the above, you have the training tools to greatly reduce the time you might otherwise be bound to spend on the managerial functions of direct supervision, expediting, and personal production.

Proper and thorough training is always a good investment for any organization.

It is a manager's honor-bound duty to protect the resources of an organization. By doing so, the public trust is served.

13
HOW TO DEAL WITH BORROWERS AND ABUSERS

Line managers may think of an organization's resources as being mostly composed of physical assets – things. It is good that line managers should think of things, for a loss of physical assets affect other assets such as money, people, and time. Organizations have systems by which they maintain control over their physical assets, but managers should develop and practice *personal* systems for the control of physical things. Your systems will offer ways to save money, to keep employees at high levels of productivity, and to free yourself and others of wasted time.

Your personal time will be worth close scrutiny. Your time management will depend upon an awareness of where time goes, who has a right to it, and what you can do about it.

In addition to protecting the organization's money, it is important that you also protect your own. Not all managers are hit upon for a loan, but should this happen to you, you should have some ideas as to what is involved and what your options are.

How to Prevent Borrowed Items from Becoming Strayed or Lost

From time to time, employees may borrow technical books, trade magazines, or business records from your office. Others may ask to borrow a pen, a stapler, tape, or whatever else is needed and available from your desk. You probably say, "Bring it back when you're finished with it," and that's the end of it. Sometimes the items reappear, sometimes they don't. Perhaps someone else wants to borrow the already borrowed item; perhaps the original borrower simply forgot to return it. When you want to use the item and it is not available, you may be uncertain as to where it is. Understandably, you will be angry when you must spend your time seeking out the missing item.

There is no monetary loss to an organization from this inner office borrowing. Items are not actually lost – they are somewhere. Someone, you think, is using the item for a good purpose.

It is an easy matter to keep a record of borrowed items. On a piece of blank notebook paper, outline a simple format that will serve your needs. Your lending control record may look like this:

Items On Loan

Date	*	Employee's Name	*	Description of Item	*	Promised Return
____		_____		_____		_____
____		_____		_____		_____
____		_____		_____		_____
____		_____		_____		_____

If people are apt to borrow things frequently, keep the record in your Hold Action tray; if borrowing occurs only occasionally, place the form in a folder in the deep file drawer of your desk.

Your control record will not guarantee that borrowed items will always be returned, but at least you will know what items were borrowed, who took them, and when you can expect them back. Just the fact that you are seen writing down the information will usually convince borrowers that items are to be returned, as promised. Later, when items are returned, people may linger at your desk for a moment just to make certain that their names are crossed off your list.

When a borrower is slow to return an item, track it down and let the thoughtless borrower understand your displeasure.

When you are forced to track down an unreturned item and the borrower explains, ''Oh, I lent it to one of the other employees, but I can't remember who,'' then you have a problem. The item is now considered missing. This is decision making time.

Inform each borrower that no one is authorized to lend a borrowed item to someone else. If anyone else wants to borrow the item, you are the person to see.

If, somehow, someone else picks up the item, the borrower is responsible for it and must track it down and retrieve it.

These two brief admonishments should prevent such a problem – most of the time.

How to Take Bad Breaks Out of Breakage

All too frequently, tools, equipment, and materials get broken. You can expect some accidents to happen. Their causes, however, can be reduced.

In every instance of damage, you must determine what happened and why. Employees may be of little help. Their explanations often come down to just three words, "It just broke."

Consider these examples:

An employee borrows a piece of equipment for personal use. Upon its return, the equipment does not function properly. "What happened?" asks the manager. "I dunno, it just stopped working," replies the employee.

A worker tosses a tool toward the work bench. It misses and strikes the concrete floor. The tool is severely damaged. "It just broke."

When poorly maintained tires blow out, engines seize, or worn out brake shoes score the wheel drums, a line manager must do better than report to a higher boss, "Sorry, they just broke." It is extremely rare for something to *just break*.

Some managers are only slightly concerned with the recovery and protection of items for which they are responsible. To encourage a greater sense of responsibility by managers, some organizations send down a strongly worded policy:

Managers may be held financially responsible for items in their care that become lost or damaged.

Managers who do not want to pay the replacement cost for a lost or damaged item will likely take strong measures of their own. To protect themselves from the costly carelessness of employees, line managers may post a simply worded notice:

You bend it, you lose it, you buy it.

Such a policy will generally motivate workers to avoid acts of misuse and to return items promptly.

In some organizations, it would be close to impossible for such a policy to be written. Without such a policy, supported by the organization, the line manager has no other recourse except to maintain close observation and awareness. It is the act of negligence or abuse, rather than the result, that will be charged against the employee.

Keep in mind, it is always better to prevent a breakdown than to point the finger of blame at someone.

Stop the neglect and abuse of things.
Use all your senses – sight, sound, smell, taste, feel; and the two other senses used by successful managers, sixth sense and common sense. Within your work world, consider what senses would you use to:
– be aware of the condition of things;
– be aware of how things are being used;
– be aware of how things are being cared for.

A shop manager, on a test drive, can feel a broken wheel bearing, can hear a rod about to go out, can diagnose some engine ills by feeling and smelling exhaust gases, and can hear the peculiar growl of an ailing transmission.

A maintenance manager can hear and smell the sizzle of a potential electrical fire.

Your awareness comes from continuous observation. Your observations will catch the little things – a burned out rear light, a dirty typewriter, food that doesn't taste right, something that feels hot that shouldn't be – but these may not provide the total picture. Inspections, systematically carried out, will give you a better view.

Create a Programme of Routine Inspections

Routine inspections will allow periodic analysis of the condition, use, and care of equipment. From your analysis, specific plans can be made, individuals can be singled out to be supervised or trained in a manner that will improve the use and care of issued equipment, and specific services or repairs can be scheduled. These planned actions will reduce the number and seriousness of irritating, time-consuming interruptions.

Routine inspections will also serve to impress upon workers the need to be more careful. Workers will take better care of the organization's property when they become sufficiently aware that you are personally concerned and actively involved in the conservation of all tools and equipment.

How to design your own inspections programme.
Programmes for routine inspections will vary according to the kinds of equipment in use. All systems, however, are prepared in the same manner.

1. List all things pertaining to a given piece of equipment that are to be inspected and evaluated.

2. Design a form to suit your purposes:
– List the pieces of equipment that are alike. For instance, six pickup trucks. Like items can be grouped on one form, or each piece of equipment can have its own inspection record. One form can record several inspections – one inspection each month for a year – or a separate form can be used for each inspection.
– Decide how often inspections should be made.
– Determine the cost of having forms printed.

3. Determine who will make the inspections.
– How much time will be spent in making inspections?
– How many inspectors will be needed?
– How much and what kind of training will be required to prepare the inspectors.

4. Determine where and when the equipment will be inspected.
– Will all the equipment be inspected in one place, at one time, or will they be inspected at various times in different places?

5. Determine just how detailed the inspection form should be.

The story of a manager who developed an inspection programme.
A manager invited several employees to attend a meeting. Those chosen employees were asked to help in the preparation of a programme for the routine inspection of the organization's fourteen half-ton pick-up trucks.

The group decided that having one monthly report for each vehicle would be too costly. Fourteen trucks would require 168 forms per year. Instead, each truck would have its own record, and that form would be used monthly, throughout an entire year. The form would be typed and 14 copies run off on a copy machine, rather than going to the expense of printing such a small quantity.

The problem of the manager's time spent in giving detailed inspections for fourteen trucks was solved when four of the attending employees volunteered to serve as inspectors.

It was decided that not all vehicles would be inspected at one time. Some trucks would be inspected early in the morning; the others would be inspected in the late afternoon. All inspections would be made in the truck parking area.

Everyone at the meeting contributed to the layout of the vehicle inspection checklist. The employees also submitted suggestions as to how an inspection should be conducted:

– All instruments must work – the speedometer and all gauges.

– The horn must work.

– The engine must start easily and run smoothly; it should be revved to determine if oil smoke blows from the exhaust.

– Oil, water, and battery must be checked.

– Gears must shift smoothly.

– There must be proper play in the clutch and brake pedals; they must engage positively.

– The steering wheel must have no excessive play.

– The windscreen must have no cracks.

– Windscreen wipers and washers must operate properly.

– Side windows must open and close easily and securely.

– The seat must have no broken springs or tears in the cover; the seat must adjust freely.

– Headliner, side panels, and floor mats must be in good condition.

– The vehicles exterior must be in good condition – body, fenders, grille, bumpers, paint, and lettering.

– There must be no dangerous exhaust leaks.

– Wheel alignments must be checked visually.

– Tyres must have adequate tread; they must be properly inflated.

– All lights must work – rear lights, brake lights, directional signals, and the headlights on high and low beams.

The manager would remain in charge of the inspection programme. Inspection forms would be filed in the manager's deep desk drawer. The manager would schedule and announce to all drivers the inspection dates and times. The manager would also analyze the reports, consult with inspectors and drivers, and arrange for all necessary service and repairs.

Finally, it was decided that the grading system would be a simple one: "G" for Good, "F" for Fair, and "P" for Poor.

Then came the design of the inspection form, which is shown in figure 13-1.

With your present understanding of how inspection programmes are conceived and used, you are capable of developing an inspection programme for any purpose, no matter what kinds of equipment you are responsible for. Some equipment is inspected and maintained under manufacturers' maintenance agreements. However, if your organization has no such agreements, this is the time to put in your own programme of inspections. Don't wait for equipment to break down.

Vehicle Inspection Checklist

Vehicle Number: _____
Year and Make: _____

Month	J	F	M	A	M	J	J	A	S	O	N	D
Date												
Mileage												
Inspector												
Instruments												
Horn												
Steering												
Clutch												
Gear Shift												
Brakes												
Windscreen												
Wipers/Washers												
Side Windows												
Window Controls												
Door Handles/ Locks												
Seat(s)												
Interior: Roof, Sides, Floor												
Engine												
Truck Body												
Paint/Lettering												
Exhaust												
Wheels/Tyres												
Rear/Brake Lights												
Directional Lights												
Head Lights												

NOTE: For any Fair or Poor rating, please provide detailed information on the reverse side. Include the date and your initials.

Figure 13-1 – A sample Vehicle Inspection Checklist.

Don't forget tools. Such simple tools as screwdrivers and wrenches are frequently abused. Many organization keep an inventory record of tools, but the condition of those tools is frequently ignored. Why can't an inventory record for tools be designed to include the condition of tools? Try your hand at designing such a combination inventory/inspection form for tools and equipment in your work area. Tools that don't work properly will not produce quality work.

To summarize, systematic routine inspections serve you in these ways:
- Help to prevent breakdowns.
- Save money and people's time.
- Bring about greater measures of safety.
- Promote employee pride.
- Improve the organization's image.
- Eliminate many of a manager's stresses.

How to Protect Your Time and Spend It Wisely

Your work time may be spent on any of the eight functions that all managers perform, on any essential work you choose to do, or on tasks that are assigned to you. Your work time may be spent by superiors who demand it and have a right to it. Your work time may be wasted by people who demand it, but have no right to it. Or, your work time may be wasted by you when you worry about things.

You have learned to set up your desk for maximum efficiency, to improve your memory, to control tasks and projects, and to analyze jobs and the time spent on their duties. You have already come a long way toward effective, personal time management.

Still, time may seem to slip through your fingers. You may feel that you just don't have enough time for personal projects, or even for your family.

Here are a few ways to help you master time:

1. Don't let friends, relatives, or employees make unreasonable demands on your work time.

2. Get to the point quickly when conversing by telephone or in person. Keep *small talk* to a minimum.

3. When conversations and meetings have ended, don't socialize for more than five minutes. Send everyone back to work. The same goes for you. Restrict social contacts – as much as possible – to break periods, lunch times, and after working hours.

4. At work, you may be faced with the *hurry up and wait* situation. This occurs when you must be someplace at an appointed time, only to learn that there will be a short delay. Delays in business are common, but

seldom short. To spend your time effectively during unexpected periods of waiting, plan for it.

– Make it a practice to have pen and paper readily available, and a clip board or notebook on which you can write.

– When you are away from your office, take along reports to analyze, letters to write, or a technical or self improvement book to read.

– Just thinking about work projects or possible solutions to problems may be time well spent. From thinking comes plans; from plans come actions. Writing down your thoughts will help you to put your plans in order. Through this process, time is made productive and worrying is eliminated.

5. When you need a period of uninterrupted time – to complete a lengthy report, to work on a project, to meet a deadline – shut yourself off from all contact with people, except for emergency situations. This is not improper if done correctly. Your reason for being unavailable must be valid, and you must convince other people of this. You will need their cooperation, not their criticism.

– Tell your boss. Get approval and support. Perhaps your boss will cover for you, take your calls, and look after your work.

– Inform the people who answer the telephone and greet visitors. Instruct them to take messages, to inform people as to when you will be available, or to direct them to other people who might help them.

– Ask your supervisors, trainers, or other trusted, experienced employees to cover for you. Instruct them as to their temporary responsibilities and the boundaries of these.

– Restrict your alone time to as short a period as possible. You should need only a half hour to return a few telephone calls. An hour should be sufficient for writing one or two important letters. Other tasks or projects may require more time. But even day-long projects can be broken up into two, four-hour retreats from business contacts.

– As soon as your office door is once again open for business, contact all persons who have been looking after your interests. Collect your messages. Find out what has been happening. Thank everyone for their support. Take care of urgent tasks before going on to any other business.

Your time applied efficiently will save seconds and minutes. It's those seconds saved – not stolen or wasted – that add up. Then you will have time to get more done, or to just have time for yourself.

About Lending Money to Employees

Lending money to employees goes far beyond the expressed responsibilities of any manager. There are many disadvantages and few, if any, benefits. Nevertheless, some managers sometimes feel a pressure to make a small personal loan to a worker.

There are different kinds of borrowers:

– There are the *moochers* – those who continually ask for a cigarette or change for the vending machine.

– There are the workers who never seem to be able to make it from payday to payday. They do, however, pay up when their pay checks are cashed.

– There are employees who have *champagne tastes* and *beer incomes*. These people want something they can't afford; something that is not essential. They can't get credit anywhere, so they seek out their bosses.

– There are workers who are faced with unexpected emergencies, with no relatives or friends to whom they can turn.

– There are the newly hired workers. They have generally been out of work for some time. Rent may be falling due, groceries are needed, and payday is still several days away.

There are no right or wrong answers to the question of whether or not you should lend money to employees. There are no fixed rules, except those you choose to make. Even though you should take a hard line against lending money, there may still be exceptions.

An employee's appeal for money is usually an emotional one. This may cause a manager some confusion and conflict. Lending institutions won't lend money based on an emotional plea. Work organizations are not likely to respond to a heart-tugging story, although some organizations will permit a payroll draw against earnings due.

It is difficult for most line managers to be completely emotionally detached. A line manager's work unit might seem as close as family. Here are people who work together, every day. Even when feeling deeply and emotionally involved with an employee's need, your decision of whether or not to lend out of pocket money should be one of reason.

If there are no right or wrong answers or rules to follow in regard to how you should deal with employees who ask for a loan, what do other managers do? Ask them.

– Ask of the times when they did lend money. Ask of the circumstances that led to their decision.

– Ask of the times and circumstances when they refused to lend money to an employee.

– Ask of the times when loans were not repaid.

– Ask about dealing with the different kinds of borrowers.

Here are some comments and suggestions offered by other managers:

"I generally lend change for the vending machines, and I don't expect to get the money back."

"I won't put up with a moocher. The other workers won't either. As soon as it is apparent that a worker never puts out money for anything, never buys for a fellow worker, and never pays back the money or cigarettes borrowed, the situation is quickly brought to a halt. People, me included, just say, 'Sorry, I'm out of change.' Some use harsher words."

"I never lend money to employees who want something that I think is not essential. A manager must be careful because some workers will lie to get what is wanted. They may say that the money is needed for something else; something essential. I ask a lot of questions."

"Lend money to one worker and all the rest will come looking for a handout. I just tell them that I don't have any money to lend. I have problems of my own."

"I've loaned out money a few times, but I look up the borrowers when payday rolls around. That's when they have the money, and that's when I get mine."

"I never ask a borrower to repay a loan. I want to know who of my team is honest and responsible."

"When I hear an emotional plea for money, I think of my family and what my wife and kids would say about my lending family income in this particular instance. Sometimes I imagine them saying, 'Go ahead,' and sometimes I imagine they saying, 'No way.'"

"I never lend money that I cannot afford to lose."

"I set aside a small sum of money for the sole purpose of making loans to financially troubled employees. Each time I make a loan, I record the date, the employee's name, the reason given as to why the money was needed, the amount of the loan, and the promised date of repayment. I keep this record away from any prying eyes. Also, I explain to borrowers that when my personal fund has been depleted – that is, all the money has been loaned out – that no further loans will be made until outstanding loans have been repaid. When the money is gone and borrowers are long overdue in repayments, I tell other employees, who are in need money, just who these delinquent borrowers are. More than once, a needy worker has gone out and collected money from fellow workers.''

"I feel sorry for new employees who can't quite make it until their first payday. I'll help when I can afford it. Usually it doesn't amount to much – maybe five or ten bucks. I feel that new workers are likely to repay their loans promptly. They're not apt to jeopardize their working relationship with a boss they hardly know.''

"Employees sometimes come to me needing a little cash for some special event – a birth, a wedding, a graduation, a funeral. These requests make me a bit angry. People have plenty of advance notice for such happenings – except, maybe, some funerals. They could have been saving their money. If they can't save money, how can they ever pay me back.''

"I don't believe in lending money to my employees. But once in awhile I do it anyway.''

"An employee may need money to pay an invoice or a doctor. Why should I lend money for such purposes. Let the worker pay the bills, not me. Let someone else wait to be paid.''

"I've had workers come to me and say, 'I know I owe you money, but I can only pay you a little of it now. I won't be able to pay the rest until the next payday.' When workers come forward like that and explain their circumstances, I know they haven't forgotten, and that they do intend to pay.''

"I've had borrowers look me straight in the eye and make promise after promise to repay a loan. They think they're making me feel better.''

"Some managers don't have the courage to say no. I don't have that problem. In my book, a boss who always lends money to anyone, for any reason, gets to be known as an 'easy touch.' They have to learn the hard way that money will not buy an employee's respect.''

"I'll give you a tip. Collect the money within 90 days

or you'll have an enemy in your midst. After that long of time, without you asking for the money, the borrower starts thinking: 'You don't really need the money.' 'Others haven't paid you back, why should I?' 'You haven't asked for it, so you've probably forgotten.' 'If the job paid better, I wouldn't need to borrow money.' 'You just like to lend money as a favor. It makes you feel important and well liked.'''

A borrower's small negative thoughts, if allowed to grow, can build to dangerous attitudes. At the same time, your work relationship with this employee deteriorates, as does the work itself. If you notice a borrower's embarrassment or avoidance, the cause may be from a feeling of guilt. If a borrower wears a scowl while in your presence, the reason may be one of resentment. When you ask a borrower to perform some work-related task, and the worker looks at you with suspicion, it may be a sign of hostility toward you. Whenever you see a negative behavior in a borrower, bring the subject out into the open. Seek out the problem.

You might get right to the point by saying something like:

"What is the problem? If its the money you owe me, let's work something out."

Chances are good that both you and the employee will feel relieved to have the situation brought to a head.

Somewhere, between the extremes – lend or not lend – there is a middle course. To find it, requires common sense. When an employee needs temporary, emergency financial assistance, to provide food, clothes, shelter, or care for family members, help should be given. Do what you can afford to do, but don't feel obligated to bear the burden alone. There are other sources of assistance. Seek them out.

To buy foolishly; to forget, neglect, and allow assets
to become stolen or thoughtlessly thrown away,
is to cheat the people who must pay.

14
HOW TO GET THE MOST FROM WHAT YOU HAVE

All organizations have systems of some sort for the management of assets. It is essential that managers understand these, for the systems are no better than the managers who use them. The systems with which managers may be involved include: purchasing, inventory, security, maintenance, repair, and disposal. As these are touched upon, perhaps you will think of ways by which you can become more involved in making the systems work.

Purchase Wisely

Some managers think they don't have a role to play in purchasing; that it is a job for the top level managers and executives. This is not true. All managers are a part of the purchasing process. Even when you submit a requisition or a request for something, you are playing a role in the purchasing programme. When you need something, a decision must be faced. To make a wise decision, many things must be understood and needs must be effectively communicated. When purchases are made from a central purchasing office, you are still left with the job of seeing that the purchases are properly received and accounted for.

Centralized purchasing may enjoy certain advantages, like tighter controls to eliminate excessive purchasing and duplication, expert counsel and support, a wider availability of suppliers, lower prices through the power of mass purchasing, and discounts for prompt payments. On the other hand, some purchasing managers have been known to be out of touch with line-level needs of an organization, especially when the organization is made up of widely scattered branches. Down-line managers must be alert to what is going on in the purchasing department.

One purchasing manager learned that a sizeable quantity discount could be earned for the organization by ordering 50-thousand employee termination forms. The organization's work force totaled slightly less than 200 employees. If all the employees were terminated and replaced yearly, it would take more than 250 years to use up the original purchase of termination forms.

Another purchasing department bought seven huge generators to provide electrical power in a small island country. Each had been purchased from a different manufacturer. The purchasing office had lost the opportunity to secure a sizeable discount by placing the order with one, carefully chosen manufacturer. Later, the small country was to learn of the considerable cost involved in maintaining large, separate inventories of parts for seven different makes of generators.

Many organizations allow their managers to purchase specified supplies, materials, equipment, and services when these things are locally available and quickly obtainable. The organization will generally keep careful watch over all purchases by managers to assure that budgets are not exceeded and that prices are competitive. Managers with purchasing powers must understand the organization's purchasing policies and procedures, and they must have sound business relationships with suppliers.

When it becomes your responsibility to make purchases for your organization, you should consider the following:

Understand the items you have in inventory.

Determine the *maximum* inventory quantity for each item. To do so, you must determine the rate at which items are used. You must also determine the maximum allowable time for the delivery of various items. Then, you can establish inventory levels and set up a system by which those levels can be controlled.

One office manager controls paper supplies in this manner:

Paper supplies are kept on shelves in a storage room. It was determined that two reams of a given form would be sufficient for one month. It was also known that re-orders would require approximately three weeks to be printed and delivered. Allowing a maximum time of four weeks for re-orders to be delivered, the office manager reasoned that the inventory should begin with four reams. After using two reams in one month, the manager would still have two reams to be used during the three to four weeks needed to replace the inventory. The reorder level, therefore, was when two reams remain.

For the sake of simplicity, with inventories of the many forms, the office manager used cards inserted into the stacks of forms. Here is an example of an inventory card:

> ## Inventory Card
>
> Description: Equipment Inspection Form
> Form Number: 1076
> Reorder level: Two packages; 1000 forms
> Quantity to order: Four packages; 2000

This particular card was inserted into the stack of equipment inspection forms, two packages from the bottom. Office employees were instructed to return the card to the manager whenever the inventory got down to the card's level.

With a similar item, you might learn that a purchase discount can be earned with the order of six reams, 3000 forms at a time. A point to consider is whether your organization prefers taking the discount even though it means tying up more money in inventory.

This card system can be used for a variety of items, but it is not applicable to all inventories. For some inventories, it will be necessary to keep a book or a file folder for inventory and reorder control. Some organizations maintain inventory control by routinely and physically counting all items; other organizations keep a handle on inventory through the use of computers. Whatever system of inventory control you employ, do not allow supplies to run out.

Determine if a purchase is really essential.

An item you need may be available somewhere else in the organization. Try to talk with someone who knows where all physical items are located and of their condition. You will need to know how a requisition or request for the transfers of an item is handled within the organization.

In some instances, it might be wise to seek expert advice as to the repair or reconditioning of an item, rather than push for its replacement.

Understand the various suppliers and learn how to deal with them.

As a manager/buyer, you should learn all you can about the lines of merchandise carried by each supplier, have an understanding of quality and availability of the merchandise, and learn about each supplier's reliability to keep promises for service and delivery.

Visit suppliers' places of business, when possible, or talk with their representatives when they call on your organization. If supplier representation is not available and you must order from catalogues, ask your questions by letter or telephone.

Listen to what other organizations have to say about their suppliers.

It is generally advisable to maintain business relationships with two or more suppliers of any given item. A little competition keeps suppliers on their toes; they'll work to maintain the quality of their services. Most suppliers are loyal to their customers, but they expect some loyalty in return. Suppliers will understand if you place an order with other suppliers when they cannot give you what you want, when you need it, at the price that was quoted by the competition. But they'll do you no favors should you buy items anywhere, anytime, for no particular reason. It is not advisable to scatter your purchases in too many directions.

Do not allow suppliers to bribe you with gifts so as to gain your business. You could find yourself with a conflict of interests. Do not be led by other managers who say that it is all right to accept a few favors and gifts from suppliers. You might hear others say, "It's the way business is done," or, "Suppliers write gifts off as a cost of doing business." Your integrity and your career are of far greater importance than a few gifts.

For your convenience, a supplier may take responsibility for keeping your stock of materials up to prescribed levels. Before you give your trust, keep close watch on how much of what is being delivered. Never permit suppliers to load you with items or services that are not needed.

Friends or relatives may attempt to influence your purchasing decisions by recommending favorite suppliers. This is a poor way to conduct business. Let everyone know that you demand fair prices, dependable services, immediate availability, quality merchandise, and prompt deliveries.

It is best not to demand immediate delivery of items or services when there is no urgency. Do you remember the story of the child who cried wolf all too often? Suppliers know when so-called emergencies are the result of poor management. When you watch your inventories carefully, and anticipate your needs well in advance, there is seldom a reason to declare an emergency. When you treat your suppliers fairly, you will receive fair treatment in return. They will respond quickly to a justifiable emergency.

Do not accept as fact a delivery date promised by a supplier. Suppliers are notoriously optimistic about how quickly they can deliver your order or render a service. If a supplier says three days, allow a week. For a promise of three weeks, count on four. For a critical item, it may help to contact the supplier a day or so before the promised delivery date and ask how the order is progressing. Your reminder may be just what is needed. Perhaps with just a bit of effort, the order can be made ready. When your order is not ready, even beyond your estimated delivery date, let the supplier know of your displeasure. Ask for the promise of another delivery day. If the supplier continues to fail in keeping promises, suggest that, hereafter, you may be forced to make other purchasing arrangements.

When several suppliers are asked to submit bids for specific orders, do not reveal those bid prices to anyone not within your organization and directly concerned with the purchase. Some managers have the mistaken notion that to tell suppliers of the lowest price submitted thus far will earn the organization the best price possible. This is not necessarily so. One bidder has only to slide under a competitor's known bid by a small amount to win the contract. Then, when suppliers learn that a manager plays games with the bidding procedure, reputable suppliers simply won't play; they won't submit bids for that organization's business. Have and hold a reputation for being fair and honorable in all your business dealings.

Express your appreciation to a supplier for prompt service. Check to make certain that your suppliers receive payments promptly. Should you learn that a supplier's payment has been held up for some unknown reason, check it out. Awaken those people in the payables department. Ask them to please process and pay the supplier's statement as quickly as possible. If you are told that the problem is with the supplier, find out what you can do to resolve it. If you feel that you do not have the authority to become this deeply involved, take the problem to your boss.

An organization may, from nothing more than habit, continue to buy a specific product from the same supplier routinely. If you learn of a supplier offering more – a better product, better service, a lower price – pass this information along to your superiors.

Understand your role in the purchasing process and give it your fullest attention and effort. From materials wisely purchased, an organization will benefit through better efficiency, longer material life, and less waste. These will add up to less human stresses, higher morale, time saved, greater productivity, and less costs in the long run.

A Forgotten Thing Is a Wasted Thing

Managers who have carefully planned for the needs of an organization and purchased needed items are understandably frustrated when it is learned that the items thought to be on hand have simply disappeared. Someone may know that an item exists and may know where it is located, but the person who needs to know may not.

To illustrate this point, consider the following:

An executive decided to visit the organization's scattered offices and shops. At one location, several pieces of damaged equipment were stored neatly on a shelf. The local manager was asked why these items were just sitting there. The manager told his boss that the damaged equipment was too good to throw away. Perhaps someday the equipment could be repaired. The executive knew that this manager had been ordering new pieces of equipment from time to time. There had been no attempt to repair and utilize the stored, damaged equipment – it had just been forgotten.

At another branch office, the visiting boss found an empty filing cabinet in a hallway, and two empty, unused desks, shoved into a corner. An old, but still workable, duplicating machine had been stored in a closet.

At still another location, in an old shed, the executive found a truck that had been gutted by fire. Perhaps the truck could be repaired, or at least some of the parts could be used.

A truck was sent to the various locations to pick up the items the executive had found. Even the burned-out truck was towed back. Somehow, the executive vowed, some value would be recovered from these forgotten items.

Accountants account for the organization's finances and physical assets. Some items are inventoried frequently. Some are inventoried perhaps only once a year, if at all. But even inventories will not tell all you should know about physical assets. Those who take inventories state the date, location, description, and quantity of each asset being accounted for. They do not, as a rule, describe the working condition of items, nor their possible utilization.

Some assets are more ignored than forgotten.

At a hospital in a so-called developing country, crates of modern medical machines and equipment – provided by foreign aid – were stored in a damp, dirty storage room. The local administrator explained with a shrug that no one could be found to install these marvelous machines. Anyway, the foreign doctors who knew how to operate them had already gone home. And there was no one to keep them in good repair. The needed expertise to solve these seemingly simple problems was never provided, nor was it ever sought. The costly, life saving medical miracles continued to sit, improperly stored, totally ignored, and soon to be forgotten.

Although the accounting of physical assets is the responsibility of administrative people, line managers should not just sit back and wait for someone to account properly for the tools, equipment, and other physical assets. The leadership and involvement of line managers – awareness, communication, problem solving, decision making, actions, record keeping, and follow-through – are the ways of keeping physical assets from becoming ignored or forgotten.

Do what you can with what you have, at the level where you are. If you haven't already done so, make your own record of physical items:

descriptions, quantities, locations – and the condition of each. Put this record in your own, personal operations manual.

How to Reduce Thefts

Stealing is a crime against the organization and against the public. It's a common crime that has been around a long time. But this crime can be substantially controlled within your organization. Here are some suggestions to help you do your part by developing your personal theft prevention programme:

1. Be aware of the assets that can possibly be stolen from your work area. Where are these things kept? How are they handled?

2. Think of the ways by which thefts might occur. This can be somewhat difficult. Since you are not a thief, you are not likely to think as a thief does.

There are people from outside and within the organization who are capable of stealing from you. Their methods may differ:

–Some thieves steal in the dark of night; some steal in broad daylight.

–Some thieves will break and enter; some will just walk in through an open door.

–Stealing can occur by someone taking something away, then falsifying the record to hide the theft. A manipulation of figures can happen right under the nose of a person being robbed.

–Stealing can occur by someone taking something away, with complete confidence that there is inadequate security, communication, or accounting. And maybe nobody really cares.

3. Examine people's privileges and freedoms. You should not set out to take away privileges or freedoms, but you may seek ways to have more control over these.

–Some employees carry shopping baskets, briefcases, or lunch sacks to and from their jobs. Do you ever wonder what might be in them?

–Some employees drive the organization's vehicles. Some are allowed to take vehicles home. Do they have permission to use these vehicles for personal business and pleasure? If employees have no right to use the organization's vehicles for personal use, and they do anyway, would you consider this stealing?

– Most organizations' restrooms are supplied with toilet paper and paper towels. Sometimes these items disappear shortly after being stocked in the restrooms.

– Some organizations allow employees to borrow small tools and equipment for personal use during non-working hours. Is there a system for signing out and signing in items that are borrowed?

– How many pens, pencils, and note pads are transported from offices to employees' homes?

– How many personal long-distance calls are placed from office telephones?

– Outsiders, too, are given various freedoms while they are on the property of an organization. Find out just how much freedom is granted to customers and visitors and what they might do with so much freedom.

4. Maintain an accurate inventory. An analysis of inventory records can tell how well items have been used and cared for, how accurately things have been accounted for, how many items are to be purchased, and what the expenses have been. An inventory analysis can also tell if things are being stolen.

Here is how the inventory accounting process works:

Throughout the month, someone in the accounting office records all figures of items received and items issued, used, or shipped out. Such information comes from daily reports submitted by various managers, along with papers that substantiate these In and Out transactions. In this way, the accounting department keeps a running inventory. At any moment, an accountant can tell how much of any item is in inventory – at least on paper. At the end of the month, columns of inventory figures are totaled. This is the final, month-end accounting inventory.

In simple terms, an accountant will explain the process with this formula: Beginning inventory, minus items sold (or issued), plus items purchased, equals the ending inventory.

But is this a true inventory? There is only one way to verify it. Each month, on the same date – generally the last day of the month – each manager must see that everything in stock is physically counted, measured, or weighed. This is the physical (actual) inventory. The final physical inventory becomes the accountant's new beginning inventory for the month to follow.

The *accounting* ending inventory and the *physical* ending inventory should be exactly the same. Often they are not. When there is a difference, it is usually the physical inventory being less than the accounting inventory. A difference between the two records is commonly referred to as *shrinkage*. Inventory shrinkage will appear for one or more of these reasons:

– Errors in accounting
– Errors in counting, weighing, or measuring
– Thefts

Accountants are responsible for the prevention of clerical errors.

Mistakes do happen, but accountants have their own systems of checks and balances to catch errors. Seldom will an accounting error be repeated.

The real control of inventory rests with line managers. A manager must closely supervise the manner by which items are received, counted, checked off against shipping invoices, and properly stored. A manager must see that items are issued only through authorized people, and that issued items are correctly recorded. These precautions will do much to bring the physical inventory more in line with the accounting inventory.

A manager must carefully train and supervise the employees who take the monthly physical inventory.

As an example, a storage building was filled with fifty-five gallon drums of expensive liquids. The manager watched an employee take the inventory. The worker kicked the steel barrels. When one gave a sound, "bing, bing, bing," the worker jotted down forty-five gallons. When a steel drum went, "bong, bong, bong," the notation made was half full. One barrel responded to hefty kicks with, "thung, thung, thung." The worker estimated that there were ten gallons remaining.

On-the-spot training immediately went into effect. The manager began with instruction on the use of a dip-stick, marked off in gallons.

An organization will decide on the items to be accounted for. It is a decision of common sense. Some small disposable items, such as paper clips, are not generally in great demand among thieves. Pens and pads of paper might be another matter. However, when usage cost is acceptable, the organization is not likely to ask for a physical count. When a manager, with the cooperation of the accounting department, begins to suspect that stealing is going on, it is time to examine all security measures.

5. Tighten up all forms of security. Most people who steal have two things in common – temptation and fear.

Something is a temptation when it attracts a person to commit an immoral or dishonest act. It may be money, food, or anything a person might need or want – especially when it appears to be free for the taking.

Fear, in this instance, refers to a thief's fear of getting caught in the act or soon after the act of theft. The extent of a thief's fear is determined by an awareness of the risks involved and thoughts of the penalty. By increasing the risk and the severity of punishment, a person's fear of being caught will greatly intensify.

The primary objective of a security programme is to prevent thefts. An organization can do much to accomplish this by reducing the temptations to steal and increasing people's fear of being caught. Some organizations take elaborate steps to prevent thefts: securely locked cabinets, safes, vaults, doors, and windows; security guards; guard dogs; electrically charged fences; alarm systems; camera or video monitors; one-way windows; see-all mirrors; and metal detectors.

In addition, these organizations are likely to have other strong deterrents:

– Rewards for a person who gives information that leads to a thief's arrest and conviction.

– Rules that control or restrict the movements and actions of employees and visitors.

– Records that account for the whereabouts of things, money, and people.

– Policies of punishment for crimes against the organization.

Deterrents to thefts can succeed only when managers cause them to be effective. Without the support of the managers – and the employees, too – the best of security measures will fail.

By way of an example, a large department store decided to test its security measures. Two private detectives were hired to attempt a theft – whatever they could steal, whenever they could get away with it. The hired thieves were given one month to carry out their mission. They could attempt a theft by any means, day or night. Only a few top executives would know of the hired detectives and what they were up to.

The next day, during busy shopping hours, the two hired thieves walked into the store. They went directly to the sporting goods department, selected a two-man canoe, loaded it with expensive fishing and camping equipment, and carried the entire load out through the front door. One of the store's floor managers was kind enough to hold the door open for the thieves. The following day, the two detectives returned the merchandise to the store's embarrassed executives.

As a manager, you can best serve you organization's security programme by taking a few sensible precautions:

– Watch people, especially strangers. Who are they? What are they doing? What is their business here? Do they have permission? If your organization doesn't have means of employee and visitor identification, check with your boss, or some responsible person at the front office. Don't be fooled by people who wear uniforms of known service organizations. Anyone can secure uniforms and tools of a trade. Watch strangers and your own employees as they arrive. Notice what they wear and carry. Watch as they leave. Does that skinny person who arrived earlier now appear twenty pounds heavier?

– Be certain that your employees know and understand the rules of security and the policies on punishments.

– See that the rules – restrictions and controls – are followed.
– Analyze all records thoroughly.
– See that things and money are not left lying around unattended.
– See that physical security devices are sound and in working order – doors, windows, locks, alarms.
– Encourage your employees to report all suspicious actions that they observe.
– Be certain that everything in your work area is locked-up before the last person leaves.

When it appears that everything is being done to guard against thefts, something may be overlooked. Thefts will occur. Each day, ask yourself, ''Are thefts occurring now in my area of responsibility?'' Mere suspicion is not enough. You must know the answer for certain.

By watching your inventories, you can know what is being taken and how much is being taken. The next step is to determine when things are being taken. Finally, you must find a way to stop the thefts.

Consider these security problems:

– A restaurant's food costs were running alarmingly high. The manager watched the food as it was received and stored. Food was watched during preparation and while it was being served. The manager saw that customers paid for their meals. Employees were watched when they left after work through a single back door. The manager could not find a single incidence of waste or theft. Yet, food costs remained high.

– Fuel costs for the four service vehicles were running slightly above normal, as were the costs of materials that were carried on the trucks. The manager assumed that higher expenses were responsible.

– At a tightly secured government construction site, gate guards checked all employees as they entered and left. At the end of each workday, a long line of workers was held up by one employee who always pushed a wheelbarrow loaded with trash – scraps of wood, old bolts and nails, small pieces of metal and wire. The guards pawed through the trash thoroughly before allowing the worker with the wheelbarrow and the other workers to proceed out through the gate.

As a manager, what do your seven senses of observation and awareness tell you about these three situations? See if the endings of these stories surprise you.

– At the restaurant, the manager searched for something that may have been overlooked. What happened after restaurant hours? Nightly, when the restaurant was closed, a maintenance crew came in to clean. The manager decided to watch the restaurant the following night, from outside. Maintenance workers were observed carrying out boxes clearly labeled as food products. The restaurant manager notified the maintenance company owner, who, in turn, notified the police.

– Higher prices for fuel and service materials were not responsible for higher operating costs. The manager's boss knew better. For each of the four trucks, fuel purchases and mileage records were checked. Records of materials used by each service worker were compared to the number of customers per route. As the boss suspected, the service person with the fewest number of service calls had the highest mileage and highest materials cost. The boss assigned a person to follow one particular service truck for a week. It didn't take long to discover that this service person was self-employed part of the day, using the organization's truck, equipment, fuel and materials to make extra money on the side. After the dishonest service person had been dealt with, the boss gave the manager a review course in ways of analyzing reports and records.

– After several years of working in government construction, the worker, who daily had taken home wheelbarrow loads of trash, quit the job and moved far away. The now-retired person finally admitted to a close friend of stealing while employed at the government. The worker had been stealing construction site wheelbarrows.

In this third story, it is not likely that a person could ever have gotten away with such a theft. Think of how managers would have been alerted to stolen wheelbarrows. The construction boss would have been aware of any wheelbarrow shortage on the job; the purchasing manager would have wondered why wheelbarrows were continually being ordered; the payables manager would have been curious about all the checks prepared to purchase wheelbarrows. These are checks and balances.

Keep in mind that it is not your job to play the part of a police officer and catch crooks. Your job is to get the most from what you have. To do this, all things placed in your trust must be kept safe and in good working order.

Systems of Maintenance and Repair Prevent Headaches

Wherever equipment is used, routine preventive maintenance is essential. Cleaning, lubricating, making minor adjustments, and replacing worn parts will do much to extend the useful life of equipment. There are four steps for you to take to begin an effective maintenance programme:

1. Prepare a detailed checklist of the services to be performed.

2. Assign those who are to be responsible for seeing that preventive maintenance gets done. Add these assignments to their job descriptions.

3. Make a schedule for all equipment to receive routine maintenance

service.   The factory equipment manuals will specify the kinds and frequency of service.

4. Supervise the results. The maintenance reports will come to you. See that the schedule has been followed and that the work has been done thoroughly. See if there are any recommendations for major repairs, or for the disposal of old equipment. Periodically, make a personal inspection of equipment, preferably after routine maintenance service has been done.

Some organizations make their own repairs. However, sometimes a needed replacement part may not be available. This is another reason why it is important to keep track of everything, even old, broken equipment. It is just possible that the serviceable parts of one piece of equipment can be used to repair the other. It is far better to have one piece of usable equipment than two broken ones.

Other organizations send damaged equipment out to repair shops. As you do with all suppliers, cultivate a close working relationship with repair shop managers. In some places, it is a common practice to retain an older piece of equipment for standby use. It is a comfort to have an extra vehicle, copying machine, or old typewriter to use while regular equipment is out for service. But some managers forget that standby equipment must be as carefully maintained as the full-time equipment.   In fact, standby equipment must be pampered. It should not be subjected to long periods of heavy-duty work. It's not meant to take abuse, but only to be of use in times of emergency. Keep standby equipment fully serviced, stored in a clean, safe place, and periodically tested. It will repay your kindness with a willingness to work at a moment's notice.

Even Junk Has Value

In time, any piece of equipment wears out, and the cost of frequent repairs will amount to more than the equipment is worth. This will be the time to dispose of it. Sometimes a manager is made responsible for making recommendations as to how equipment should be disposed of. Here are actions to consider:

1. Equipment that is still in near working order may be sold *as is*. Or it can be repaired before being sold – if the higher sale price will be greater than the repair cost.

2. Equipment that is not economically feasible to repair can be stripped of all usable parts. Then, the parts can be sold, or retained and used by the organization.

3. Equipment, or what remains of it, might have some value as scrap. No matter how little you believe the item to be worth, you can never tell who might want it, or for what reason.

Nothing should just be thrown away to rot or gather dust.

Managers who account for their assets, who protect and care for them, and who get the last possible bit of value from them, are likely to be assigned the organization's newest and best equipment.

We are born with two ears and one mouth.
It would appear that we should listen more and talk less.

15

HOW TO BE AN UNDERSTANDING AND AN UNDERSTOOD BOSS

In practicality, we should listen, so as to understand; and speak, so as to be understood. Some employees might say that their bosses don't do either one.

Some managers could voice the same complaint of their employees. Whatever the case, interpersonal communication can be improved to everyone's satisfaction through a bit of know-how and practice.

How to Be an Understanding Listener

Listen to what is said and understand what is heard.

Speaking without listening is similar to a bird trying to fly without feathers. Most people who have normal hearing will insist that they do listen. Too many apparently do not understand what they hear.

There is a game sometimes played at parties where one person is elected to whisper a message – instructions or information – to another person, who, in turn, whispers what was heard and understood to another person and so on around the room. The last person to receive the message repeats it aloud for everyone to hear. Not surprisingly, everyone begins laughing because the last saying is a mangled interpretation of the first message. A message begins as, "All supervisors are to report to the personnel manager, at eight o'clock, A.M., and bring whatever is necessary to help in the discussion of improving employee morale." The message is finally related aloud as understood by the tenth person to hear it. "All the supervisors are invited to the boss's house tomorrow night at eight . . . and bring your own bottle."

Most of us have misunderstood something, in some small way, at some time or another. But small misunderstandings, when passed along, generally become repeatedly misunderstood in small ways, until suddenly there is one BIG misunderstanding.

Awareness through listening requires continual concentration and a practice of habits that managers generally know, but sometimes forget. Check yourself out on the following.

Be available and approachable.

Throughout almost any working day, people will frequently *drop in* to see the manager. Many will bring information, or problems; some will just stop to visit.

A manager should be available to callers. Everyone expects it. But there are times when you, as the boss, cannot allow interruptions to happen. Priorities of the work at hand must be quickly weighed against the importance and urgency of what has just dropped in. When an interruption is unacceptable, you must politely say so. Follow this by saying when you will be available. An arrangement can be made for a specific time; the visitor can be asked to return when it is more convenient; or the person can be contacted later by telephone. You are making yourself available.

Employees frequently catch the boss away from the office, on the way to somewhere. The advice is the same. If you are in a hurry, and if the employee's business can wait, make an appointment for later. You are making yourself available.

While visiting work areas, you should always be readily available and easily approachable. That is one of your main reasons for being there. In most instances, workers are seeking your opinions, advice, decisions, instructions, or orders. These, you can deal with instantly on the spot.

Most managers do try to make themselves available to their employees. Yet, employees are all too frequently led to think otherwise. The employees who work closely with the manager – those who greet visitors and answer the telephone – may turn workers away with thoughtless comments: "The manager is in a meeting," "He's busy," "She's not here," or "I don't know where anyone is. Nobody tells me anything."

When you are away from your desk, or locked in your office with paperwork or meetings, people still must be told just when will be the right time to talk with you. Your close employees and associates must be trained to write down the names of people who call, to take messages, and to give reasonable explanations as to why you are not available at the moment. When callers are treated with sensible courtesy, they will know that you really care about seeing them.

Have your people say something like, "The manager will be in a meeting most of the morning. May I have her call you back when she is available?" Or, "He should be back by 3:30. Could you return then?" Or, "The manager is away for the day. May I take a message?" Or, "The manager just stepped out of the office for a few minutes. Would you like to take a seat and wait?"

While most managers are readily available, some are not easily approachable. A rude greeting will not encourage a worker to speak up. An approachable manager will put a visitor at ease: "Come on in. Sit down, here. Now, what can I do for you?"

Out on the work site, a manager may be busy with someone else when a worker comes up and interrupts. Instead of exclaiming, "Don't bother me! Can't you see I'm busy?" the manager who practices being available and approachable will say, "Hold it for just a minute. Don't go away."

Attempt to prevent interruptions from the outside.

A worker hears the boss tell someone out front, "We don't want to be disturbed." The employee feels important. The boss really wants to listen, without interruptions. Unfortunately, you cannot always guarantee complete privacy. The day may be unusually busy with urgent problems arising unexpectedly. Under these conditions, apologize for the interruptions. When an interruption has passed, encourage the speaker to continue, "I'm sorry. Now, you were telling me about . . ." The employee will understand and will be impressed with your willingness to talk during such a hectic day.

Don't spend time thinking when you should be listening.

A remark is made that starts the manager thinking about a suitable reply. While thinking, the manager's listening system fails to grasp the speaker's explanation that follows. The point of the message is missed while the manager's thoughts block what is being said. It is, of course, important to think before speaking, but not while you are plugged into the listening mode. Wait until the speaker has finished, then take a moment to digest the information and plan your reply.

Some managers simply lose interest in what is being said. They begin to think of other things. A speaker can sense a person's inattention. Don't let it happen to you. Know that even a dull person has something to say. Actively stay alert as you listen. If seated, sit forward on your chair; lean toward the speaker. Use appropriate facial expressions to let the speaker know you are listening. Avoid looking out the window or at your watch.

Listen closely to words, and for their meanings.

When a speaker skips lightly over or around a subject, and when pertinent facts are evaded or omitted, there can be no clear understanding. A manager must seek clarification. Seek clarification when a person appears to be exaggerating.

– A supervisor reports that there is a worker who is always late for work.

– Another supervisor reports that the crews never finish jobs on time.

The words *never* and *always* are exaggerations of the facts. It is difficult to believe the entirety of such statements. Nevertheless, the meanings are clear – the supervisors have problems. Now, it is up to their manager to learn the facts. From the facts, the seriousness of the problem will be determined.

Watch the speaker's facial expressions and body movements; listen to voice inflections.

Observing the mannerisms of a speaker is one thing; being aware of their meanings is another. You may observe a speaker's anger, fear, joy, nervousness, or suspicion, but what would it mean?

– Why is a worker so nervous while explaining how a piece of equipment became broken?

– An employee expresses understanding of the company policy, but his eyes hint of a lingering confusion.

– Your most dependable worker says there is no way that the small task you assigned can be completed by the afternoon. But there is a twinkle of mischief behind those eyes.

Laughing excessively, heavy breathing, needless perspiring, shifting about as if in discomfort – these and other unusual mannerisms won't necessarily reveal the truth behind what a speaker is saying, but they will alert you to seek the truth. And knowing your people well will be most valuable in determining whether or not such concern is even necessary.

Ask appropriate questions at the proper time.

It is essential that a manager learn all facts pertinent to a conversation. For the facts to be known, a manager will likely need to ask questions. Ask them with respect for the speaker. Do not interrupt while a person is speaking. The speaker's train of thought might become lost. This would be the speaker's loss, and yours as well. Be courteous, let the speaker continue. Something may be said that will answer your question before it need be asked.

Should it be necessary for you to ask a speaker to clarify a statement, wait until a sentence is finished or a thought has been expressed, then ask your question. Ask only questions that pertain to what has been said. Don't attack a speaker with questions about things that have not yet been mentioned. It is not unusual to forget essential parts of a presentation momentarily. In such instances, a speaker may welcome an appropriate question or statement. Something, then, is needed to put the speaker back on the track so that views and facts can be more completely stated.

Evaluate and filter what is being said.

An employee storms into the office swearing angrily. The manager is momentarily alarmed but allows the worker to unload the anger and wind down. Then the boss slips in a few pertinent questions. From the employee's responses, facts are brought out and evaluated. The manager discount's the initial furious behavior and filters out the loud, abrasive words that were said. What remains is the worker's understandable complaint.

Do not ridicule what an employee says.

Words of ridicule are often unintentional. Perhaps this is why some managers find such retorts difficult to curb. Words that should not be said tend to slip out unexpectedly, sometimes in anger, sometimes in humor, sometimes because of a manager's resentment. Whatever the reason, there is no excuse for causing an employee to feel inferior, embarrassed, or insulted. Avoid the following and any similar expressions:

– You ought to know the answer to that. I've told you a million times.

    – Why can't you do it right for once? A child could do it.
    – Are there anymore stupid questions?
    – Just do it my way. Leave the thinking to me.

Practice replacing outbursts of ridicule with habits of leadership that will create followers. Listen to every question no matter how often it is asked; to every complaint; to every request for an instruction, a decision, or a confirmation; and to every story of a worker's accomplishment and achievement. And always listen with a logical, quiet mind. Praise any improvement, regardless of how small. Encourage each worker when appropriate.

Satisfy the speaker's need.

There is always a reason why an employee comes to a manager. It may be to ask for something – a personal favor, an answer, a loan. It may be to say something – a complaint, a report, an idea, a bit of gossip. Whatever it is, the employee expects some sort of satisfaction. A worker does not always expect to have his or her own way, but every employee expects to be heard. A manager who listens gives the employee this satisfaction.

When a manager listens but cannot give an employee what is sought, a need still remains to be satisfied. The employee needs to know why. The boss must patiently explain the reasons, and the employee's level of satisfaction must be determined.

"Now do you understand the situation and our position at this time?"

The manager will continue to listen until it is known that the worker does understand. The employee may not like an answer, but the need to know why will have been satisfied.

Practice the techniques of listening.

While you listen to a speaker, you may find your own needs and purposes changing somewhat. You may need to:
- gather additional facts
- encourage the speaker to explore all sides of the subject
- understand the worker's thoughts and feelings better
- show that you are interested and attentive
- encourage the person to continue talking
- bring the subject to a close successfully.

Here are some suggested comments and questions that might well be used for your purposes:
- Can you say that more clearly?
- Is this the problem as you see it?
- As I understand it, you plan to . . .
- This, then, is your decision, and these are your reasons . . .
- I see. Uh-huh. Yes, I understand.
- That's an interesting point.
- I was (shocked, angry, disappointed, elated, etc.) when I learned that . . .
- So, what are your intentions now?
- You seem to have covered the subject. Is there anything else?
- Shall we leave it at that until I can give you an answer?

Keep your responses neutral. While listening, do not take the employee's side; do not show your side. Stay neutral until it is appropriate for you to take a stand and say what you think. There is a time for your views to be understood.

How to Be an Understood Speaker

Much has been taught on the subject of public speaking. Line supervisors and managers, however, do most of their speaking one-on-one or to small groups. Orders and instructions are given quickly. Often, little or no time is allowed to respond to a confused employee who asks, ''What do you mean?''

Rather than our learning how to speak effectively before a large, captive audience, most of us would benefit more from frequent reminders on how to speak in specifics when in the office or on the line.

Capture the listener's attention.

Consider this old story:

A man borrowed a mule from a neighbor. The mule was cooperative until it was fully loaded. It then became stubborn and would not budge. The man pleaded and yelled; he pulled and he shoved; but the mule continued to stand there.

Finally the owner was summoned. He listened to the man's complaint. The owner then picked up a stout stick and gave the balky mule a resounding blow, right between the eyes. A few words were whispered into the mule's ear. Obediently the animal walked off carrying the heavy load. The owner advised the astonished man, ''First, you have to get his attention.''

It is not advisable for a manager to get an employee's attention by such a drastic action as a blow to the head (although a few managers may sometimes be tempted to do so). A few appropriate words will generally serve as suitable attention-getters:

– ''Listen-up . . .''
– ''Now hear this . . .''
– ''Excuse me, but . . .''
– ''Would you like to hear this?''
– ''Let me explain it . . .''
– ''Here's how it works . . .''

Control your physical expressions.

Just as when you are in the listening mode, your moods when speaking are expressed, in part, by your physical movements. It is therefore understandable that employees will quickly give you their attention when a feeling is shown. You briskly walk up to people with purpose, rather than shuffling up to them in slow motion. You sit up straight in your chair, rather than slouching in a manner of indifference. You smile or you scowl to impart your feeling. You gesture emphatically, rather than just twiddling your thumbs. You may not even be aware that you are communicating with physical mannerisms. Nevertheless, the listener is reading your movements.

When you share what is meant to be good news, the employees believe you. They not only hear your words, they see your enthusiasm and happiness.

When you are explaining how and when a job must be done, you are not smiling. Your workers are not smiling either. Your words are being understood.

A manager may occasionally bring personal problems to work, accompanied by feelings of anger, frustration, worry, or some other negative emotion. Be careful to store away such feelings when communicating about work. Employees should not have to suffer from a manager's dark mood.

Should you be carrying around a non-productive emotion, take whatever physical or mental action is necessary for you to shake a grouchy behavior. For instance:

– Take a brisk walk. Walk around the building; walk anywhere. Get away from your work and your employees, even if for just a few minutes. Treat yourself to some time alone.

– Get close to nature. Use your senses to experience the sky, the earth, the sun, the wind, the rain. Listen to the sounds of life. These may help to put you in tune with what is truly real.

– Visit a friend. Perhaps you know someone – maybe another manager – who has successfully coped with a personal unhappiness similar to yours.

– If you can't shake your mood, it may be advisable to let your workers know that your mood is of a personal nature and has nothing to do with them. They'll feel better, and chances are they will do whatever they can to support you throughout the day.

– If a work-related problem involving your employees is the cause of your unhappiness, let them see your worry or displeasure. But be fair. Keep things in perspective. Don't let a small disappointment blow-up into a bitter, stormy one.

Use voice inflections.

All the emotions that can be shown with facial expressions and other physical mannerisms can be communicated through voice inflections.

A voice inflection is a change in the pitch or tone of the voice. Shouting is a voice inflection. It is similar to the physical action of pounding on a desk. Either method, shouting or pounding, will serve to gain attention and lend intensity to what is being said. Generally, they go together. Shouting and pounding are bullying tactics which are best left to the dictatorial sort of manager. Democratic managers learn more effective ways to use inflections so as to speak with authority.

A point to remember is that the inflection must fit the message.

A well-liked supervisor gives instructions to his workers: orders that have come down from top management as to what, how, and when a task is to be done. The supervisor's voice is casual, a bit light-hearted, almost as if it were all a joke. What kind of performance can be expected from the employees? More than usual, the same as usual, or, perhaps, less than usual?

Another popular supervisor gives the same set of instructions to a work team, but the message is given in a strong, firm voice and a slow, measured delivery. It is likely that these workers will get the message and that great effort will be put to the task.

Don't forget to show your feelings over the telephone. All too few people at work really lend feelings to their words when talking on the telephone. They generally sound dull and impersonal, unless they are speaking with friends or relatives. No one can see you over the telephone. No one can see your physical mannerisms – a smile or a frown. Only the voice is heard.

Practice adding more zest to your telephone conversations, even when speaking with strangers. When you answer the phone, make your greeting sound as if you are glad to receive the call, even though it may be a complaint or problem call. As you continue to speak, use your voice inflections to express the feelings that are appropriate to the conversation.

For yourself, or for any employee you have who sounds flat on the phone, practice with a tape recorder. Set up simulations for receiving calls from work superiors and the general public; respond to given information, requests, and demands. In the beginning, you may think that your inflections sound exaggerated. Listen closely to well known announcers on radio and television. Their inflections, too, sound a bit exaggerated. But they are enjoyable to listen to and they sound convincing. That's what you want – for people to enjoy listening to you and feel convinced.

Speak in a thorough and orderly manner.

In your mind, outline what you want to say. It may be smart to use your thought hangers. Keep track of all the facts and details. While speaking, you may become momentarily distracted by something or someone. You'll want to get back on the subject as quickly as possible.

Be certain that your message is understood.

A manager will ask the workers if they understand. The workers will usually indicate that they do. The manager will ask, "Are there any questions?" Most likely there will be none. A manager may not be satisfied with these responses.

Experienced managers know that some employees may sometimes hear only what they want to hear. What they want to hear may be somewhat different from what the manager wants them to understand.

When in doubt, it may be advisable to use a direct approach to measure a worker's understanding of what you said. Ask questions of your employees so they can let you know they understand.

- "So, tell me what you will be doing on this job?"
- "So, how are we going to handle this problem?"
- "What will you do right after that equipment gets here?"

Don't antagonize or belittle your experienced workers when you have no doubt as to their ability to understand your words and to get the job done. You will know from experience that when reliable workers don't understand something, they will ask. Avoid earning the reputation of never trusting anyone.

How to Bring a Conversation to an End

After the end of all your listening and speaking, you, as manager, will likely be responsible for bringing a conversation to a close. Sometimes this also means getting a visitor out the door.

Any conversation that is not going anywhere, or not solving anything, should be terminated at a given point. Perhaps your visitor was not well prepared. You might suggest what information would be constructive at a later meeting. Perhaps you, too, need time to gather facts. Re-schedule the meeting, then and there, if possible, while you are both together.

You may still have a problem of getting the visitor to leave. This person may feel no sense of urgency to leave. Pleasant conversation in your comfortable office certainly beats working.

When a guest has stayed beyond acceptable welcome, take action.

1. Stand up. The visitor will likely stand up, too.

2. Say something to let the guest know that the meeting has ended:

"I've enjoyed this meeting with you, but I must let you get back to your job. I know you have work to do."

Or, "I'm sorry that I must get back to work, now."

3. Walk toward the door while you are saying your final words. The visitor should follow you. At the door, shake hands and lead the guest through the doorway. "Have a nice day."

4. Walk over to where the guest is seated, offer your hand, pull the

visitor out of the chair, continue to shake the hand as you lead this person to and out through the door. This is very effective.

By listening and speaking effectively, you understand your employees and they understand you. Problems can be resolved. Conversations can be concluded effectively. Solid working relationships are in the making. Your other functions of management should come more easily.

The best of leaders
have the respect of their followers.

16
HOW TO EARN THE RESPECT OF YOUR EMPLOYEES

A successful manager knows how to get along with people. It's a matter of *leadership*, an acceptable *style*, and skills in *communication*. Consider the meanings of these terms:
– Leadership: The guiding, conducting, directing, influencing of followers.
– Style: The manner in which a manager acts and communicates.
– Communication: Making known; exchanging thoughts and messages.

A tree should be judged only by its fruit.
A manager is a leader whose primary responsibility is to bring workers together to work in harmony. A manager cannot afford to make generalizations about people who differ in age, sex, race, religion, or whatever else. Prejudices cannot be allowed to enter a manager's mind. Employees must be looked upon as individuals – each one's qualities must be seen in a way that best serves the organization.

Relationships need time to grow.
A manager once spoke out, "Management trainers are always trying to tell me how to get along with my employees. When is someone going to tell the employees how to get along with me?"
The most likely answer is that no one ever will. Employees will

learn about their managers, but they will need time, just as a manager will need time to know and understand the workers. The most difficult period is at the beginning when a manager and workers are first thrown together. This may be a time of considerable change. Given an opportunity, the workers and manager will learn of each other's strengths and weaknesses, their individual mannerisms, and habits.

It is not necessary for a manager's style to change. If thoughts and messages are exchanged and made known, and actions are taken in all fairness, it will make little difference whether a manager is loud or quiet, temperamental or easy going, quick to take action or slow and cautious. Eventually, the workers will learn what to expect. Thus, in time, the managers style – including idiosyncrasies – will be accepted.

The story of a manager who ranted and raved.

Everyone on a job site could hear the boss yelling at the workers. They stood around in a semi-circle with sober faces as the supervisor yelled, screamed, and gestured while underscoring the errors of the work crews. One worker, in all seriousness, leaned over and whispered to a companion, ''We have a very smart boss, I think.''

Indeed, this manager was a very smart boss. Everyone from the workers on the site on up though top management knew it. The manager's loud, abrasive manner was shrugged off; the boss was respected and loud outbursts were accepted. Messages were understood.

It is more important for a manager to be respected than to be liked. Workers, too, expect the same. How quickly and successfully this mutual respect is formed depends largely on how soon the manager and workers are seen by one another to be competent, and how quickly and wisely a manager puts into action a few common sense practices.

A Dozen Common Sense Ways to Earn the Respect of Your Employees

1. Continue to do what you do best – manage.

Satisfy the requirements of your job description; give proper priorities to the eight functions of management. You and your office are well organized; you don't forget things; you keep your promises; you observe, you are aware, you act; you are an understanding listener and an understood speaker; and you are learning more about management as you go along.

2. Delegate sensibly.

Some managers think they must do everything themselves. They appear to trust no one. Perhaps these managers are insecure and feel that their work is sacred, that their positions remain strong only through the giving of personal attention to all tasks. Perhaps some of these managers simply feel that they can do the work faster and better than anyone else. They actually enjoy competing with the workers and bettering them. Whichever the case, such managers generally become inefficient and ineffective in a growing organization.

Let others on your team participate. For example, assign someone to put on part of a training programme. Watch morale improve as you get workers involved in what are generally thought to be supervisory tasks.

Keep in mind that delegating is similar to asking a favor. Most employees like to do favors. What they don't like is being ordered to do things that are not actual parts of their jobs. And they like to know that their favors are appreciated. When asking someone to do something, say, "please"; when the task is finished, say, "thank you."

You can delegate a responsibility, but you cannot delegate accountability. You are still accountable. It is essential that you follow up on tasks you have delegated. When the task is lengthy and complicated, check the work as it progresses. For a brief, simple task, give the employee a time or date for its completion, and ask for a report when the work is finished. Never stoop to spy on workers to see how delegated tasks are coming along. Keep your interests and concerns out in the open.

Don't over delegate. Don't let workers think that they are being taken advantage of. Keep your own job description and functions of management clearly in focus. Do delegate to expedite your work, to develop the skills of your workers, and to enhance employee pride and self esteem.

3. Give praise in public; give criticism in private.

When a manager heaps praise upon a deserving employee, right out in front of everyone, the worker – even while blushing with embarrassment – will feel honored.

It is a dishonor to severely criticize or scold a worker when witnessed by other people, even when employees are used to such treatment. When your criticism is given privately, an employee feels less embarrassed and somewhat appreciative that the issue is just between the two of you. The corrective action will be more easily taken.

4. Give the credit to your employees; keep the blame for yourself.

When the work has been running smoothly and the goals have been met, tell your superiors that the results were largely due to the workers' efforts. If a superior offers congratulations for work well done, share these good words with your employees.

When work fails to achieve the expected results, and higher management complains, accept total responsibility. Don't offer excuses or point a finger of accusation at any employee. Present the facts to top management that pertain to the situation, nothing more. When the workers learn that their manager has accepted all the blame for a failure, they will be more likely to accept whatever actions you must take.

5. When you are wrong, admit it.

What does it cost to admit to an employee that you were wrong? Nothing. What you will gain is the employee's respect. Employees respect a manager who will honestly admit a mistake. If employees tease you about your goof, take the teasing good naturedly. Their humor means that they trust you. They think of you as one of them, on the same team. Later, when an employee makes a mistake, it will certainly be readily admitted.

6. An apology costs you nothing; the rewards are beyond measure.

If a disagreement between two people is to end, one of them should apologize. It really makes little difference who is right and who is wrong. The sad fact is that there is a separation between two people who should be working together in some manner of harmony. The person who has the courage to lead begins by saying, "I'm sorry for anything I might have said to hurt your feelings. Let's get this straightened out by someone who can give us the facts."

An apology will work even when there is no argument.

A young supervisor approached an old time machinist with a list of needed repairs.

The machinist was in a foul mood: "What's wrong with everyone? They all act like babies, they can't take care of anything, they break things, and they expect me to make everything right again. Boss, you and the others can go t' hell with these repairs. I've got other things to do, today."

The young boss bristled at this outburst from the older employee. Still seething, the supervisor stared hard at the machinist. Then a youthful grin spread across the supervisor's face. "Hey, ease off. I'm sorry."

"What are you sorry about?" barked the old machinist.

"I don't really know," replied the supervisor, "but I must have said something wrong or put it the wrong way to ruffle your feathers so much."

The machinist's eyes softened. In a quiet voice he said, "You got time for a cup of coffee, boss?"

Over coffee, the old-timer told the young supervisor of problems at home. The supervisor quietly listened, understanding, at last, the reason for the employee's outburst. The young boss was glad that no angry outburst had been made in retaliation. After coffee, the machinist assured the young supervisor that the needed repairs would be made as soon as possible.

This young boss apologized from strength, not weakness. By taking a role of leader, the supervisor came away a winner by using logic, rather than emotion, to deal with a potentially difficult situation.

7. Let the employees sometimes have their moments of humor and fun.

In one office, upon seeing two employees talking, the office manager would move immediately to stand between the two workers, arms folded, saying nothing, just glaring. What kind of morale could anyone expect in an office run by such a person?

Don't be a grouch. When work is flowing smoothly, don't worry about a bit of horseplay, friendly banter, or a few socially acceptable jokes. The employees are showing their high spirits, their pride, and their confidence in being able to get the job done. Keep in mind that a spirited race horse can be reined-in when necessary. But a cart horse can't be whipped or spurred to win races.

In another office, when workers were tense from work pressures and tempers were strained, the manager walked into their midst and declared a National Underachievement Day. After everyone had shared a few minutes of fun and relaxation, the work proceeded smoothly.

8. Utilize your employees's strengths; support their weaknesses.

There are generally some job tasks that employees like to do best. Other tasks may get done, but with less skill and enthusiasm. Try to get the most from what employees like to do, and what they do best. When possible, allow a worker to do fewer tasks where weaknesses are apparent.

In one office, two workers did everything: they typed, answered the telephone, collected money, took complaints, and attended to the ever-mounting pile of bookkeeping. The manager noticed that one employee enjoyed the variety of tasks – everything except bookkeeping. The other person liked the bookkeeping and typing, but seemed to avoid talking to customers or taking messages over the phone. The manager wrote separate job descriptions that allowed these two employees to do what they enjoyed most. They would, of course, be expected to help one another when work loads demanded it.

9. Let the employees know of changes before they happen.

Many employees do not like sudden, unexpected changes. Inform your employees when top management announces planned or anticipated changes. When you are thinking of making a change, tell your workers about it as soon as you feel confident to do so. Ask them to give it some thought. This is your opportunity to explain, in advance, how and why the change will take place. Invite comments. A few worthy comments could cause you to alter your plans somewhat. But the outcome will remain your decision, not the employees. By involving the workers in the planning, you are giving them time to get used to the change before it happens.

One manager had been thinking for some time of rearranging the layout of the work space. The objectives were to improve the work flow, reduce walking distance, and make it easier for workers, whose jobs were related, to communicate more readily. The manager did not want to upset a working day, so a crew was asked to come in at night and make the moves.

The next morning, the workers were understandably surprised. Some were pleased; a few complained. One long-time employee quit – just walked out the door. Later, when this person returned for a final pay check, the manager was told that the move was taken as a personal insult. The former work space, near the window, had been just fine. No one had asked for an old hand's opinion.

10. Be fair with everyone.

You may frequently give preferential treatment to one employee or another, and for good reasons. What other employees might believe to be an act of favoritism may be nothing more than their ignorance of those reasons. Preferential treatment cannot be considered as favoritism if it is given fairly, and if it is understood by everyone. You must convince your workers that they will all be treated alike.

Consider these thoughts:

– Anyone who is self motivated and exceptionally capable will be directed for better opportunities.

– Anyone with a special aptitude will be assigned work where this aptitude can be better utilized.

– A worker who is ill and deemed incapable of performing assigned duties, or who's illness jeopardizes the health of other workers, will be sent home.

– A worker who is just sleepy will not be allowed to go home.

– Workers who are lazy or troublesome will earn the displeasure of the immediate supervisor and will be so informed.

– If personal, family-oriented favors are granted for one employee, such favors should be granted others in similar cases.

Add whatever rules of fairness you can think of, but don't make them up, instance by instance, as you go along. If you do, your ideas of fairness will be seen as inconsistent.

11. Speak up for your employees.

Most of your employees are undoubtedly capable at their jobs. They deserve to be defended when uninformed people question their worth. Defend your employees and they will defend you. Morale will reach a high mark when you and your employees support one another. Usually only a few words of explanation are needed to set the record straight.

If a worker misunderstands your order and makes a mistake that costs time and materials, admit to your boss that you did not explain the order properly.

12. Judge yourself truthfully.

If you are not feeling well and you're not getting everything done that you should, accept it. If your employees or your boss mention your inadequate performance, don't con them. Level with them. You don't have anything to be ashamed of. You'll be respected for not trying to fool the people who are close to you.

Then there are days where you might be exploding with energy and managing in a most creative and effective manner. Even though others do not take notice of your performance, you can still judge yourself as successful. At day's end, you can walk away from the job with a glow of satisfaction. Be satisfied with that.

If you are working in a planning mode, with your feet on your desk, as you think of plans for a new project, and others kid you about having nothing to do, take such teasing in good humor. Chances are they really know you have something big on your mind. Certainly you know it. No explanations are necessary.

To earn the respect of your employees, be the leader in establishing a solid and acceptable relationship. Be consistent. Workers will become accustomed to your behavior and style. In time, a mutual bond will form with links of understanding, tolerance, respect, and trust.

The boss and I, we get along fine.
He does his job and I do mine.

17
HOW TO GET ALONG WITH YOUR BOSS

Knowing how to get along with your boss can prevent unpleasant misunderstandings and managerial snarls at your level. Moreover, a solid subordinate-boss relationship can add greatly to the broadening of your work experiences and to the development of your management skills.

Why Some Managers Dislike Their Bosses

Here are some complaints frequently heard from managers:

– "My manager pokes questions into everything, interferes and asks stupid questions without knowing anything of the work we do."

– "The boss doesn't seem to care what or how we are doing, and doesn't bother to find out."

– "Most of the time the boss isn't available. What can I do when my manager seems always to have someone in the office, or is off at a meeting somewhere, or just disappears?"

– "The boss is smart enough and seems to know the job, but wants to do things without telling me or anybody else what's going on."

– "The boss is two-faced, insincere. To my face, I'm praised; behind my back, I'm criticized."

– "My manager complains about everything. Nothing is ever done right or fast enough."

– "My boss won't raise a finger to help when the rest of us are way behind in trying to get our work done on time."

– "When one of us in the group comes up with a good idea, or when we do something really worthwhile, the boss figures out a way to take all the credit.''

– ''My manager may give me permission to make a decision and take action, but if something goes wrong, I'm out on the limb, alone. The boss tells everyone that the way I did it was wrong and never approved.''

Your boss may have one or more of these faults. If so, what will you do? It is obvious that your boss is not one of your workers. You can't fire an immediate superior. You can't even take disciplinary action. There are ways, however, by which you can work with, through, or around your boss.

Be of Value to Your Boss, and the Organization Will Value You

How you function best as a manager will depend, in part, on your knowledge of the boss's style of management and your ability to deal with it. Here are some suggestions:

1. Do not attempt to make your boss appear incompetent or foolish. Do not permit your workers to do so, either. Disobedience or harmful action to discredit the boss will eventually only hurt you.

2. Keep any ill feelings about the boss to yourself. Let the boss's actions speak for themselves. Don't let your workers push you into making an emotional outburst against your boss that can be held against you later.

3. If you hear that your boss is unreasonably poking into things at the work site and interfering with the workers, get involved. Get out there on the site and be of assistance. Show the boss around and answer all questions. Invite your manager to go with you on rounds of inspection. As long as you keep the boss occupied, the workers won't be bothered. Keep your boss informed by telephone and with memos. In time, your superior will be thoroughly familiar and satisfied with the workings of your unit. At this point, your manager's attention will be directed elsewhere.

4. If your boss appears not to care about the work, the employees, or the accomplishments, put the facts in writing. Send memos and reports. Occasionally, in-person, ask for feedback. Don't be overly sensitive by what you regard as disinterest. An apparent lack of interest may stem from

feelings of complete trust and confidence in your ability to keep things flowing smoothly and produce expected results.

There are some managers who simply don't show much emotion. As long as you get logical answers and workable advice, you can do your job. If you are not getting these, and it becomes evident that your boss is truly disinterested, keep careful records. Someday, if you should suddenly be asked to account for the organization's failings, your carefully kept records could prevent your boss from making you the scapegoat.

5. Do everything possible to help your boss to become successful. By doing so, you will come to be recognized throughout the organization as a competent, supportive manager – a team player. Top management likes this kind of line manager. With this recognition, you will undoubtedly be allowed to learn more and do more.

6. Keep confidential information to yourself. By keeping the boss's trust, more bits of valuable information may be revealed to you. Your boss needs someone trustworthy to whom private matters can be discussed. Let it be you.

7. A boss who is of a jealous and possessive nature does not quickly share information, does not like what might be interpreted as competition, and does not like independent thought and action by subordinates. This is the sort of boss who might take credit for your ideas and accomplishments. To claim your rightful credit would likely cause this person to find ways to embarrass you and put you in your place. Just keep a log or diary of your accomplishments and file them in a secure place.

8. The boss who is away and out of touch much of the time will provide you many opportunities to make decisions, take actions, and grow as a manager. Be careful how you assume these rules of authority.

From someone of authority, seek whatever your need – information, advice, decision, confirmation. Explain your boss's absence and the situation that requires a prompt response.

Be cautious of advice from peer level managers. It is questionable that your boss would accept their advice as authoritative.

Inform your boss, in writing (even though you make an oral report), exactly what decisions were made and actions taken during the manager's absence. State the name and position of the person who advised and confirmed your actions, if any. Include known results in your report. Ask if, in the boss's opinion, the decisions and actions taken by you were correct.

9. Do not brag to friend, family, employees, or other managers of how successfully you are running your group with little or no help from your boss. Such talk could earn you a job cleaning toilets.

10. There are a few unscrupulous bosses who will go to higher executives in an organization and attempt to discredit their subordinate managers. Such bosses may falsely blame others for failures that are rightfully theirs. In these rare instances, managers should know how to protect themselves.

Should you, for any reason, feel that one day you may need to defend an action or explain the truth of some matter, then it would be wise to document everything you do. You should keep dated records of your boss's orders and instructions, when and how you made decisions, and from whom you received confirmation, both written and spoken. Keep dated records of all ideas and suggestions you submit to your boss. Be sure your files are secured. There have been known instances where sensitive files have simply *disappeared*.

11. If your boss repeatedly ignores the valid complaints of workers, write a report, supported with facts, and personally submit it to your boss. When complaints are of a non-personal nature – such as unsatisfactory equipment, or poor office lighting – names of complaining workers must not be mentioned. Your boss may demand to know who is making a complaint.

"Who made this complaint?" the boss may ask angrily.

As the manager, you might reply, "The complaint comes from the group. I think it is worth looking into, so it has become my complaint."

A fair boss will respect such a straight-forward reply.

It is important to remember that you must not earn a reputation of being a trouble-maker. Results count only when they are brought about through ways acceptable to the organization. As previously mentioned, you may find it advisable to keep accurate notes and records. Thus, should your boss continue to ignore legitimate complaints, you will find another way to make the complaints known in the right places.

12. Treat your performance review with respect. It becomes a permanent part of your personal record.

– Do your best to meet established goals and standards.

– If a rating is less than expected, find out why. Seek advice as to how you can improve.

– Work according to priorities that you and your boss have agreed upon.

– Make notes of your progress and accomplishments. Honestly

recognize any shortcomings you might have. Be ready for your next performance review.

– Don't feel bad if your performance review is less than perfect. Don't be argumentative. Just be prepared to offer your records in a logical manner. Again, ask your boss what specifically is wanted of you.

– Even if your rating is superior, don't be content. Treading water is not good enough. Work to improve and grow in knowledge and experience.

Bosses, bad and good.

Bosses, just as you, are subject to performance reviews. An appraisal is loaded with many checks and balances that will ultimately sort out the good bosses from the bad.

Be patient and be a bit tolerant. Give some credit for the thinking and reasoning to the people at the top. They may be allowing an old-timer who has slowed down a bit to retire with dignity. Perhaps there is a transfer in the works for a boss who is presently mis-slotted. And maybe there is a termination being considered for an incompetent manager, just as soon as sufficient evidence has been gathered to justify such an action.

Those who would be considered bad bosses are, by far, very few. In truth, there are far more capable, considerate, and supportive bosses. This majority knows that organizations continually look for promotable people. They know that by helping their managers to improve, they are furthering their own careers.

When the Boss Calls You into the Office, Be Prepared

Some managers are uncomfortable when seated across the desk from their bosses. They should be. These are managers who are unprepared to make intelligent comments. They respond to the boss's probing questions only with a shrug or blank stare. They take their tongue lashings in silence and wait patiently to be told what to do. These responses are not what bosses want. They expect more from their managers.

To help eliminate uncomfortable meetings with your boss:

1. Try to find out the purpose for being called into the boss's office. You can't just come out and ask, "What do you want to see me about?" But it will help to ask if there are any records, reports, or information you should bring to the meeting.

2. Prepare for the meeting. Use your sixth sense and your common sense. You should think of what questions might be asked. This is not a

simple step. Questions tend to become complex – one question leads to another. The questioning may go like this:

"How many man-hours have been lost due to accidents?"

"How serious have the personal injuries been?"

"What has been the extent of damages to equipment?"

"What actions have you taken to prevent a re-occurrence of these types of accidents?"

A boss will be keenly disappointed when a manager does not have factual answers. Consider, too, that perhaps you are being tested. The boss may already have the answers. In any event, before a discussion can begin, the boss will expect you to know exactly what is going on. The only way to know the facts is to collect and review the records.

3. Listen to the questions, think out your answers, then respond quickly, clearly, and concisely. Don't waste the boss's time while you shuffle through papers. Have them organized. Be able to recognize each record at a glance and know what facts are included.

4. Keep in mind that one record may not be sufficient to cover the subject. For instance, a boss wants to talk about production. A manager and the boss each have their own production figures for the past three months. The figures show that there is an obvious production slump. But they do not specifically show where, nor do they show the reason. Production records, by themselves, will not provide the answers.

The boss will undoubtedly ask questions regarding absenteeism, accidents, and shortages. Documented facts will be expected, not answers such as, "There have been several people out sick," "There have been several accidents," "Breakdowns have slowed our production," or "We can't do anything about shortages." Such answers are worthless. Have all records and facts that pertain to the boss's subject of investigation.

5. After the boss's questions have been satisfied, ask permission to offer your own thoughts and ideas relative to the problem. The boss may have already asked for your views. The boss, of course, will have the final word.

There is no reason to fear a meeting with a boss. Armed with hard facts, knowledge of the job, and personal confidence, you should welcome such an opportunity. Only at a meeting with the boss can a capable and prepared manager, such as you, become recognized as a partner in management and not just a taker and giver of orders.

This is what getting along with your boss is all about.

How to Welcome a New Boss

As soon as the appointment of a new immediate superior has been announced by a reliable source, begin preparing your welcoming mat.

- Inform your employees.
- Be alert to their moods, attitudes, and behaviors on the job.
- Be alert for false rumors.
- Assure your workers that they will be informed as soon as more facts are known regarding your new boss and future operations.
- Check all files to see that records are current and readily available.
- See that the physical properties are in good order.
- Maintain a spirit of welcome for your new superior and a respect for management's decision.

You and the employees know that the newly appointed manager comes with delegated authority, but none of you may know what sort of person will appear on the scene. There may be a tendency for you to hold back, to wait and wonder. True, it may be wise to not implement new plans at this time, but routine work should flow as usual.

Upon arrival, a self introduction should be made by the new boss. The new manager should inspect everything and ask questions. Intentions should be announced as to how the unit will be run. Leadership should be quickly established by the new boss. This should happen, but it might not.

There might be an instance when a new boss will quietly come into the unit, find the assigned office, sit back, and wait for something to happen. This could happen. This manager may assume that everyone knows of the change in command and that everyone knows what has to be done. Too often, everyone else in the unit does the same thing – waits for something to happen. Where, then, is the leader?

If you should experience such a situation, assume the non-delegated role of leadership for the purpose of establishing a proper relationship with the rightful leader, your new boss.

Wait a few days to see if the newcomer will want to meet with you. If nothing happens, respectfully ask for a short meeting. Explain that you have a few questions that will require immediate answers so as to prevent delays in the work.

When you do meet with your new boss, and after your questions have been dealt with, ask if the boss would like to meet with workers, or be introduced during a tour of the facilities, or whatever you believe to be appropriate for your situation.

Perhaps the new boss would like to examine work records; to learn about the employees – their training, knowledge, skills, experiences, performances. Would the boss be interested in hearing of present problems facing the work unit, or outstanding achievements? Ask such questions.

Ask your quiet, retiring superior about any proposed changes of objectives, goals, and plans; any new policies, rules, or procedures. You may learn much from this first encounter which you have initiated. Perhaps you will learn that the new manager has already examined the work records, reports, and personnel files. These actions, in themselves, will let you know that your superior is on the ball, that he knows how to search for facts and will likely continue to do so. You may learn of the boss's personality, and the degree of willingness and ability to communicate. You may learn of future plans for the work group – facts that you can share with the employees, as promised.

There is something comforting in having
the facts of a matter in writing.

18

WHERE, WHEN, AND HOW TO WRITE EFFECTIVELY

A written message is an inexpensive form of communication which requires less time to prepare and deliver than it takes to make a series of telephone calls or to conduct a meeting. A written message can be read at a time that is convenient to the person for whom it is intended, can reach several individuals in scattered locations, can be copied with exact consistency, and can remain on file indefinitely.

For these reasons, many managers find letters, memos, reports, newsletters, and bulletin boards to be a most effective form of communication. They have learned that what is silently read is often more *clearly and loudly received* than what is heard.

Most business writing is done in the form of letters, memorandums, and reports. These serve a variety of purposes:
- seeking or providing information
- requesting or granting favors
- offering or accepting invitations
- issuing or acknowledging orders.

How to Write Letters, Memos, and Reports Effectively

There are managers who run into difficulties when writing. Some managers complain that they can't think of what to say; their minds become as blank as the paper before them. Some managers know what to say, but they can't express themselves in writing. Some managers are not familiar with the proper format of a written, business communication;

some believe that their knowledge of grammar, punctuation and spelling is inadequate.

Many colleges and universities teach courses in business correspondence. Your local bookstore is likely to have one or more books to suit your writing needs. Either way, by taking a course or reading some books, you can learn from educators or business professionals.

If these ways are too expensive or inconvenient for you, there is another way. It isn't really an easier way, but it won't cost you anything, you won't have to go to school, and it is practical and applicable. Naturally, there is some effort involved.

Learn to write business letters, memos, reports.

Here are a few suggestions to help you develop your own writing course and overcome any writing limitations:

1. Go to a manager whom you admire, or a secretary who writes the boss's business correspondence, and ask to see correspondence file copies of the form you need to learn right now – business letters, memos, and reports. Don't be embarrassed at revealing your lack of polish as a writer. Chances are you will be much admired for your desire to improve this managerial skill. Remember, look for the copies of correspondence that are similar in purpose to the ones you probably will need to write.

2. Study the layouts.
– Notice how much space is allowed for top, bottom, and side margins.
– Notice where the date is positioned, how the letter is addressed, and the placement of these at the top of the page.
– Notice the forms of salutation: some are formal, others are informal; some are personal, addressing a person by name; others are impersonal, as with "Dear Sir:" or "Dear Madam:". Sometimes the "Dear" is eliminated, especially when the sex of the recipient is unknown. The salutation may be directed only to the title or classification of the recipient: "To The General Manager:", "To The President:".
– Notice that a colon follows a business salutation. To a friend, you would follow the salutation with a comma: "Dear Pat,".
– Notice that the sender's name is signed. The sender's name and title are generally typed underneath the signature.
– Following the closing signature, you may find the initials in capital letters, then a slash, followed by initials in small case: DAW/kr. The first initials are those of the person who composed the correspondence; the second set of initials are those of the person who typed it.
– Following the initials, you will occasionally find the abbreviation,

"cc:". This stands for *carbon copy*, copies of the correspondence sent to others who might have interest in the matter. Following the abbreviation will be the persons or places where copies have been sent.

    Example: cc: Executive Vice President
                     Department Of Human Resources
                     File

   – You may also sometimes find the abbreviation, "Encl.:", which stands for *enclosure*. This means that other material accompanies the letter, memo, or report.

    Example: Encl.: Copy of employee's Ideas For Profit

   3. Carefully study the contents of the correspondence copies. Sometimes the purpose is stated in the opening format, above the text.

    Example: Date:
                To:
                From:
                Subject:

Without such a formal format, the purpose is generally stated in the first paragraph.

    Example: This letter is to inform you . . .

   When a business letter is written to a friend, however, the first paragraph may contain a note of common, personal interest.

    Example: We heard of your daughter's graduation with
                honors. Congratulations to the daughter and
                the parents. Drop us a line and let us know
                what she has planned next.

   A friendly opener would then be followed with the main purpose of the correspondence. Here is where you get into the lessons of written expression. Choose one paragraph, or just one sentence. Put the letter aside and see how closely you can write that thought – not memorized words, but the thought in your own words. Most famous writers began their careers by imitating the styles of other writers. Everyone learns some things from the school of imitation. Continue to practice writing other thoughts of other writers. Compare each of your written expressions with the original versions.

   4. After you have had sufficient practice at imitating other writers, begin to express your own thoughts.

   – Review the purpose of your message.

– Gather your facts.

– Arrange your thoughts in logical, outlined order.

– Know the person to whom you are writing: If the person is a friend, be friendly; if the person is a stranger, be polite; if the person is an enemy, don't write.

The rest should be easy:

– If you want information, ask for it.

– If someone asks for information, give it.

– If someone extends an invitation, say how delighted you are to accept, or how disappointed you are to decline.

– If someone has experienced a misfortune, express your feelings. Put yourself in the other person's place. Imagine what that individual will think and feel when your letter is read. Be as considerate as you would be if you were talking directly with that person.

5. Express your thoughts as simply as possible. Write short sentences: they are less likely to have grammatical errors, they will require less punctuation, and they are easier to read and understand.

6. Keep a dictionary handy. Look up a word when you are unsure of its spelling or meaning. To find a word in the dictionary, you will need to know approximately how it is spelled. If you cannot find that word, don't use it. Think of another word – one that will be easier to spell. If you can't think of another word that conveys the same meaning, rewrite the sentence. There is more than one way to express a thought.

7. Read your letter aloud. Or better yet, have someone read it to you. If a sentence has to be read more than once to be understood, you can bet that the sentence structure needs improving. Once again, say the thought aloud. Say it in a manner that will be more clearly understood. Rewrite the sentence. Don't think of yourself as an inferior writer when you find it necessary to cross out words, erase mistakes, and rewrite entire paragraphs. Professional writers take these same corrective actions.

How to know when a message is received and understood.

You will want to know that information, instructions, or orders sent by letter or memo have been acted upon. In these instances, you might close with a statement similar to one of the following:

– ''Please initial and return on or before (date).''

– ''Please reply by letter no later than (date).''

– ''Please give me a call by (date), and let me know what you think.''

It is always wise to state a deadline for any reply that you want to receive.

A manager will sometimes send one letter to be read by a chain of people. Underneath the address, the word *Attention:* is followed by a list of people to receive the message.

In the letter or memo, the last paragraph will instruct each recipient to initial next to his or her name at the top of the page. The last person on the list is instructed to return the letter to the person who wrote it. It is often wise to follow a written message with an oral one. With a brief telephone call, you can learn if your letter was received, you can answer questions, and you can reinforce the importance of what was written.

The opposite is also true. You may find it of value to send letters following conversations that were made in person or on the telephone. A follow-up written message is a clear and specific reminder of what was said.

Influence Your Employees Through the Organization's Newsletter

A regularly published paper is a favorite method of communication for large organizations where employees are widely scattered throughout several departments.

Through most newsletters, employees' unity is strengthened because the publication is for the employees, not for the general public. Much is written of what the employees are doing.

From the organization's newsletter, employees learn what management is doing. Management can bring about greater employee pride and faith in the organization and can counter speculative rumors with truthful facts. An announcement of new equipment to be purchased; plans for expansion; opportunities for new jobs, transfers and promotions – all these can be brought to the workers through an organization's newsletter.

Some progressive organizations allow employees to be heard – to ask questions and to air complaints.

Although workers are interested in what goes on in management and what is happening in other work areas, they prefer to read about themselves and their own work unit. It's your responsibility to report what is newsworthy throughout your own work area. When you promote the successes, the interesting happenings, and the humorous instances of your employees through the organization's publication, you will be seen as a responsible, caring leader. This is a role you must constantly promote for yourself – being a leader worth following.

Begin by contacting the organization's newsletter editor. Let it be known that you are interested in being a regular contributor. Learn the

paper's format, the deadlines for contributions, and the sections that appear regularly. These sections may include such topics as:
- notices of promotions and transfers of employees
- employment anniversaries and years of service
- employee marriage notices
- announcements of births to the employees of the organization
- organization sponsored sports scores and standings
- cartoons and jokes appropriate to the organization
- news and information about departments and units
- letters to the editor: questions, opinions, complaints from the employees, with answers or comments from qualified leaders in the organization
- contributions of a technical nature: how to do it better, faster, easier, and cheaper.

Encourage your employees to help in making their work group better known throughout the organization. Try to have various employees mentioned by name in each issue of the newsletter.

As a reporter, you need not worry about your writing style. Simply provide the facts. The editor will see that an article is suitably written for publication.

How to Use a Bulletin Board Effectively

The display of messages at specific locations is one of the oldest, simplest methods of communication. Long ago, people cut marks on trees, or arranged piles of stones to signify a message. Whoever might pass by would understand these messages. Similar trail markings are still being used throughout the world.

As written languages developed, leaders of communities and recognized organizations began to post messages where people were likely to gather. Bulletin boards were eventually established at key locations as permanent message centers.

Today, well-managed bulletin boards continue to be popular gathering places. People can read the information that comes down through the organization as well as use the bulletin boards, themselves, to exchange messages. In work organizations, there are specific licenses, posters, and bulletins that, by law, must be displayed. Such permanent notices should be displayed in prominent locations, but not necessarily on the same bulletins board that is used by work unit managers and their employees.

What can a bulletin board do for you?
You may want to display such items on your bulletin board as:

– Posters and bulletins that come from the central office.

– Your instructions, announcements, and reminders to workers.

– Messages written by employees. These may include notices of things to sell, trade, or wanted to buy; requests to share transportation or living quarters; or announcements of social and sports events.

– Jokes, cartoons, and humorous stories.

The benefits derived from your bulletin board will include:

– Time saved. A single message for the bulletin board requires less time to prepare than writing several letters or memorandums. A posted message frequently eliminates the need for a meeting. Employees can read the bulletin board at their convenience.

– Improved morale. Cartoons, jokes, humorous stories, and personal messages will give the workers a sense of sharing, participation, and belonging. The bulletin board will encourage the employees to communicate freely and openly.

– Improved productivity. Workers who post personal messages on the bulletin board will have less reason to wander away from their work place just to pass the same personal message from person to person. The bulletin provides a means of contact with other employees whom they may not personally know, or who are difficult to reach during working hours.

– Fewer rumors. You can prevent rumors, or put a stop to rumors that are going around, by frequently posting factual messages of what is happening.

If the organization won't give you a bulletin board, make one.

Organizations will usually provide bulletin boards for unit managers. However, if your organization cannot or will not provide you with a bulletin board, you can easily and quickly make your own. The board should be of a soft, porous material in which pins or thumb tacks can be easily put in and removed without leaving ugly holes. The size of the board is determined by the anticipated number of items to be displayed.

How to manage a bulletin board.

As with all other personal systems of management, the bulletin board must be well managed to be effective. Here are a few suggestions:

1. Locate the bulletin board in a well traveled and frequented area near a drinking fountain, main door, or time-clock; or in a place where workers eat and rest. Avoid locations such as hallways and work areas where a gathering of employees would interfere with normal people traffic or with other employees at work.

2. It is advisable to have one person delegated to manage the bulletin board. This person will be responsible for:

– Seeing that all messages and humorous contributions are clearly worded and not offensive to other employees. In many organizations, messages written by employees must be submitted directly to the bulletin board supervisor to be approved and posted. Unauthorized messages are to be removed.

– Determining the dates that items are to be removed. The date of posting should be written at the top of the message. The content of the message will often determine the date of removal. An announcement of a coming event, for instance, should be removed as soon as the event has taken place. Humorous items and personal messages should remain no longer than a week or two. An employee may complain that an advertised object has not yet been sold after two weeks. Encourage the worker to write a new message; one with more sales appeal.

It is important that messages not be allowed to get stale. Keep employee readership high with fresh copy.

– Keeping the board, neat, attractive, and orderly. Removing and posting messages is only part of the job. Arrange key messages for maximum exposure. Rotating messages from one position to another will draw added attention.

3. Orders, instructions, and other important messages from various levels of management should include the statement, "Please Read and Initial." This will allow you to determine quickly who has read a message and who has not.

4. Include the location and the purpose of the bulletin board in your orientation of new employees. Also, explain how the bulletin board can be used by the employees. While you may delegate the responsibility of caring for the bulletin board, you are not delegating your accountability for its effectiveness. Check the bulletin board yourself frequently. See that it does not become messy with old, tattered, and faded bulletins tacked over one another. To develop pride in your employees, give them things to be proud of.

Write your own ticket to success.

Managers are expected to improve their managerial talents. Writing is one of these essential talents. Become familiar with the various forms of written communication used within your organization. Continue to study how writers of these communications express themselves. Use your own written messages to make clear and lasting impressions. Remember that skills are born from practice. Whatever the business form of written communication, whatever the thought to be expressed, you need only to write in a manner that is simple, expressive, factual, courteous, and in a logical order.

Meetings and medicines are prescribed to cure ills.
Each can leave a lingering good taste when pleasantly coated.

19
HOW TO USE MEETINGS TO GET RESULTS

Some managers are accused of having too few meetings; some are accused of having too many. Some meetings are too long; others are too short. Some meetings are dull. Nevertheless, meetings are essential. They are more personal than other forms of communication; results can be obtained quickly; and information given through systems of meetings can filter upward, downward, and sideways.

It is important for supervisors and managers at every level to be able to conduct meetings that hold people's attention and, even more important, get results. Only meetings that get results are successful.

Ingredients of a Successful Meeting

The ingredients of a successful meeting are purpose, goal, method, and leadership.

The Purpose

Meetings come in variety of purposes:
- to determine and prepare rules, policies, and procedures
- to prepare informative bulletins
- to issue work assignments
- to offer encouragement and raise enthusism
- to present new plans or methods
- to demonstrate new equipment or new products
- to learn of employees' problems, feelings, opinions, and ideas
- to settle disagreements

– to hear reports, evaluations, and proposals
– to explore and solve complex problems.

The purpose will be the key in determining who will be invited to a meeting: workers, other managers, executives, or specialists.

The Goal

Every meeting must have a goal. The goal is the stated final accomplishment. Think for a moment of goals in relationship to the purposes: a purpose may be to write rules that will correct a problem within the organization, while the goal would be for these rules to be workable, enforceable, and agreed upon. A purpose may be to issue work assignments. The associated goal would be to get the job done quickly by putting the right people in the right slots.

Method And Leadership

The method of conducting a meeting and the manner of leadership employed are determined by the purpose for having a meeting and by the ease or difficulty anticipated in attaining the goal. These are best understood by taking a look at the two general classifications of meetings: informal and formal.

Informal Meetings, Brief and Simple

You may have need to call your workers together quickly and unexpectedly. The meeting may be held anywhere, indoors or outdoors. To accomplish a result (goal), you may have a reason (purpose) to make announcements, give reminders, give work orders, or arouse some enthusiasm. Informal on-the-job gatherings for such purposes should last no longer than three to five minutes. Control this time; don't allow open discussions. Should employees have personal views to offer, invite them to see you in your office, after the meeting.

At other times, you may call a few of your reliable employees to your office for a more complex purpose, to ask for their opinions on a work related matter, or just to kick around some ideas. These meetings can also be informal, but you will want it to be in the privacy of your office, or some other place where you can talk without interruptions. You'll also want to allow sufficient time for everyone to express their views and bring the meeting closer to achieving the result you are looking for.

How to Prepare for a Formal Meeting

A given purpose may be better accomplished in a formal meeting. This form of meeting, however, requires more than just a hoot and a wave of your hand to a few workers close by. Preparations must be made well in advance.

Begin by asking yourself questions. Your answers will equip you with a list of step-by-step preparations to be made.

1. What are the subjects to be covered?

Sufficient knowledge of these subjects is essential to planning an agenda and scheduling within a time frame. Generally, a meeting should last no longer than one hour. In that hour, an agenda of only one to three items should be presented. No meeting should have more than five topics. Too many subjects within an hour will create confusion and cause participants to lose interest and forget much of what was said. If one subject requires nearly all of an hour, schedule any remaining subjects for another meeting period. Additional one hour meetings can be scheduled for later in the day, or for another day. When you hear talk of an organization holding day-long meetings, that is what is meant – a series of one hour meetings held throughout the day. Even what are said to be meetings lasting two or three hours are usually broken into hourly segments by calling for break periods of 10 to 30 minutes.

2. Who should be invited to the meeting?

Your invitation list will depend largely upon the purpose of the meeting. Some meetings are of a general nature. Other meetings are of limited concern. But even when the subject is of interest to many employees, only a few may be invited.

For instance, the purpose of a meeting may be to consider the purchase of a new piece of equipment. Many employees may be interested, but only those who can make valuable contributions to the subject should be invited to attend as participants. In this instance, you might choose to invite someone who understands the technical aspects of the equipment, a person who can discuss its operation, someone who can talk of cost analysis, and another who understands the purchasing process.

There are instances where your boss and bosses of higher rank may be asked not to attend a meeting. You may feel that their presence would tend to intimidate the participants. Many valuable thoughts and opinions might remain unsaid. If this should happen, the meeting could fall short of its goal. You may suggest to these bosses that once the facts and opinions have been gathered, and a recommendation has been made, you will provide them with a complete report, either in writing or at a meeting for their benefit. Have the courage to keep out the people whose presence is not required, no matter how much rank and power they have. Level with your boss; explain why you feel that results can best be obtained through a closed session. Most likely, your boss and other higher-ups will respect your request for the reasons you state.

3. Where and when should meetings be held?

Formal meetings should be held in a room that is well lighted, properly ventilated, free from outside distractions, and where the members can be seated comfortably. A private office may be suitable for a small group of people. For large groups, a special meeting room is needed. Where organizations have no special meeting facilities, you can generally rent a meeting room at a restaurant or hotel if your budget will allow for it. Some managers hold meetings in their homes, or at the homes of participants.

Choose a meeting date and time that is most convenient for the participants. You might find it advisable to poll the group as to their preferences before setting a date and time. If it is impossible for one of your chosen participants to attend, you'll just have to find a substitute – someone of equivalent knowledge in that particular specialty.

4. Do the participants know one another?

People are more willing to participate in group discussions when they know the names and jobs of other participants. Don't let your guests be strangers. If they do not already know one another by name, provide them with name tags. Name tags are not expensive. Some organizations, such as banks, will give them to you for free. Name tags also can be made simply by writing names on pieces of paper and using pins as fasteners.

Depending upon how and where participants are to be seated, another idea is to make name signs to be placed at the front of the tables or desks in front of the guests. Take a piece of 8½" by 11" heavy stock paper, cut off about 4 inches from the top. Fold in two, length ways, and you have an A-frame name sign, standing approximately 2 inches high and 8½ inches long. You can use a broad tip marker pen for printing names and titles.

It's also a good idea to introduce the participants, or let them introduce themselves, at the first meeting.

5. How should the seating be arranged?

When little participation is expected from individuals – as in a training meeting – the seating can be arranged in school room fashion. For open discussions, when everyone is expected to voice contributions, a conference table might be more suitable. For somewhat larger groups, several tables can be arranged in a U-shape, with the participants being seated on the outside facing inward. If tables are not available, simply arrange chairs in a semicircle.

6. What will the participants need?

Inform the participants of any specific records or reports that they are to bring to the meeting. When participants are required to take notes, writing materials should be provided by the organization, or the members should be advised to bring their own.

If smoking is to be permitted, a supply of ash trays should be made available. If smoking is not to be allowed during the meeting, let the members know of this policy in advance. Tell them, too, how long the meeting will be. If your meeting is held to an hour, smokers will probably find no problem abstaining from smoking for such a short time. Should the meeting be a lengthy one, let the smokers know if there will be break periods and a place where they can light up.

Refreshments are sometimes provided when meetings continue through a half day or even through an entire work day. Light refreshments generally help to keep the participants' energy levels up. If you feel that refreshments are called for, be sure you have the approval of the organization – not only for the kind of refreshments, but for the cost as well. It is not smart to serve beer, wine, or hard liquor at meetings. Sound decisions and proposed actions do not come from bottles. When choosing refreshments, never serve any beverage or food that will offend customs or religions. Refreshments are seldom provided for brief (one hour), routinely scheduled meetings.

7. What will you or other featured speakers need?

Review your subjects for the meeting. How can these be best presented? What presentation aids are available? Some of the options are: blackboard, chalk, and eraser; flip chart, easel, and marking pen; film or slide projector; tape or record machine; a table for displays. Also, you might need certain papers to be copied and handed out during the meeting.

8. How and when should the participants be notified?

Give invited people sufficient time to plan for their attendance. Decide how they will first be notified – a written notice, a telephone call, or a personal contact. Make an outline of the essential notice information so that everyone will receive the same general information.

The notice should include the purpose of the meeting, subjects to be covered; the date, time and place; the approximate duration of the meeting; and any materials or records that the members are to bring.

A reminder should be given to each invited participant on the day before the meeting, by the surest and quickest manner.

Making a meeting preparation checklist.

Now that you have gathered the answers to your questions, you are ready to outline a meeting preparation checklist. By using the list, you can assign specific tasks for others to do. You will also be able to keep track of other peoples' progress as they work on their assigned preparations. Here is a sample format:

Meeting Preparation Checklist

A. General Information

    1. Purpose of the meeting:

    2. Subjects to be covered:

    3. Names, titles, locations of persons to be invited:

    4. Meeting Location:
        Date: Time: Duration:

B. Preparations

    Task Assignments   Assigned To / Complete By

Don't let assignments become forgotten. Some of your people may need to be reminded and nudged to get assigned tasks completed on time.

How to Conduct a Formal Meeting

Don't allow a lengthy delay to spoil the results of your planning before the meeting begins. If all participants are not present a few minutes before the meeting, have someone put in a call to any people who are missing. Come as close as you can to starting your meeting on time, with or without the absent members.

If you are fairly new at conducting meetings and feel just a little bit nervous, don't mention it. You'll warm up to the task at hand as the meeting gets underway and any thoughts of nervousness will be forgotten.

During the meeting, your main job will be to keep the discussions moving forward, on track and on schedule. As the meeting progresses, your watch will tell you how much time has been used. Your meeting outline will tell you what subjects remain. Here are a few suggestions to help you maintain control of your meeting:

1. Do not allow one person to dominate the meeting. Listen carefully to what is being said. A speaker may get carried away with the importance of an opinion. If it takes too long to get a point across, if the same thing is said over and over again, or if the speaker strays away from the topic under discussion, wait until a sentence has been said then quickly interrupt, ''Can you briefly summarize your thoughts as they pertain to the subject being discussed?'', or, ''Your point is well taken, but it does not pertain to the question at hand? Please hold that thought until later.''

2. Pull the quiet members into the discussions. They were invited for what they have to offer. Do not assume that they, who are now just sitting and listening, have nothing to say. A quiet member may be waiting for you to say who is to speak next. Another quiet member may be intimidated by individuals in the group who are of much higher rank. Still another quiet one may be turned off by the loudness and interruptions of other group members.

When a subject touches upon a quiet person's field of expertise, jump in and ask that person a direct question: ''What do you think are the most common, on-the-job breakdowns, and why do you think they occur?'' Or, ''What is your opinion as to how the other operators will feel about the proposed changes in procedures?''

When quiet members are asked to speak, when you have made certain that they will have the group's attention, they will participate. They may speak quietly and briefly, but what they say will be of importance.

3. Do not allow a speaker to be interrupted. If someone does interrupt, or begins to talk aloud to another participant, stop it with an interruption of your own: ''Okay, let's listen to what this speaker has to say, then I'll ask for your comments and questions.''

4. Do not allow dead issues to be brought up again: ''That business is finished. We must now resolve the question before us.''

5. Do not allow yourself to be intimidated. The conduct of the meeting is your responsibility. Throughout the meeting, you are the boss. If someone outranks you and jumps in with uncalled for comments, treat

the remarks just as you would those from anyone else. (Perhaps you might use a bit more tact and diplomacy.)

6. In a really good meeting, participants can sometimes become overly enthusiastic, loud, and aggressive. You and others might find it difficult to hear or be heard, but don't shout. Instead, try lowering your voice while continuing to talk. The chances are good that the loud ones will quiet down, one by one, as they become aware that perhaps something of importance is being said. It sometimes is equally effective to just stand quietly, without saying anything, until the loud ones take notice of your silence.

7. In a meeting where members sit silently with owl-like stares, little can be accomplished. It is preferable to conduct a meeting of enthusiastic participants. Be enthusiastic, yourself. Display a sense of humor. In a good natured way, scold the group for appearing as statues. Go around the group asking each individual the same question. Sooner or later, someone will say something worthwhile, something that will provoke others to respond.

How to Record a Formal Meeting

It is the purpose of a meeting, rather than its length, that determines the need for a written record. Minutes of a meeting are generally written when the purpose is any of the following:
- prepare rules, policies, and procedures
- explore and solve complex problems
- plan new projects or programmes
- propose strategies and actions
- make decisions
- examine reports and evaluate works in progress.

Some managers encourage participants to write their own notes during meetings. Personal notes may be adequate for a brief, informal meeting, but not for an in-depth, formal meeting. When participants write their own notes, you have no knowledge as to what is written. The minutes written by a recording secretary, on the other hand, will be complete, accurate, and consistent.

If you do not have someone with the training and experience to record meetings, all you need is someone who can write notes quickly and legibly. Your recorder will write notes only when instructed to do so. During the meeting, your responsibility will be to dictate all essential information to be recorded. The recording secretary's job is to take notes, not to participate in the meeting.

If prefer to have a member of the meeting keep the minutes, remember that this person cannot do two things at once. When you have something to be recorded, all talking except your own will have to stop, allowing your recorder to concentrate on writing without missing any of the meeting. The rest of the time, the keeper of the minutes can serve as a group participant without having to worry about writing notes.

Here are some guidelines for creating a meaningful, workable record of your meeting:

1. Instruct your secretary to record the time, day, and date. Record the names of the participants. Note those persons who are absent.

2. Choose the manner in which you wish the meeting notes to be written. Some managers choose to have minutes written in the simplest form. Notes are written only after a subject has been presented, discussed, and decided. A manager then dictates a summary statement to the secretary. This form stresses results, rather than details of how results were obtained. For example:

> "The proposals from the Blue Equipment Company and the Green Equipment Company for the purchase of a new backhoe were discussed by the members present. The factors for comparison were: capacity, performance, maintenance, cost, terms, and delivery time. The members of this committee voted unanimously to recommend the acceptance of the proposal as offered by the Blue Company."

Other managers prefer to record the pertinent contributions of each participant. The advantage of this form is that a reader will know the identity of persons who offered specific information or comments. Should further details be required, the proper person can be contacted. Here is an example of this form:

> "The project engineer expressed need for equipment with sufficient capacity to dig 28 miles of trenches within the contracted time. The purchasing manager distributed copies of the purchase proposals and technical specifications. The heavy equipment foreman asked about maintenance support. The purchasing manager stated that the Blue Company would send a person to show mechanics the new, simplified maintenance procedures for their advanced backhoe design."

3. Stop the meeting whenever you want to make a statement for the record. Only you, the chairman, will instruct the recorder to write. When the secretary has finished writing your statement, ask that it be read aloud. After the group has been asked to approve or correct the statement, you will move on to the next topic.

4. Instruct the secretary to make note of any assignments that are given to members. It is frequently necessary for someone to seek further information or take some action following a meeting. Any assignment written into the minutes will serve as a future reminder of what must be done. In the same manner, those absent will also be informed or reminded of who is supposed to do what.

5. Should another meeting be necessary, try to schedule it before you adjourn. It will be easier to get members to agree to a time, date, and place while you have them all together. Instruct the secretary to include information in the minutes of the next scheduled meeting.

6. Have the secretary note the time when the meeting ends.

7. Following the meeting, the recorder, or someone you assign to do the typing, will type the minutes and have copies made. These copies will be distributed to all members of the committee, including those persons who were absent, and to any other individuals who are entitled to receive them.

One more word about your recording secretary. Much time can be saved during meetings should you be fortunate enough to have a professional secretary with experience in keeping records in the format of your choice. But until a secretary's skill in writing notes has been proven, continue to dictate your statements. Accuracy, completeness, and consistency are more important than time saved.

How to Rate Your Meetings and Yourself

–Did you feel that your meeting was adequately prepared?
–Did the meeting begin on time?
–Did you limit your topics to five or less?
–Did you control the participants – encouraging the quiet ones to talk, and stopping those who talked too much?
–Did you adhere to the time limit you set?
–Did you speak from the heart and mind rather than just from notes?
–Did you determine the need for the meeting to be recorded? Was the information clearly and concisely written in the format you prefer?

–Did the meeting accomplish its purpose? Did you attain the desired results?

As you attend meetings of other managers, listen and watch. How would you rate them? Learn what you can from managers who conduct meetings successfully. Practice what you learn. Your ability to prepare and conduct meetings for various purposes – meetings that will be stimulating and productive – will serve to advance your career in management.

How to Speak Without Notes

As a manager, the chances are good that you may be called upon to stand before a group of people and speak on a specific topic. There is no reason to stand before an audience with your head held down as you read from notes in your trembling hand. People watching a speaker read from notes are distracted from what is being said. Some might wonder if the speaker really knows the subject. Some might think it a bother to listen when they could read the same material if copies of the notes were made available.

You do know your subject. If you didn't, you wouldn't have been asked to speak on it. So, you don't need to write down what you already know. You do, however, need to begin with a simple outline that puts the parts in order. A successful speaker knows how to keep an outline out of sight.

Here are some ways to make your outline invisible.

1. Write a detailed outline of your speech. Study it.

2. On a smaller piece of paper, reduce your outline. Use only topic headlines and a key word or two, to trigger your memory.

3. Reduce these headings and words to an even smaller piece of paper; one that can be held in the palm of your hand without being seen by anyone else.

4. Put those abbreviated headings and key words in your mind, on *thought hangers*.

5. Practice giving your speech – once, using the abbreviated outline; then, again, without the outline.

6. Just before you give your talk to an audience, you should be able to throw away your *crutch* – that tiny scrap of paper. Not having the paper in your hand will force you to think of the logical flow, rather than read from an outline.

As you speak, let yourself enjoy the feeling of sharing what you know with others. And remember this: no one except you will know if you should forget some small part of your talk. During the question and answer session following your presentation, the audience will have ample opportunity to learn what else they want to know.

There are answers to every question.
The trick is in finding the right answer.

20
HOW TO MAKE SENSIBLE DECISIONS

Managers occasionally may feel that their job is one continuous series of problems, and that blame will come down heavily on the managers who do not solve those problems. They may wonder, perhaps, if there are some uncontrollable problems – problems for which they cannot be held responsible.

There are some problems, of course, for which they will not be blamed. Nevertheless, they are expected to cope with problems that affect their work groups, even though problems occur through no fault of their own.

Most problems respond to procedure. As you understand and practice a decision making procedure, problems will appear not so much as obstacles, but more as opportunities for accomplishments. A discussion of how procedure replaces obstacles with opportunities will include: problems, decisions, actions, progress measurements, and the evaluation of results.

Recognize a Problem for What It Is

1. Expect problems to arise. Seek them out. Listen to people, ask questions. Observe the actions that are taking place in your own organization and throughout the world. Read articles, stories, news items. Be aware of the happenings around you that may affect changes in your organization and your work.

At a time when the country is in an economic recession, it should be no surprise that money, from all sources, may be less available. There may be less work; fewer, if any, pay raises; and a rash of lay-offs.

In times of low interest rates, organizations borrow money for capital expansion; people borrow money to finance houses and automobiles. Prosperity is at hand; good paying jobs are plentiful. Prosperity brings problems in new forms – there are workers to hire and train, equipment to install, orders to fill.

Seasoned managers have a sense of what is coming and they prepare themselves for whatever crunch will occur, good or bad.

2. Consider the problem. Ask yourself a few pertinent questions:
– Does the problem originate at a source that is far removed from your work place?
– Does the problem come from within your area of control?
– Is it a problem that you can prevent?
– Is it a problem that has happened, is happening, or one that may happen?
– Is it essential that you act quickly, or do you have time to plan and prepare?

Before you reach for a sensible decision, it is essential to shine a light of understanding on the subject of your concern. A decision does not mean the end of a problem. It is merely the beginning of a solution.

How to Reach a Sensible Decision

There are three ways to reach a decision: intuition, judgement, and system.

Intuition

You may know that an occurrence will take place, that a chosen action will be correct, that the situation is bound to end successfully. You may, however, be unable to explain your reason because reasoning is not involved. You just *know*. Perhaps you've had a strong intuition about someone you've just met. Impulsively, you've wanted that person as a close friend, maybe even a spouse.

Intuition is knowing without using conscious thought processes. Intuition is frequently referred to as a hunch, or a *gut feeling*, and may stem from a person's moral principles and strict convictions of what is right and wrong. These intuitions are worth heeding. On the other hand, what a person believes to be intuition may often be nothing more than wishful thinking. Most people who gamble – who bet on horse races, a show of cards, or a turn of the wheel – unwisely depend upon their hunches. Most intuitive gamblers lose.

If a time comes when you cannot offer a sound explanation for your chosen decision, other than to say it is just a hunch, you will likely fail in convincing your superior that your decision is, indeed, a sound one. It is also unlikely that you will persuade your boss to your way of thinking.

Judgement

Fully ninety percent of all decisions are based upon judgement. Managers will say, "It is my judgement that we will . . ." These managers assume that their judgement is superior to those of their employees. They have, they reason, more knowledge and experience from which to draw, therefore their decisions should be correct. They might be right if those managers have sufficient, current knowledge and experience.

Most judgement decisions come easily and quickly. This is what is expected of managers. Occasionally, managers will need time to remember what it was they once knew, or the experiences they once had. Some managers might say, "Let me give you a decision tomorrow. I want to think about it." These managers feel need to question their own judgement-calling abilities. They admit that some time is needed to recall what they once knew and to tap into current knowledge and experience. There is nothing wrong with taking time to think before expressing a judgement. Taking time to base a judgement on today's happenings is a wiser course than snapping off judgements based on "the ways we did things back in the old days."

Your Decision Making System

Imagine that you have been made aware of a problem. You have no intuitive thought that will inspire a solution. You may feel somewhat unknowledgeable and inexperienced to make a judgement regarding the problem at hand. You will need to turn your decision making over to a system.

This decision making system can be broken down into nine steps:

1. Collect and analyze all available information.

Depending upon the nature of the problem, you may choose to collect and analyze information yourself, or you may delegate all or part of these tasks to others.

Information may come to you through conversations, meetings, books, reports, or records. If the information you need is perhaps technical in nature, it is advisable to enlist the aid of a specialist. Specialists know what to look for, where to look, and how to explain what they find. It is not considered smart for a manager, without knowledge of medicine, to dig through medical books and then prescribe and treat a serious illness. Play it smart. Seek counsel of those who have professional expertise in the field of your concern.

2. Look for the real problem.

This step is frequently forgotten. Some managers are so concerned with what is obvious, that they overlook what may be less apparent but more serious. The information you gather and analyze should alert you to a previously hidden problem, if it exists.

The following stories illustrate the point:

Fights were occurring in a warehouse nearly every day. The manager learned that one person was always involved in the fighting. The snap judgement was to fire the employee, as called for by company policy, but the boss took time to check personnel records and found that the accused trouble-maker was from another country. Letters of recommendation from that country showed that the person was considered as a loyal, trusted, capable, hard-working worker. The boss snooped around a bit more. One of the old-time warehouse workers, who had not been involved in the fighting, told the manager that there were several workers who had been making problems for the *outsider*. This, the manager believed, was the real problem – racial intolerance. Putting a stop to that would be a wiser decision than firing the newcomer.

A manager was made aware that the small, five-horsepower engines that drove the pumps were burning out at an alarming rate. The workers suggested that the engines be purchased from another manufacturer. The boss called on a small engine mechanic to look into the problem. The mechanic told the manager that there was nothing wrong with the engines and that the problem was with the workers. It seemed that the workers had simply been neglecting to change the oil, as specified, or even add oil when the level was low.

3. Recognize known restrictions.

Since there are things a manager can and cannot do, you must realistically determine all the limitations that are imposed by the organiza-tion and the public that can restrict your proposed solution to a problem. Realistic, in this context, means your appreciation for the situation as it stands now.

Don't use restrictions as excuses for doing nothing. Too frequently managers have been heard to say such things as:

"It can't be done."

"We tried that once before and it didn't work."

"This is the way we've always done it."

"We can't afford to change."

"We don't have enough."

"The boss won't let me."

"That's the way it is; that's the way it's gotta be."

It is common for organizations to create restrictive policies which help prevent line managers from making unwise decisions. Sports have their restrictions, too. What you do is learn the rules of the game, then you go out and play to win. So it is in the procedure of decision-making. Know the restrictions, learn the rules, and make decisions that score within these boundaries. Here are a couple of instances where managers were forced to accept specific restrictions, but were still able to reach decisions that satisfied their purposes.

During hot weather, the young, outdoor workers at a retirement community would take off their shirts, as was customary. The community manager soon learned that the retirees of the community loudly protested this sort of undress. The community organization subsequently ruled that workers were forbidden to shed their shirts while working on the property. The line manager made the decision to purchase light, loosely woven cotton shirts for the outdoor crews. This decision was acceptable to the organization and to the residents.

A manager was fed up with an employee who continually caused trouble. The organization, however, did not permit line managers to hire or fire employees. The manager met with his boss and learned how to build a case against the errant worker, in writing. In time, the line manager presented a record of misdeeds that led to the troublesome worker's termination of employment.

4. Think of two or more workable solutions.

When only one solution is offered, there is no need for a decision. That's it. Then what happens when that solution doesn't satisfy all the criteria?

Accept the fact that some solutions may not be practical or fully workable at a given time or place. You need several possible solutions so as to find the one that best fits present circumstances.

As an example, if a pump that was critical to your operation gave a groan, a last gasp, and quit working, as the manager, you would be faced with three possible decisions:

– order a new pump immediately

– send the broken pump away to be rebuilt

– take parts from other old, broken pumps now stored in the parts shed with the hope of salvaging one workable pump from the lot.

Obviously, in this situation, more information would be needed.

5. Collect new information, specific to each proposed solution.

Solutions are likely to have their particular advantages and disadvantages. To make sensible comparisons, you must have sufficient and current facts. Here is some additional information that's needed to resolve the broken pump problem:

It would take several weeks to get delivery of a new pump. Furthermore, the purchase of a new pump at this time would exceed the manager's allotted budget for the quarter of this year. Sending the broken pump off to be rebuilt would also result in a delay of weeks. It was learned that the cost for a rebuilt pump was only slightly less than the price of a new pump. Two mechanics assured the manager that they could get one pump to function within a few hours by taking parts from the old, broken pumps.

6. Make your decision.

This should be the easiest step of all. The steps you have already taken, now come together. The decision you are about to make seems to be the only sensible one.

In the case of the broken pump, your immediate concern should be to get a pump back on the line as quickly as possible. So, you would likely tell the mechanics to go ahead with the salvage of the broken pump. Soon, they would have repaired the pump with old parts – but the pump would be working. This decision would be a good one. Another decision would follow: you should order a new pump, charged to the next quarter's budget, retaining the old pump as a workable standby.

7. Get other people's approval and support.

It is essential that you have the approval and support of all persons who will be affected in any manner by your decision. This is sometimes the most difficult step to accomplish.

As you collected information, you may have been made aware of some questions, doubts, and resistances in the minds of some people. Now that your decision has been made known, these thoughts may rise up to be full-blown objections or obstacles. There may be people who think their ideas are better. Some may believe that your plan is doomed to failure. Others may simply protest in ignorance, not really understanding the reasons for your decision.

To win the approval and support of those who will be affected by your decision, give them the total picture of the problem and all the facts that contributed to your solution.

Send a detailed report to your immediate supervisor and to any other superior who may be concerned with your decision. Start with the problem. Outline the steps you have taken. Include the information you have considered, and the source. List all possible alternative decisions. Clearly express your decision and summarize your reasons. If you are asked to present your report at a meeting, be prepared to answer probing questions.

It is equally important for you to have the approval and support of your employees. You may wish to call a meeting for this purpose, or you may find it suitably effective to state your justifications for the decision in a newsletter, or with a notice on the bulletin board.

Supervisors under your command especially must understand, approve, and support your decision, because they are the ones who will influence the workers under them. As much approval and support as possible should be gained before your plan goes into effect.

8. Test the solution when it is possible to do so.

It may be advisable to begin a plan on a small scale. For instance, a manager may intend to buy ten new computers of the latest technology. For the moment, only one is ordered. It will be on trial for a period of time. If the computer meets all the demands of the job, nine more will be ordered from the same manufacturer. Or the manager may order one computer from each of two leading manufacturers. After a period of comparison, the manager will order additional computers from the manufacturer whose computer has proved to be superior. This process of comparison and testing is often referred to as *benchmarking*.

A test will serve as a safety switch. If, as a test progresses, the records indicate that the results will be less than satisfactory, you can alter or discontinue the plan. You may need to back up a few steps and begin again. It is wiser to learn from small mistakes and then search for a better decision, rather than to waste additional time, money, and energies on an unfulfilled decision.

When it is not feasible to test a solution, investigate decisions that have been made by other organizations in situations similar to yours. Let their experiences serve as your testing ground. Learning from other people's experiences is inexpensive, smart management. The lessons learned from others will help you to avoid their mistakes and adopt their successes.

9. Listen to other people's opinion.

Decisions seldom please everyone. Some people are creatures of habit; they do not take to changes easily. Some people see the best in any situation, some see the worst. Those who see the worst tend to be natural complainers. Try to get quiet workers to give their opinions. Listen with an open mind. Filter out those comments that sound shallow, insensitive, selfish, or illogical. Listen politely and attentively to whoever voices an opinion.

By listening carefully and asking questions, you will hear sensible remarks. Even critical comments might offer something constructive. Sometimes, new suggestions will be offered. Consider these as if they had been offered when you were first seeking alternative solutions. These new suggestion will need to be investigated, just as you did with the others. There is nothing wrong with adjusting a plan to make it more successful. First decisions should not be engraved in stone.

If the decision making system is so good, why are nearly ninety percent of all decisions made from judgement?
The answer is – the decision making system has limitations:
– It is time consuming. An urgent problem may necessitate an immediate decision.
– It invites criticism, and criticism leads to delays.
– The decision maker may be subjected to unexpected pressures from powerful, influential people.

Nevertheless, for decisions of great importance and widespread impact, you will do well to treat them with patience, investigative thoroughness, and careful consideration.

Don't Let Misleading Reports Sabotage Your Decisions

Managers' decisions are frequently based on what other people write or say in reports. Managers cannot be everywhere and they cannot see everything, so reports are their eyes and ears. However, managers must treat reports with caution and respectful attention.

Be alert not only for what is reported, but also for what is not. Reports may reveal more than the progress of a job or the status of a situation. They may lead to hidden, seldom suspected problems.

There are three kinds of reports to watch for – incomplete reports, inaccurate reports, and falsified reports.

Incomplete Reports
These are the easiest to catch. There are blank spaces. When asked about these omissions, an employee may offer some sort of excuse:
– "I was in a hurry and I forgot."
– "I had nothing to enter in those spaces, so I left them blank."
– "I didn't know what I was supposed to write there."

These excuses are not acceptable and should be treated as possible problems.

To understand the problem, you must gather the information that will lead you to understand the cause. It may be sufficient to tell a lazy or thoughtless employee to take back the report and fill it out completely, or it may be necessary to give an employee a little extra training, right then and there.

Inaccurate Reports

Mistakes are not intentional, but they do indicate that a person is not thinking properly.

Inaccurate reports are more difficult to detect than incomplete reports. On the surface, a report may appear to be correct. At least all the spaces are filled. Often, it will be the systems of checks and balances that help managers to spot the inaccurate reports, as the following three examples demonstrate.

A worker was assigned to take a physical inventory of office equipment – desks, tables, chairs, filing cabinets, office machines, trash baskets. In three buildings, the report stated, there was a total of 33 desks. The manager suspected that this figure was wrong since the previous inventory report had listed 52 desks. After questioning the worker, the manager learned that the second floor of the last building had been forgotten.

A telephone employee reported that eight telephones had been disconnected and two connected. The manager checked a copy of the morning work ticket and found that there were eight telephones to be connected and two disconnected. Either the morning report or the technician's report had to be inaccurate. The technician admitted that, in haste, the numbers had been transposed.

Just before going off duty, a nurse wrote on a patient's chart that one gram of medication was given at a specified time. The on-coming charge nurse had to know immediately if the report was accurate or not. If one gram was given, an emergency code must be called at once. Fortunately the off-going nurse was caught before leaving the hospital.

"Sorry about that. I forgot to put in the decimal point."
The medication given was for a safe, one-tenth gram.

Notice that, in each example, a system of checks and balances served to detect an inaccurate report. In the first example, it was a previous inventory report. In the second example, it was the morning work ticket. In the final example, it was a charge nurse's medical knowledge.

The cures for inaccurate reports are similar to those for incomplete reports. Learn the real causes, then take appropriate actions. In addition, let your employees know of the consequences that can result when information is reported inaccurately.

Falsified Reports

When a report is falsified, it is intentional. There is no mistake, no lapse of memory. The report is meant to deceive and mislead. It is an act of dishonesty.

Again, systems of checks and balances can serve to bring falsified reports to your attention.

If you suspect an employee of falsifying reports, you may not want to announce your suspicion right away, since a single incident may not provide you with sufficient proof. The employee, of course, would say that this particular report was not falsified, but only inaccurate, and certainly not intentional.

In addition, premature accusation will cause a dishonest person to discontinue the falsifying of reports temporarily in favor of some other form of dishonesty of which you will have no knowledge.

The three most common reasons for falsifying reports are:

– A person wants performance to appear better than it is.

– A person wants to hide a mistake or error.

– Someone is attempting to cover up an even more serious act of dishonesty – perhaps theft.

Decisions reached through careful analysis of reports can only be acted upon successfully when these reports are written completely, accurately, honestly, and submitted promptly.

Don't Let a Committee Undermine Your Decisions

As ruling bodies and decision makers, committees generally have a poor reputation. A committee is sometimes compared to a cross breed of a horse and a mule. One half wants to carry a load and run; the other half wants to bray, kick up its heels, and balk when there is work to be done.

When you enroll a committee in your decision making system, try to hold the participants to two particular tasks:

– To collect and analyze information.
– To offer fresh ideas and suggestions.

There is no harm in allowing members to vote on proposed solutions. In this manner, you will know of their views and where they stand. However, if you are the person responsible for a decision, accept that responsibility – make the final decision – for it is you who will be held accountable.

There is one committee that will never give you any trouble – a mind-appointed committee to help you reach a sensible decision. Think of people, living or dead, whom you have long admired for their sound judgements and successful actions. Visualize them sitting around a conference table, with you at the head. Imagine what they would say to you – the questions some would ask, the answers others would give; the decision or stand they would unanimously take. Consider how those who have gone before you would handle a similar situation.

In your daily business affairs, you will make many decisions. Some decisions will be small ones, made on your own; some will be made with the help of other people. Solutions will be reached through any one of the ways by which decisions are made. Decisions may be arrived at in moments, days, weeks, months, or even years. The importance placed on problems, or the time needed to reach decisions, is not the main issue. Every problem deserves your fullest attention. Every decision deserves to be a sensible one.

A person's complaint may be the seed of improvement.
An employee's idea may be the seed of invention.

21
HOW TO FIND OUT WHAT YOUR EMPLOYEES REALLY THINK

Progressive organizations encourage their employees to speak out by submitting their opinions, complaints, praises, and ideas that relate to their jobs.

Some managers resent the complaints and ideas of workers. They seem to regard these expressions as attacks on their leadership and the ways of the organization. When the expressed thoughts of workers are laughed at or scoffed at by managers, the workers naturally become discouraged. They lose enthusiasm for their work. Suggestions for improvements no longer flow from workers to managers and the organization loses one of its most valuable assets – the thoughts, feelings, and ideas of the employees.

Employees should be encouraged by managers to express their views of their work and the workplace.

The Sound Off Questionnaire:
How to Construct Your Own

Before designing an employee opinion survey, consider the following:

1. A brief introduction is needed to explain the purpose of the

opinion survey form and to instruct the employees as to what they are to do. Here is an example:

> The organization wishes to improve its efficiency of operation as well as the working conditions of its employees. Your responses to the following questions will suggest the areas where improvements might be made. Please mark the responses that best express your thoughts and feelings towards each of the following questions.

> 2. There are several ways in which employee responses can be made.
> – Written narrative
> – Multiple choice
> – True or False

Your form may use one or all of these.

The written narrative response allows employees to explain their views and opinions fully. However, some employees find it difficult to express themselves adequately in writing.

Multiple choice is most popular form, but you must decide how the choices are to be worded. Here is one method:

> (Please circle one answer for each question) - What is your opinion of the Code Of Conduct For Employees?
> a. It should not be changed.
> b. It should be changed.
> c. It should be done away with.

Here is another way:

> What is your opinion of the Code Of Conduct For Employees? (Unsatisfactory) (Poor) (Fair) (Good) (Excellent)

In the first example, you must prepare the answers for each question. You'll need several different answers to each question. In the second example, the answers to all questions are always expressed in the same manner. You will need to write your questions so as to be compatible with the choice of answers. With the five choices shown in the second example, a question would not appear as, "How did you learn to do your job?" None of the answers would make sense.

Multiple choice answers can also be expressed as numbers. In the instructions, direct the employees to respond with one of the numbers representing: 1 – Unsatisfactory; 2 – Poor; 3 – Fair; 4 – Good; 5 – Excellent.

Employees occasionally are asked to respond to questions with a "Yes" or "No." Yes and no answers are like black and white in that they don't tell you much about the shades of feelings between the two extremes. Still, questions calling for the simplest of all responses have their place and purpose.

3. Write your questions to serve either general or specific purposes. You might ask questions pertaining to employees supervision:
    – How do you rank your immediate supervisor's knowledge of your job?
    – How do you rank your supervisor's assistance with work-related problems?

Ask how they feel about their performance reviews:
    – How do your rank your supervisor's fairness in giving performance reviews?

Ask employees about pay and work:
    – Do you think that your pay rate is equal to or better than the pay of workers with similar jobs in other organizations?
    – Do you consider your work load to be reasonable?

Ask employees about their personal satisfactions:
    – Do you feel a sense of accomplishment from your job?
    – Does your supervisor give you credit for doing exceptional work?
    – Do you feel free to offer ideas or complaints to management?

Ask about working conditions:
    – Do you observe and experience cooperation between work units?
    – How would you rate the sanitation facilities?
    – Are lighting and ventilation adequate?

Ask employees how they feel about top management and the future of the organization:
    – Are promotional opportunities made known when they occur?
    – Do you have confidence in the decisions of top management?
    – Do you feel secure regarding the organization's future prospects?

Ask employees about their personal ambitions:
    – Are you interested in further training and advancement?
    – Is there any information relating to your personal qualifications that you think should be brought to the attention of management?

– Do you feel that opportunities for training and advancement are available to you?

In specific instances – after there has been a major change of managers, policies, rules, procedures or any other important change that directly affects the workers – a Sound Off Questionnaire should be constructed with questions that pertain exclusively to the change:
– How well have you been trained to operate the new equipment?
– How well does the new equipment improve production?

4. Following the questions, have space for remarks. This section may appear as:

Remarks: (Please write your comments for any answers you have given that require additional explanation. Use the reverse side of this form, if necessary.)

5. It is quite common for the chief executive of the organization to offer a few words. The message may read:

The organization is continually working to develop a more competent management staff and to improve working conditions and benefits for employees. Your views are essential to the planning of worthwhile programmes toward these purposes. The organization sincerely appreciates your participation in this survey.

The chief executive's statement may be located either at the beginning of the form or at the end. First or last, it is intended to show employees that what they 'sound off' about will be carefully considered by top officials in the organization.

6. Finally, there should be a line for the employee's signature. It is common that some employees will choose not to be known for the answers and remarks given. Therefore, beneath the signature line, add a brief explanation such as the following:

Signature of Employee_____
Job Title _____ Work Location _____

Note: You are not required to sign this opinion survey. However, if you wish to discuss any of your responses, comments, or other work related subjects, it will be necessary for you to give your name, job title, and work location. Your identity and conversation will be respectfully held in confidence.

When an employee's identity and responses invite further discussion, a meeting should be arranged between that employee and a person best suited to deal with the subject of concern.

Before getting too far into designing your Sound Off Questionnaire, it would be smart to look around and ask other organizations for copies of their opinion survey forms. You'll find that there are wide differences in form and content. From these differences you can select the most appropriate inputs that will go into the creation of your own questionnaire.

How to Pinpoint a Specific Problem

A large number of responses from satisfied employees, with only a few from dissatisfied employees, may cause management to believe that the organization is operating smoothly and efficiently. In a relatively large organization, this can be deceiving. There could be a serious personnel problem waiting to explode. Here is an illustration as to how this might happen:

A hospital administrator was delighted with the fact that one hundred employees had returned the opinion survey forms. Of these, 92 percent had given answers that ranged from fair to excellent. Only eight people had expressed a serious dissatisfaction, and six of those had not bothered to sign their names.

One of the administrator's assistants was suspicious of the results. The answers and comments from the six unsigned responses were too much alike. One month later, the administrator was persuaded to distribute another questionnaire composed of different questions. This time, there was to be a special set of numbers typed in the lower left hand corner of each form. The numbers, a code, looked like a printer's form number, but, in fact, identified the specific work area, job classification, and work shift of each employee in the hospital. Only the administrator, the assistant, and a trusted secretary knew of this code.

When the questionnaires were returned, the administrator was surprised to learn that the six unsigned questionnaires came from the total staff of nurses assigned to the same ward, on the same shift. The administrator had been happy with a record 92 percent of the employees being satisfied. But now, with an employee rate of 100 percent dissatisfaction in one location, there was immediate cause for alarm.

During the following few days, the administrator and other key staff personnel made unannounced visits to the troubled ward during the shift when the six unhappy nurses were on duty. The reasons for the nurses' dissatisfaction were soon brought to light. The problems were quickly resolved.

Without the coded keys to work areas and job classifications, the serious personnel problems in such a critical area would never have been made known until after serious consequences had occurred. The six nurses would likely have quit before anyone had an opportunity to correct the situation.

How to Invite Employees to Sound Off

A dissatisfied worker is already a problem. The longer a dissatisfaction remains, the greater the problem becomes. It is not this programme's purpose to have a questionnaire handed out each time a worker appears unhappy. There are occasions, however, when it is appropriate for employees to *sound off*.

Here are some suggestions as to when opinion surveys should be distributed and to whom.

– All employees, annually.

– New employees within three months from their date of hire.

– Employees who are affected by radical organizational changes, within one to three months from the date of change.

– Employees of a work group whose productivity is below standard, following three months of recorded evidence.

How to Protect the Employees' Trust

Employees generally need the assurance that they can speak out without fear of reprisal – without punishment. Not all managers will give that assurance.

There are a few managers who believe that the organization's Sound Off Questionnaire is a *sneaky* method used to check up on them. There are some managers who will attempt to discourage workers from responding truthfully to the questionnaire; some will attempt to learn what the workers wrote or to intimidate workers into writing responses favorable to the managers.

For an opinion survey to succeed, an organization needs confident, competent managers. It is these managers who can best explain the programme to the workers and encourage their participation.

– Tell how workers, and the organization, can benefit from the complaints and problems that are brought into the open.

– Tell how the workers' responses and identities are kept confidential.

To insure the success of the questionnaire, the organization should take actions in support of the programme.

An orientation should be held for all managers, explaining the purposes and values of the programme, the manner in which the questionnaires will be distributed and collected, and how the questionnaires will be analyzed. It is important for managers to realize that the questionnaire is for their benefit. Managers who do their jobs well will gain favorable recognition; those who have problems of which they are not aware will be informed and the organization will help those managers to correct unsatisfactory situations.

The Sound Off Questionnaire should be distributed in a manner that will avoid embarrassment to the workers.

When it is practical and economical to do so, the survey form should be mailed to the workers' homes. Stamped, self-addressed return envelopes should be included.

When it is impractical or too costly to use the mail services, the questionnaire can be distributed with the workers' pay checks, in sealed envelopes. A return envelope should be enclosed with each one.

There are other ways to distribute the survey forms. The main thing to remember is that you want to avoid embarrassment to the employees. Choose a method of distribution that will serve your purpose and circumstances.

The opinion survey forms must also be collected in a manner that avoids embarrassment to workers. Questionnaires that are returned by mail – the return envelopes having been addressed to the chief executive of the organization – pose no problem.

Questionnaires that are not returned by mail must be collected at locations that are accessible to the workers. A large box in a shop or office might do. However, one person should be appointed to see that no one takes completed questionnaires from the container. This responsible person should deliver the returned forms to the office of the chief executive on a daily basis.

It is generally not a good idea for line managers to handle returned opinion surveys.

The chief executive will usually assign one or more executives or executive secretaries to the task of tabulating and analyzing the employees' responses.

The chief executive should assign qualified persons to correct known problems, and explain the reasons for specific conditions. These person should work directly with line managers.

The line managers might not be told specifically what the survey results revealed and will never be told the names of those who disclosed certain information. Only the conditions should be discussed. In some instances, the chief executive's appointee will talk directly with workers who have asked for help. These will be private conversations, away from the work place.

How to Tabulate and Analyze the Responses

Consolidating the results of the questionnaires is a simple process. A blank questionnaire serves as a worksheet. The person doing the tabulating makes a mark for each answer from each questionnaire in the appropriate column on the worksheet. The marks for each question are totaled and the number is written down and circled. (Note: The questionnaires from workers who asked for personal attention should be set aside after they have been recorded on the worksheet.)

Below is an illustration of how the worksheet of tabulated responses might look.

	Fail	Poor	Fair	Good	Excellent
1. How effectively has the training prepared you to perform your job?	I ①	⊬Ш I ⑥	Ш Ш I ⑪ 85%		III ③
2. How do you rate the equipment and tools that are essential to your work?	⊬Ш IIII ⑨	Ш Ш I ⑪ 100%			

In this illustration, a picture is beginning to form. It appears that the workers are more impressed with their accomplishments in developing skills than they are with their tools and equipment. It seems that workers are ambitious and wanting even more training. This would indicate that morale is good, but that the employees may become frustrated and discouraged if they continue to work with inadequate tools and equipment.

Can the organization afford to buy better equipment? Can they afford not to? Is there an explanation that will be acceptable to the workers? What new training programmes should be developed? These are the kinds of questions executives will ask and the answers they develop will hopefully lead to corrective actions.

Accumulated Sound Off Questionnaires will show, in most instances, that an organization is operating smoothly, managers are competent, employees are motivated, and morale is high. This is as it should be. But there is always a certain amount of tinkering for managers to do, and small improvements to make. It is like a mechanic who works on a fine running machine. The engine is tuned continuously and other fine adjustments are made. In striving to make a machine run perfectly, a mechanic finds personal purpose in life and a special pride in the work done.

One final word. There should be no place in an organization for egos that get bent out of shape. Even though a manager, at any level, is personally criticized, every manager is considered to be big enough to survive any attack with an open mind, understanding, and tolerance.

Every manager's motto should be: Get it said; get it resolved; get it over with. Even under the most severe criticism, a manager should express appreciation for the input. The easiest worker to deal with is one who loudly, if not eloquently, expresses a criticism of management. The most difficult is the quiet worker who harbors frustration, resentment, and rebellion without a word. It is indeed sad when a top-rated, quiet worker turns in a resignation with the simple explanation, ''I've had it!''

Most worthwhile advances of civilization have come, not from managers, but from inspired workers.

22

HOW TO HARVEST PROFITABLE IDEAS FROM YOUR EMPLOYEES

Employees have more to offer than constructive complaints. Because they do the work, workers frequently have ideas as to how the work should be done. These ideas can be highly profitable to an organization. Harvesting ideas is not automatic.

There are various reasons why some employees are hesitant about sharing their ideas with management:

– Some people have been taught throughout childhood not to think on their own and not to speak out.

– Some people do not know how to express themselves.

– Some are afraid of being ridiculed.

– Some are afraid of what their friends may think.

– There are employees who let it be known that they are not being paid to think.

– There are those who believe that bosses steal employees' ideas for their own personal gain.

– Some employees see no means of communication with the managers who can put their ideas to good use.

Successful managers can deal with these reasons. They do not pretend to be know-it-all bosses, they ask for ideas, they never laugh at an employee's suggestion, and they credit the contributor for a profitable idea.

There are three methods commonly used by managers to draw upon the profitable ideas of their employees:
- Seeking ideas while on the job.
- Seeking ideas in meetings.
- Seeking ideas through a formal programme.

Seeking Ideas While on the Job

Small problems frequently arise on the job. An involved worker may have a solution. A manager has only to ask for it and the problem will be solved.

An often-told story is about a heavily loaded truck that stood an inch too high to go under a concrete overpass. The manager knew it would be impossible to remove the obstacle, and that there was no alternate route. Unloading the truck was a discouraging possibility. The harried manager asked if anyone had any ideas. The driver's assistant suggested letting some air out of the tires. It worked. The truck was lowered a fraction more than an inch, just enough for the load to go under the overpass.

Seeking Ideas in Meetings

Managers will occasionally have operational problems similar to these:
- Maintenance costs are too high.
- Equipment breakdowns are excessive.
- Contracted work is behind schedule.
- Tools are in short supply, as is the money to buy them.
- Replacement parts have been delayed in shipment.
- Customers are continually complaining.

Executives and staff managers are not likely to offer quick, magical solutions. Line managers must cope with these operational problems as they occur, until problems are overcome. When problems occur, successful line managers seek the help of their employees.

When an operational problem arises, a manager may call a meeting of his most knowledgeable and experienced employees. There, the problem will be presented in detail and there will be an explanation of what may happen to them all if the problem is allowed to continue. Then, the gathered employees will be asked to help solve the problem.

After the manager and employees have hammered out a workable solution, it is common practice to forward a report to the manager's immediate boss. The report will generally include the names of the participants, along with their contributions to the solution. A copy of the report will be given to each participant. Depending upon the difficulty of the problem and success of the solution, the manager may wish to give some form of recognition or reward to the participating employees.

Experienced workers generally feel honored when they are asked to help bring about operational improvements. Aside from their personal feelings of accomplishment, and their valuable contributions, the manager derives an even further benefit. When solutions are put into action, those employees will defend the manager's decisions because they helped form them.

Seek Ideas Through a Formal Programme

Most progressive organizations have some method of seeking profitable ideas from employees. Still, the managers are the ones who must make the system work.

The suggestion box is now history. This rather old-fashioned method had one serious drawback. Workers were apt to throw trash into the suggestion box, including petty complaints and selfish suggestions. A better way to learn of employees' opinions of the organization has already been offered.

The subject of *employee ideas* has its own identity and a separate treatment. Employees' suggestions should be profitable to the organization. Their purpose should be to improve efficiency and to produce better services and/or products. The words *Ideas For Profit* express this purpose.

An Ideas For Profit programme requires careful planning and continuous attention. The planners must develop a system that:
  – solicits ideas from the employees
  – collects the ideas
  – selects the ideas that are workable and profitable
  – provides methods of recognition and reward
  – puts the ideas to work
  – publicizes the programme.

Following are the steps that should be taken to implement an Ideas For Profit programme.

1. Organize an Ideas For Profit committee.

The committee members should represent all levels of specialization within your organization, including labor. Some committees have as many as twelve members; some have as few as three.

A large committee has a wide representation of knowledge and experience from various fields. A small committee can gather its members together more easily, and the members are likely to accomplish more in less time. A small committee can call upon other specialists as needs arise.

The responsibilities of the committee should be divided among the members. While the programme is being developed, the members should meet frequently for the purpose of planning. The actual task assignments should be independently done by members, between meetings.

Only later, after the programme is in motion, will members meet for the purpose of processing and appraising ideas that have been submitted.

2. Design and print a form that the employees will use to submit their ideas.

This form should ask for such information as:
– month, day, and year
– employee's name
– work location
– description of the idea
– purpose and benefits
– supportive information: statistics, technical data
– cost estimates
– employees' signature.

It would be wise to write the form in duplicate. The original copy should be sent directly to the Ideas For Profit committee, while the second copy should be retained by the employee. In some organizations, a third copy may be sent to Human Resources to be filed in the employee's personnel file.

3. Decide how the forms will be made readily available to all employees.

Many organizations display their Ideas For Profit forms in racks, or by hanging them on hooks, nails, or clips. These are displayed where employees are likely to gather and be reminded of the programme. Consider that some employees might vandalize the forms. It happens. Some organizations leave the forms in the hands of line managers to be distributed as requested. Certainly this method might reduce the waste of forms. But remember, out of sight, out of mind. So if you choose to have managers control the form supply, remind them to make announcements of the Ideas for Profit programme frequently at their short, informal meetings.

4. Teach the managers to understand and support the programme.

Lessons should include:

– Encouraging the workers to submit profitable ideas.

– Helping workers to put their ideas in writing, but only when the manager is asked to do so.

– Directing employees to specialists who can provide technical advice, when needed.

– Keeping the employees' ideas confidential; not discussing ideas with anyone, without permission.

5. Establish a system of recognition and rewards.

Some organizations determine the long range worth of an idea – how much money it will save or earn. The successful contributor is then rewarded with a percentage of the calculated amount. The plan is fair, but complicated.

Other organizations reward their employees with flat sums of money. The same amount is paid for each usable idea, regardless of its importance. This practice can discourage people from submitting better, more profitable ideas.

Yet another plan may be to have a range of monetary rewards, with the committee voting on the amount to be paid for any given idea.

Whatever method of recognition and reward is chosen, the amount should run according to the idea's value to the organization. In other words, an idea that will save the organization ten thousand dollars should earn the contributor far more recognition and reward than an idea worth one hundred dollars.

6. Publicize the Ideas For Profit programme.

This is important, not only in the beginning, but continually. The employees need reminders that this programme is for them, as well as for the organization. Use all available means of communication.

7. Maintain direct contact with each employee who submits an idea.

Those who submit ideas will be anxious to know how their contribution is progressing. Notify the worker when an idea has been received by the committee, and again when the idea is up for consideration.

A technical idea may require lengthy periods of review, research, or tests. Inform the employee of any delays.

When the committee has reached a decision, notify the employee as soon as possible. Whether an idea is accepted or not, thank the employee, in writing, for the interest shown. Encourage each contributor to submit additional ideas. Win or loose, ideas submitted by employees should eventually wind up in their personnel files.

8. Direct winning ideas to where they will become profitable.

Along with an idea, send the committee's report. The report will present the committee members' opinions and arguments favoring the idea.

Don't allow profitable ideas to wither and die. Check to see that the idea has been successfully put to use and continues to be of value.

Your knowledge of what employees think – of you, the organization, and their jobs – is essential to your successful management of the work unit and its work. Knowing of justified complaints and constructive suggestions and ideas can only help you to make sensible decisions before taking actions.

The difference between being a hero and a sucker
is knowing when to quit.

23
HOW TO HELP TROUBLED EMPLOYEES

Employees' personal problems are sometimes apt to hinder work performance. Troubled behaviors are also likely to interfere with other employees. In your organization, you cannot allow these situations to happen. Not for long.

You can try to reduce an employee's stress, or eliminate the employee's problem altogether. Or you may be forced to remove the employee from the work scene. No manager wants to fire a worker who is already burdened with a serious, personal problem. Your first alternative, then, should be to provide help. But do so carefully. Know what you are doing and what you are getting into.

Anticipating and Recognizing Personal Problems

The personal problems that can affect employees' work are many and varied. Still, it is essential that some thought be given to as many of these as can be anticipated. Having done so, you can quickly recognize a worker's personal problem as it arises.

Anticipating an employees' problem.

How many personal problems can you think of that might affect an employee's job performance? Check out the following, then add others that come to mind.

– An employee's spouse runs off with no forwarding address.
– An employee's spouse suddenly demands a divorce.
– An employee learns of a spouse's marital affair.

– An employee is surprised with an unwanted pregnancy.

– An employee learns of a family member addicted to drugs (or alcohol).

– An employee is addicted to drugs (or alcohol).

– An employee learns of his own or a family member's serious illness.

– An employee, without funds, is in desperate need of legal advice.

– An employee frequently suffers from aches and pains.

– An employee has talked to other workers of committing suicide.

– An employee is being harassed by phone and mail by an unknown person.

Recognizing an employee's problem.

The sooner a problem is recognized, the sooner steps can be taken to prevent further unhappiness for the employee and harm to the work performance. Look for physical evidence, changes in habits and routines, and behavioral changes.

– An employee has bruises on the face and arms.

– An employee, on the job, smells of liquor.

– An employee's eyes appear red and swollen, as if from crying.

– A normally happy worker now appears sullen and withdrawn.

– A worker begins to borrow money from other employees.

– A worker begins to arrive at work late and leave early.

– An employee now receives an unreasonable number of telephone calls.

There are other clues that you may observe. Awareness of what you observe, however, is the real key to recognizing a worker's personal problem.

Before you talk with a troubled employee, it may be helpful to learn what you can from the employee's friends at work. Understand that workers may respond differently when asked to talk about a fellow employee. One worker may be glad to share knowledge of a friend's problem. Another may act as if a friend has no problem at all. Still another employee may tell a story that isn't true. Each person, in a personal way, simply wants to protect a friend. Some employees may step forward and tell what they know of a worker's problem, because their own patience is wearing thin. Too, there are employees who enjoy inventing rumors and stirring up problems. Ask the same questions of several people. Compare and filter the answers. Convince the workers in your unit that your only intent is to help a fellow worker. When they trust you, the truth you seek will generally come out.

Be careful that your cooperative workers don't have the mistaken notion that once the problem is learned you will just forget about the troubled worker's unsatisfactory performance. Poor work cannot just be forgiven. To correct the worker's performance, the problem must be successfully resolved.

Getting the Troubled Employee to Talk

Learning of an employee's problem from others is merely a preparation. The most reliable source for getting at the true facts is the troubled worker. Knowing that you are already aware of a problem, the employee may willingly discuss the situation. That would be a good step forward. Yet, another employee might be embarrassed and hesitant to talk. To get this person to open up, there are some steps you can take.

1. Meet with the employee in a comfortable, quiet place where you will not be interrupted.

2. Tell the employee what you have observed and heard. Do not give the sources of your information.

3. Assure the employee that whatever is said at your meeting will be held in confidence. Only those persons who can be of help will need to know, and even they will not be told without the employee's permission.

4. If appropriate, tell it like it is – that this person's job is on the line.

5. Explain that you have an obligation to protect the organization and a right to dismiss the worker if the situation is not corrected. But you also have a duty to help a worker in trouble as best you can.

Finding Sources of Help

First, check with your personnel or human resources office. They may have a list of available sources of social assistance. Second, call your library and ask if they have a reference book of community services.

If your community has no such publication, this would be someone's opportunity to put a group together for the purpose of locating and listing various sources of help for people with problems. This is not an easy project. You might expect a doctor, a lawyer, or a religious leader to be aware of help that can be found elsewhere. Most likely, though, you and the members of your group will have to dig deeply to develop a meaningful referral list.

Before beginning your search, make an outline of the pertinent information to be included on your list or card file:
– name of the social service organization
– name of individual(s) to contact
– address and phone number
– business hours (and how they can be reached in an emergency)
– description of service or aid
– cost of the service or fee structure
– requirements for eligibility.

Here are a few suggestions as to where to begin searching:
– In the telephone directory, check the list of government agencies that identify sources of information and assistance.
– Call your colleges, universities, and public school system. Ask about the various services and aids they offer to troubled students and to the general public.
– Most churches provide help for unfortunate people.
– Civic clubs frequently support selected causes.
– Check with professional service organizations: Red Cross, Salvation Army, the various disease-fighting organizations.
– Your community professionals – physicians, psychiatrists, psychologists, attorneys, accountants, and others – may refer you to sources of free or low fee, specialized social services.

This worthy project is not one to be done in a day. But once completed, you may be able to talk the local Chamber of Commerce or a local bank into publishing your references of social assistance.

What Can You Do About Someone's Problem?

Most often, employees are capable of solving their own problems – their unacceptable behavior or slack performance being only temporary. In other instances, employees may seek you out just to listen without wanting you to offer advice or pass judgement. Then there are those who will attempt to push you into taking action of some sort.

In some instances, an employee's problem requires nothing more than everyone's understanding.

As an example, a young man who worked in a warehouse began coming to work more than an hour late each morning. He was a shy, quiet new employee who preferred to keep to himself. The manager confronted the young man with the record of recent tardiness. The young man lowered his head but said nothing. The boss was patient, but insistent.

Hesitantly, the employee explained that his wife had gone to the hospital for a serious operation. Each morning, before coming to work, the children were taken to a relative's house. This side trip caused him to be late. But, he continued, his wife would be out of the hospital in just four more days.

The manager decided that no disciplinary action would be taken. The employee was asked, however, for permission to explain the situation to the other employees. The warehouse workers were grateful for the information and volunteered to do extra work so that the young man could arrive at work late and leave early to pick up his children. They also took up a collection and sent flowers to the worker's wife.

It is often within a manager's power to solve an employee's problem.

In another situation, a hospital aide was looking more tired and unhappy with each passing day. More than one nurse complained, in private, of the aide's inattention to work. The charge nurse asked the young woman what was wrong and was told of how the aide's husband had been assigned to the night shift where he worked: they didn't get to see much of each other. The charge nurse asked if the aide would like to work the night shift at the hospital. The charge nurse, knowing there was an aide on the night shift who wanted to work days, was certain that the transfers would go through. The young woman was pleased with the solution.

Employees who have more serious personal problems should be referred to the organization's human resources office. In some cases, the people there can offer assistance. If you have your own referral list, write down the information for the troubled employee. Ask the employee to check back later and tell you of the results. Make a note to yourself to re-establish contact should the employee fail to report to you within a reasonable time. Continue to observe the worker's behavior and work performance closely.

Take the First Step When Necessary

An employee who is extremely ill, filled with pain, overcome by grief, or confused by stress, may find it nearly impossible to make a decision or take an action to relieve the problem. It will help if you quickly become aware of the worker's helpless condition. Perhaps you can suggest a solution. But don't be surprised with responses such as these:

– "I don't see how they can help me."
– "Nothing else has helped. What good would that do?"
– "I'll be all right. Just leave me alone."

No matter how negatively the troubled worker replies to your suggestions, there is one final thing you can do. Take one more step. Do something that will make it easier for the employee to take your suggestion than to resist you.

Here are some examples:

– "I'm going to take you home right now. You are in no condition to work. Don't worry about the job. We'll take care of it. You just take care of yourself."

– "I've made a couple of telephone calls for you. It's all arranged. Here's a paper with the location, time, and the person to see. One of our people will take you there and bring you back. Is this okay with you?"

Don't Become a Victim

A manager must learn to recognize the thin line between helping a victim and becoming one. It is a simple matter to become a victim. Unfortunately, becoming a victim begins with being thoughtful and kind.

This was demonstrated to a group of managers:

One person was instructed, in private, to collapse to the floor. The *victim* was told to remain totally limp. After the volunteer victim collapsed, the other managers were told that their colleague could not get up without assistance. One manager volunteered to help. The rescuer's arms went around the victim's chest. As the lift got underway, the victim's arms flopped overhead and the body slipped from the grasp. Another volunteer was recruited to help get the victim upright. It worked. The victim was standing on two feet, but the body buckled at the knees and at the waist. For several minutes, the two volunteer helpers continued to support a helpless body. They didn't know what else to do.

After a time, the two rescuers displayed embarrassment, then anger – not with the victim, but with themselves. Finally, with an understanding glance between them, they let the helpless victim drop back to the floor.

There are employees who repeatedly return to their managers expecting a sympathetic ear to problems that never seem to end. Some managers continue to give help or seek help for these seemingly unfortunate workers. The managers are apparently unaware that their troubled employees do nothing on their own to compliment the help that has already been given them. These managers become transformed from rescuers to victims.

You should pull back from attending to an employee's personal problems when one of the following conclusions has been reached:

– The employee once again feels confident, independent, and productive.

– You feel that you have done everything possible to set the employee on the road to recovery. From then on, the problem must be solved by the worker or through the help of someone else.

Remember Your Motives

For some people, it is natural to help a troubled stranger. There is no other motive than to help a fellow human being. With a troubled employee, the situation is different. There are other motives:

– You have a managerial responsibility, as well as a moral one.

– You must reduce or eliminate stresses – your own and those of others in your work group.

– You must protect the efficiency and morale of your work group.

– You must do what you can to prevent labor turnover. Replacing a trained employee is time consuming and expensive.

– You are the one to answer to the authorities for the doings and wrongdoings of your employees.

Be satisfied with your efforts to help a troubled employee. Accept no credit for a person's return to happiness and productivity; take no blame for a person's failure. You also have a responsibility to protect your own happiness and productivity.

How to Deal with an Angry Employee

What does a manager do when an angry employee blows into the office like a raging hurricane, making loud accusations, demands, or threats?

The manager may also become angry. The yelling becomes a duet. The angry manager may attempt to throw the angry worker out of the office. The worker may try to stuff the manager into a filing cabinet. Physical violence frequently results in bodily injury and broken furniture. And, after the dust has settled, the employee and the boss are bitter because nothing has been resolved.

Although an angry outburst may come as a surprise, a manager cannot allow a personal emotion to erupt before determining what led to the employee's anger in the first place. Accept the fact that – surprised or not – you cannot learn the facts and solve a yet unknown problem when an employee is having a fit of bad temper. You must first gain and maintain control of the situation. Then, try these suggestions to help *defuse* your employee's anger.

1. Remain relaxed.

If a big dog should come bounding toward you baring its teeth and barking furiously, you would likely freeze in your tracks and carefully watch the animal's behavior as you tried to determine it's intent. Your angry employee is not a dog, of course, but for the moment this person is behaving like one. Watch, but do not react to what is, now, nothing more than angry *barking*.

2. Take away the fire.

This step won't work with mean dogs, but it can work with loud, angry people. Treat the angry employee as you would a kettle of boiling water. Take the kettle away from the fire and the water will quickly simmer down. The water will still be hot, but it will stop making all those hissing and gurgling sounds. Anger will remain at the *boiling point* until the employee has your attention and has convinced you that there is a problem and that the problem is serious.

Begin with something like this: "Hey, I hear you. Whatever your problem is, I'm glad you brought it to me. Now listen, just sit down and give me a minute to get this paper work out of the way. I've got to get it finished, first. And close the door, will you, so we won't be bothered."

If you don't really have any work to do, make some. Grab a piece of paper and begin writing, or study a report – any old report will do. Look busy. Tell someone that you don't want to be interrupted during this meeting. Now, your hot-headed guest should feel convinced that you are willing to listen, and you feel better that you are bringing the situation down to a simmer.

Anger cannot continue to erupt for long, unless it is fueled. You have not added fuel to the worker's anger by being angry yourself. When you think that the worker's anger has sufficiently subsided to be discussed rationally and quietly, open up the sore subject: "Okay, now tell me about it – slowly, from the beginning."

3. Listen attentively.

Among those angry sounds, you may hear something sensible – the reason, perhaps, why the worker is angry. Carefully consider the worker's point of view. To this person, there is a serious wrong that must be made right.

The employee was correct in bringing the problem to you, even though the manner was a bit noisy and unrestrained. Whether or not you agree with the employee's argument, it is important to show that you understand how the person feels and thinks about the situation.

4. Take the lead.

You will have your turn to reply when the worker feels that the problem has been convincingly dumped in your lap. Keep in mind that, when dealing with an unhappy or dissatisfied person, you must take control. If you think that you are now in control then this may be the time to bring the situation to a satisfactory conclusion.

You may not yet feel confident. The employee may continue to be irrational and express hostility. You may need time for further investigation of the problem – to sort out conflicting statements and to see the other side of the coin. Convince your employee of your interest and intent to get to the bottom of this matter.

> "Okay, I understand what you have told me. Now here is what I'm going to do . . ."

One or more other people may be brought together for a final confrontation. Certain records may be brought out to back up a decision. It may be beneficial, in some instances, to schedule a private meeting away from your office. Such decisions on your part will depend on the circumstances of the situation that provoked the employee's anger and the personalities involved. There's an old military axiom that reads, "Fight on the high ground." In terms of management, this simply means pick your time, pick your place, and know your plan and course of action.

The person who was angrily trying to lead you is now being led by you.

The key to dealing with a clique is to become its leader without anyone knowing it.

24
HOW TO MAKE A CLIQUE CLICK

A clique is an exclusive group of people. In a work force, they are the employees who have set themselves apart from others. Chances are there is a clique within your own work unit. Before jumping to conclusions, making quick judgements, and taking hasty actions, take a few moments to check out your understanding of cliques.

How and Why Cliques Get Started

The formation of a clique is a natural occurrence. Wherever employees work together for any extended period of time, it is only natural that cliques will form. Two or more workers will find that they have interests in common. They think and feel the same way about their origins, experiences, professions, skills, their manager, the organization, or any other bonding factors. They begin to exclude other employees from their personal conversations. Later, other workers who share similar interests may become accepted by the clique.

As a members of a clique, workers attain some personal satisfactions:

– They are accepted for who they are and what they can do.

– They can express themselves freely.

– A feeling of group power encourages them to behave as the others do. They may dare to do as a group what they would not do as individuals.

A clique has no organized structure and no stated goals. A clique does, however, have a leader. Without any form of election, a worker who is respected for knowledge, experience, and charisma will be accepted by the other workers as their leader.

There are many managers who want to break up the cliques within their work forces. Their assumption is that *all* cliques are harmful to management. This assumption, of course, is false. Most cliques are loyal to their work groups and to their organizations. Their members are efficient and productive. The successful managers have learned to understand the roots of a clique. They respect individual differences while continuing to maintain leadership and standards of performance.

Successful managers have also learned to create cliques – exclusive groups of workers. They encourage cliques to work competitively with one another, yet in harmony.

Six Steps to the Successful Management of a Clique

You can prevent a clique from spreading harmful rumors and inciting disharmony. You must. Here are six steps to make this happen.

1. Identify the clique that is responsible for unsatisfactory performance or harmful actions.

Most managers have known instances when they had the materials, the equipment, and the manpower to do specific jobs, yet the work standards had not been met, and the jobs had not been completed as scheduled. Not one person could be held responsible. These managers, whose jobs depend upon meeting established standards, learned the hard way that it is not uncommon for a clique of workers to set its own standards as to what a full days work should be. The workers of one clique may exceed the performances of other employees. Another clique may fall far short of established standards. Is one clique good and another bad? Maybe. Maybe not. Know and understand the reason for standards; know their purpose.

Two, young, athletic high school students were hired to unload a railroad boxcar on Saturdays. The foreman told the two part-time employees that it would take them all day to unload the freight car. By noon, the boxcar had been emptied. The following Saturday, the youngsters were *promoted* to a job, upstairs, scheduling outgoing shipments on various freight carriers.

Why were these part time youngsters relieved after doing a superior job? The foreman knew that a person's energy, especially young energy, can be exploded during a short span of time. Part-timers do not expect to remain at any particular job as a career. What, then, should be the standard for full-timers who have the task of unloading a single freight car every day, Monday through Friday. The organization had established a standard that one boxcar per day was enough for full-time employees. A clique of two, young high school students should not have exceeded established standards.

2. When your goals are not being met, examine every possible cause.

Through the process of elimination, you may come down to only one: a specific group of employees is managing the work. Be cautious. It is not always a simple matter to identify the offending clique.

Cliques can and do exist, even in under-developed areas, where modern equipment may be lacking and work projects are considered small by modern standards.

A young bricklayer was known to set a fast pace. Every work day, this youngster laid more bricks than any other bricklayer. Suddenly there was a drastic slow down. The manager noticed that all the better bricklayers had slowed down. "What has happened to that fast pace you were setting?" the manager asked. The young bricklayer replied, "I'm putting down all the good bricks that are brought to me. A lot of the bricks are broken."

At first, the manager had wondered if the bricklayers were setting their own production standards. Now, perhaps, there was reason to suspect the hod carriers – those who carried bricks to the bricklayers.

Then, something caught the manager's attention. The oldest of the bricklayers had joined the young workers. Here was the oldest, most experienced bricklayer being greeted warmly by the younger, less experienced and slower producers. Could this be the clique behind the problem, the manager wondered?

3. Learn the reason for the clique's behavior.

First, analyze your systems of management. What systems are missing or inadequate? Why are the needs of some employees not being met? Are they well informed with current news of the organization? Do all employees have opportunities to express themselves to management? Do the workers know where they stand – their worth to the organization, their job security, their opportunities for advancement? Have they been properly trained?

Next, open the lines of communication. Distribute opinion survey forms. Talk with the workers you have identified as being part of a clique. Listen to what they have to say. Realize, however, that these workers may be hesitant to talk with you. They may distrust your motives. They may feel that you are prying into their affairs. Under direct questioning, they may give evasive or dishonest answers. Be patient. Don't expect one worker to reveal a clique's unsatisfactory performance. Be content with bits of information – threads of truth from various sources.

Talk with workers who are not members of the clique. Ask for their opinions of the present problem. They have watched what has been happening and have heard what has been said. These employees may have done nothing to harm or help the situation, but they know what is going on and they have an interest in the outcome. Generally, the majority of workers do not want the organization to be harmed through the actions of a few disgruntled employees. Most of the workers privately want work disruptions corrected.

In the situation with the bricklayers, the construction manager talked individually with the young bricklayers as they worked. The manager mentioned that one of young bricklayers, the fast one, didn't seem to be a part of their group, but the oldest, most experienced bricklayer did seem to fit in with them. The general opinion was that the young bricklayer was thought of as a hot-shot, a show-off. The manager was puzzled. How could jealousy cause such a slow down?

The old-time bricklayer was called into the manager's on-site office. Together, these two had worked together on many jobs throughout the years. Now, the old friend admitted that working on the high walls was becoming tougher. It was impossible to keep up with the other experienced workers. The young bricklayers didn't mind having an old, slow worker in their group. They were slow, too. The old bricklayer expressed concern for the young workers' lack of adequate, on-the-job training. No one in the organization seemed to care about them.

Lack of training and inadequate performance reviews are two more possible reasons for a clique's misbehavior. Still, the manager wondered how an old-timer and a small group of young, inexperienced workers could be responsible for the failure of the hod carriers to deliver unbroken bricks promptly to the faster bricklayers.

One of the better bricklayers, who also had worked with the manager on previous jobs, admitted to a rumor going around that when this job was finished, there would be no more work. The construction manager learned nothing more from the hod carriers. They all continued to repeat the same excuses.

The foreman was called in for another talk. This time, the manager tried a different approach. "There are no broken bricks in the storage area. I can only think that your people are purposely breaking bricks and withholding bricks from the more experienced bricklayers. If you ever want to work for me on another project, you had better give me a truthful explanation."

The shaken foreman admitted that the hod carriers had heard talk that there would be no more work after this job. Someone had suggested that if the hod carriers could slow down the top producers, then everyone would be working at the same slow pace, and the job would last longer.

Lack of current information about the organization's future was still another reason for poor performance. If the hod carriers hadn't started the rumor, who was responsible? Not the experienced bricklayers – the manager had worked with them before. Not the young, ambitious brick-layer – this one wanted to be recognized for superior performance. The manager was convinced that the rumor originated with the clique of young bricklayers.

4. Identify the clique's leader.

The loudest and most aggressive member of a clique may not be the leader. The leader may be a quiet person who prefers to let other employees take the actions and the risks. This person's power is an ability to persuade workers. Look for the worker in a clique who is respected by the others for knowledge, skills, experience, and charisma. This is the leader.

Of the young, inexperienced workers, the manager suspected the old bricklayer as the group's leader. Here was a respected leader whom the young bricklayers would follow. If the old-timer told them a story of tough times ahead, they would pass it along.

The manager had never seen hod carriers breaking bricks. The evidence was there, but not the proof. No one would ever admit to starting or telling a rumor. There certainly was not sufficient evidence to fire the old bricklayer. The manager even had some doubts that the rumor had been started intentionally. Furthermore, every bricklayer and hod carrier would be needed to finish the project on schedule.

5. Within reason, satisfy the needs of the clique members.

Clique members have similar attitudes. They will usually share the same grievances. Thus, the elimination of a commonly held grievance should satisfy most clique members.

– Become personally involved with employees' work related prob-lems.

– Tell the clique's members that you are aware of their actions, and that you know the cause. You also know who is the instigator of their attitudes and conduct.

– Let these workers know that further misconduct will not be tolerat-ed.

– Ask clique members about their thoughts and feelings. Listen attentively. Offer no arguments.

– Tell the workers that you will do what you can to better the situation, and that they will be further informed as to the results of your efforts. Make no promises that you cannot keep.

– When a solution, a compromise, or an explanation has been decided upon, seek the support of the clique's leader. The leader's satisfaction will influence the other workers to agree, also. The leader's support is not absolutely essential; the support of the workers, as a whole, is far more important. Don't back down to the unreasonable demands of anyone.

– Inform all workers – not only the members of the clique – of the information you learn, the changes you will make, and the results you expect to achieve.

With the majority of the workers respectful of your leadership and appreciative of your actions and explanation, the few remaining disgruntled members, if any, will have even fewer workers to whom they can complain. Further rumors will find fewer listeners.

In the example, the construction site manager had understood that the hod carriers had reacted to a rumor that their jobs were nearly finished. They had unwittingly allowed themselves to be manipulated by another clique. By resorting to sabotage, they had put themselves in jeopardy. The hod carrier foreman must have known of this situation. This is where the slow down could have been prevented.

The manager called for the hod carrier foreman and instructed him to tell the workers that bricks were to be carefully and quickly delivered to bricklayers according to their demands, and that bricklayers had been told to report any hod carrier who delivered broken bricks. The foreman was to tell the workers to read the bulletin board regularly. The manager was to be notified of any further rumors.

A notice was placed on the bulletin board announcing that the manager had been selected to manage the next building project. Those workers who worked hard to bring this present job to a successful completion, on schedule, would likely be hired for the next project. The manager called the old bricklayer to the office and explained that there would be no more work on the high walls. The old-timer was to spend morning work hours instructing the inexperienced bricklayers in the techniques to improve the quality and speed in their work. In the afternoon hours, the old master bricklayer was to work on bricklaying jobs around the grounds, the low walls bordering the property, the area around the fountain: all the brick work that people would look at most closely. The old-timer was quite pleased with this new assignment.

The manager held a brief meeting with the young bricklayers and let them know that they now had an opportunity to learn from a master bricklayer. They could become as good as any other bricklayer on the job. The successful ones would go with the manager to the next construction project, while those who failed or made trouble would be out of work.

6. Control the members of the clique.
When all the steps have been taken to correct the problems created by a misguided clique, watch the members closely. Performance evaluations might be given frequently. Do not hesitate to write incident reports on workers who misbehave. You have satisfied the needs of a clique, now let those employees satisfy yours.

Once again, remember that cliques are not necessarily harmful. On the contrary, many cliques are created by management – to set some people apart – so as to maximize their potential talents, and, perhaps, to foster a competitive spirit within other groups.

Cliques created by you will always be easier to manage. You are a part of the clique; you are its invisible influence; you are its leader.

Precious stones are frequently hidden beneath common rocks. A successful miner will find them, dig them out, and assess their value. A successful manager will search for workers of high value in the same manner.

25

HOW TO MEASURE AND IMPROVE EMPLOYEE PERFORMANCE

A group of managers was asked, "What do performance reviews mean to you?"

The unanimous answer was, "Pay raises! We're going to get more money."

Another group of managers was asked the question, "Why do you have performance reviews regularly, once a year?"

The reply was, "We don't know. We always have to fill out performance evaluations. Human Resources tells us to do them."

An employee was asked why performance evaluations and reviews were used. The employee said, "All this organization wants us to do is work harder."

There must be better answers than these.

What Are the Real Reasons for Performance Reviews?

First of all, it is important to know the meaning of performance. An employee's performance stems from a combination of the person's motivation, knowledge, skills, and experience. Without a person's job-directed motivation, training and experience will have little or no effect.

On the other hand, if job-directed motivation is high, but training and acquired skills are lacking, the end result will be equally disappointing.

In addition to knowing the meaning of performance evaluations and reviews, it is also important to know their purposes.

1. Periodic performance evaluations provide a tracking record of the workers. Performances, behaviors, attitudes, wants, and needs can all be recorded. By comparing a worker's present evaluation with past evaluations, trends become apparent. Improvements, declines, achievements, failures, and feelings that swing either way between negative and positive, can be compared, noted, and addressed during a performance review.

2. A performance review provides an opportunity to develop and maintain good communications. The performance review session is the ideal time to focus on specific problems and to bring situations to a head. It is a time for a boss to offer warranted criticism and give deserved praise. It is also a time for the employee to air complaints and to express needs, hopes, ambitions, fears, or frustrations.

Essentially, the worker may be thinking, "What do you expect from me? How good do you think I am at my job? What do you think I am best at? What don't you like? How can I do better? What's in it for me?"

During the performance review, the manager must draw out the employee and be an understanding listener and an effective speaker.

3. Discussing the possibilities of performance improvements is, of course, a purpose of the evaluation and review session. A manager cannot simply demand performance improvements from workers. Ways and means must be pointed out. Both boss and worker must work together toward an agreed-upon plan. Any programme for performance improvement will require follow-up supervision, counseling and support.

4. Problem solving may begin at the performance review. Either the manager or the employee may bring a problem to light. It will be better to solve it now, or work toward its solution, rather than to let it fester and become a crisis.

5. Performance evaluations provide essential information for decision making. A pay raise is only one of these decisions. Equally important are the decisions involving employees who are being considered for transfer, promotion, disciplinary action, termination, or further training.

6. As workers are rated, so shall managers be measured. If workers

are rated uniformly high, and the unit's performance is less than great, top management will surely question the ratings and proceed with an investigation of the manager's abilities to train, inspire, lead, and utilize the unit's employees.

Should the boss of a work group rate workers uniformly low, so as to let top management know of all the difficulties and obstacles there are to being a manager, the executive level will rightly expect those situations to be corrected, and soon.

The Performance Evaluation Form

Most large organizations use some system of performance evaluation. Most small organizations don't.

In organizations, large or small, every supervisor and manager should know the construction and use of a performance evaluation form. For those leaders whose organizations do not have performance evaluations, a form that is workable and easy to use can be created easily. This will require some thought, time, and effort, but the results will be worthwhile.

First, sketch out the top part that identifies the worker and purpose of the form. The introduction might look like this:

EMPLOYEE PERFORMANCE EVALUATION

Name: _____ Date: _____

Job Title: _____

Work Location: _____

Some headings also include such information as Date of Hire; Date of Last Performance Review; Purpose of This Review (annual, or other stated reasons); Special Instructions, such as, "any rating of Excellent or Unsatisfactory must have a written explanation."

Next, think carefully about the subjects you will use for the evaluation of your employees. As you think about measurements and judgements of the employee at the job, ask yourself these questions:

– Is the subject for which the worker is to be rated relevant to the job?

– Is it really measurable, or simply based on feelings?

– Can the subject to be rated be related accurately to the time covered by this rating period?

– Will the ratings on these subjects be helpful for the development of a worker?

Here are some subjects you might use on your evaluation form:
– quantity of work
– quality of work
– attendance
– punctuality
– willingness to accept work assignments
– cooperation with other employees
– attention to costs
– attention to safety.

You might think of many other categories for which to evaluate your workers, such as: job knowledge, job skill, job attitude, time management, self management, initiative, leadership, reliability, interpersonal relationships, communication, problem solving, decision making, compliance with company rules, policies and procedures, use and maintenance of equipment and property, personal appearance, ability to plan and coordinate, and ability to train. The list of subjects for employee evaluation can be as broad and as detailed as you wish it to be.

If you are developing an evaluation form for the first time and for your own use, keep it simple to begin with. Get some feedback from key employees. List only those subjects that are most applicable to the workers at the jobs you supervise. As all organizations do, you can revise your evaluation form as needed.

Add a section for your written comments. These might include:
– Employee's accomplishments since last performance reviews:
– Actions to be taken by the employee:
– Other remarks:

Some forms ask questions to be directed to the employee.
– What parts of the job are most enjoyable?
– What parts of the job are least enjoyable?
– What parts of the job offer difficulties?
– What can the supervisor do to improve the employee's knowledge, and skills?
– What talents and skills do you possess, outside of work, that might be of value within the organization?

Finally, provide lines for signatures and dates:

Employee's signature: _____ Date: _____

Manager's signature: _____ Date: _____

The next step is to determine what method you will use for grading.

The Rating System

There are as many different ways to rate employee performance as there are different performance evaluation forms on which to rate them. Here is a sampling of rating systems:
- Satisfactory or Unsatisfactory (S or U)
- Excellent – Good – Fair – Poor (E, G, F, P)
- Exceeds expected standard (E) – At expected standard (A) – Below expected standard (B) – Under expected standard (U)
- 5 – 4 – 3 – 2 – 1 (5 is high, 3 is average, 1 is low)

On some forms, the range of grading choices is listed for each subject. The rater need only mark the appropriate rating. On other forms, the rater enters the grade – a number or an abbreviation – into a blank space.

Choose a system that is easy to use, serves the purpose of expressing your measurements of an employee, and is easily understood by all persons concerned.

When Should Performance Evaluations Be Made?

A new employee should be called in for a performance review after the first one to three months of employment depending on the settling-in time required for a given job. There may be little known of performance from which to base an accurate evaluation, so the main purpose of this meeting is to open up a meaningful communication. Ask questions. Find out how the employee feels about the job, fellow employees, the organization, and what the employee wants and expects from here on. Probe for what are thought to be problems and attempt to solve them or explain them to the worker's satisfaction. With this initial performance review, you are showing your interest in the employee's feelings, expectations, and performance.

You might find it advisable to conduct another performance review after three to six months of employment. Somewhere within this time frame, a new employee, even at the most difficult job, should be up to speed.

Should an employee's performance evaluation prove to be unsatisfactory, reviews should be conducted in periods of from one to three months, until all ratings are satisfactory.

Performance evaluations and reviews should be made whenever an employee is being considered for transfer or promotion, or for a disciplinary reason.

All employees should have a performance evaluation and review at least annually.

Getting Ready for the Performance Evaluation and Review

Be certain that you are thoroughly familiar with the worker's job description.

– Review the employee's training record.

– Review past performance evaluations.

– Review any observations you may have noted since the last evaluation regarding the employee's performance, such as quality and quantity of work, special accomplishments, on-job behavior, absenteeism, or tardiness.

Using the materials which justify your ratings, complete the employee's performance evaluation form. Use the rating standards you have chosen.

When an employee has completed a special task or project, or made a noteworthy improvement, note this under *Employee Accomplishments*.

Under *Actions To Be Taken By The Employee*, note any tasks, projects, corrections, or improvements to be completed before the next evaluation.

Focus on some goal – what you expect the employee to attain at some future time.

Develop some short-range objectives that will serve as targets and measuring sticks for the worker. Set them to be reasonable, attainable, and measurable.

Overcoming Resistance to Performance Reviews

Performance reviews are only as valuable as you make them. You will understand the reasons why performance review programmes sometimes slide down to uselessness when you learn to recognize attitudes that can interfere with the purposes of performance reviews:

– A manager may feel embarrassed. It may seem senseless to make an issue of an employee's performance evaluation when any question of performance is brought up on the job as the need arises.

– Employees may believe that the only purpose of performance reviews is to get them to work harder.

– A manager may think that performance evaluations and reviews are just a lot of extra paper work – work that has no purpose.

   – A manager may be under continuous stress. This is just something else to do in a hurry. The manager just wants to get it over with.

   – A manager may believe that the evaluations should be critical of the employees. The executives should understand how difficult it is for the manager to accomplish all the objectives with these workers.

   – A manager may believe the employees should receive high marks. The manager wants the executives to understand that this is the best work group in the entire organization.

   Don't let these or similar attitudes destroy your performance evaluation programme. Keep the purposes firmly in mind. Share these purposes with your employees. Consider ways to get employees to participate in the performance review.

   – "I know we've worked together a long time and we talk about work every day, but this review is for the record. Look over this evaluation and tell me if you think it is fair."

   – "Sit down and relax for a few minutes. I'm not going to send off my opinions about you without you knowing what they are. You may have some opinions of your own that I should consider."

   – "Besides discussing these ratings, I want to ask if you are happy at the job you are doing. Are you interested in further training? Do you have any immediate plans for yourself? What are you doing to get what you want and get to where you want to be?"

   – "I'm certainly satisfied with your work, but I'd like to hear your views about the number of rejections we have been having."

   – "Let's go over these ratings together. I know we both want them to be fair and honest."

Conducting a Successful Performance Review

   To accomplish its objective, the performance review must have privacy and, if possible, be conducted without interruptions.

   You can either fill out the evaluation forms before meeting with your employees, or you can discuss each subject with the worker and add your rating to a form as you go along.

   The worker's participation will do much to make a review successful. One way to do this is to have the employees make out their own performance evaluations. Try it. You write your ratings on separate forms. At your individual meetings, compare each employee's ratings with your own. You may be surprised to see how conservatively the employees rate themselves. Often, the workers' ratings are lower than yours. This method of conducting a performance review reduces stress. An employee becomes as interested in the ratings as you.

At this point, focus your views only on those ratings where you and the employee differ, especially those where ratings differ largely or where scores are dangerously low. A small difference is not worth an argument. If a worker puts down *poor* and your rating is *failing*, no harm will be done if you upgrade your evaluation to a rating of *poor*. The employee has received and understood the message. Together, at this time, you can get to the root of the problem and work out a manner by which performance can be improved. This will impress upon the employee the importance of an assigned action.

Occasionally, you may have a situation where the employee says *good* and you say *poor*. This is a wide separation; one of you is wrong. It could be you, but it is the employee's responsibility to defend the self rating by offering accurate facts. If the employee's rating cannot be realistically substantiated, your evaluation must be accepted. You may have reason to compromise, settling for fair. The worker will feel a bit better and may be willing to cooperate with you in planning a course of action to achieve the desired improvement.

Let it be known that the success of all employees in your work unit is your sincere interest. You want each one of them to be rated as better than good. Your own success depends upon being surrounded by capable employees.

Under *Actions To Be Taken*, note any tasks or projects to be completed or any necessary improvements to be made by the employee. Three steps will impress upon the employee the importance of an assigned action.

1. Time Limit

State the time allowed for the employee to complete the assignment.

2. Agreement

There must be an agreement between the employee and you that the assignment is reasonable. Let the employee offer a reasonable solution if it is believed that the task cannot be performed or completed within the time allowed. If an alternative action is found to be to your satisfaction, let it become the agreement.

3. Follow-up

Make a note on your calendar to see that the employee's promise is kept. The employee might possibly think that you have forgotten the agreement. Don't. It may be advisable to call the worker in for further discussion as to the status of the promised action.

During the performance review, discussions should not be restricted only to your measurements and opinions of the employee's performance. You should also encourage the employee to offer opinions, feelings, wants, and needs regarding the job, you, and the organization. These observations and findings should be noted on the evaluation form under *Remarks*.

Ratings aside, employees will not all react alike to the way you conduct your performance review meetings. Be prepared for differences.

– The employee may react defensively.
– The employee may pass the buck.

These two are closely associated. Listen attentively and focus on factual, recorded evidence. Get a partial acceptance of the correction or action you propose and let the worker know that the next review will speak for itself.

In a way you are saying, "Okay, I'm not pushing you this time. I'm letting the subject pass for now. But it better not happen again."

– The employee may be unresponsive.

Ask a question. Sit back and wait for an answer. Say nothing. If there is still no response, ask another question, one that might turn up the heat a bit. You might go so far as to ask, "Do you want to talk about this and come up with some sort of a solution or do you want to let it stand on this evaluation, as is?"

– The employee may become belligerent.

Don't toss out praise. It won't do any good. Be calm. Buy time to let the employee cool down. Just listen until the hurricane winds and tidal waves pass over. Don't go down to the employee's level of belligerence. Gently lead the employee, with understanding, up to your plane of reason.

– The employee may be in total agreement.

Don't buy what the employee sees as an easy way out. Be specific and repetitious. Let the employee know that problems will be solved, actions will be taken, and that follow-up checks will not be forgotten.

Thank the employees for sharing in these performance evaluations and reviews.

Something Else to Think About

If you think, because you rated all your employees at the poor or failing levels, that top executives will be impressed with how hard you work and with all that you have to put up with, think again. The executives are going to ask why you let them become this way and what you are going to do about it.

If you think the top-side executives will be impressed with the super-high ratings that imply that your people are all high achievers, the executives are going to dig into your production figures. If the work results don't equate with the employee performance ratings, you will be considered a loser, and a blind one at that.

The performance reviews should stimulate a new beginning. Your observation and awareness levels are now current. Your seven senses are keenly alert. Plans of what needs to be done with the people in your work unit should be formulated as quickly as possible. It's time for action.

*From within each individual swells an urge to do something
– or nothing.*

26
HOW TO MOTIVATE YOUR EMPLOYEES

One of the qualities managers want from their employees is motivation. To most managers, employees are said to have motivation when they have the self discipline to seek and begin work without being told, and have the patience and persistence to finish their work, quickly and thoroughly. Falling short of this definition, employees are said to be unmotivated. The key word, here, is *unmotivated*, for it puts the blame back on the managers for those employees who lack motivation. For employees to have motivation, managers must motivate.

Before tackling the subject of how to motivate, take a look at the words *motive, motivate, motivation.*

Motive

A motive is an impulse that causes a person to take an action. But within any individual, what is the desired action and what is the impulse that spurs the action?

People are different and so are their motives. Although workers may have different motives for doing a job, managers generally find no fault with their motives, as long as the job gets done.

Many years ago, a traveler was walking down a dusty road. He came upon a worker who was sitting beside the road chipping away at a big rock with a chisel and hammer. On the left were more big rocks. On the right side were big stone blocks.

"What are you doing?" the traveler asked.

"I'm making blocks out of rocks," replied the worker.

The traveler, satisfied with the worker's answer, went on down the road. Soon the traveler came upon another rock cutter – chisel in one hand, hammer in the other – making rock chips fly. Here, too, were piles of rocks and stone blocks. Again, the traveler asked, "What are you doing?"

"I'm earning a living," the worker replied.

A most sensible answer, thought the traveler. Further down the road, the traveler came upon still another rock cutter working with chisel and hammer to chip rocks into blocks. "And what are you doing?" the traveler asked.

The busy worker paused and looked up with a pleasant smile. "I'm building a cathedral." The traveler sat down in the shade of a tree to reflect upon the motives of those who work.

Motivate

To motivate someone is to stimulate them to take action, providing an incentive or motive.

Managers give orders: "Go get it." "Get to work." "Do it this way." They expect their workers to do something.

Or managers may want workers to do nothing: "Stop talking." "Don't do that."

To get workers to comply, managers seek ways to stimulate them to take the desired actions, providing the workers with incentives or motives.

Fear, backed with guns, whips, and mean dogs, is not presently popular in most civilized countries. However, fear in more subtle forms is still widely used to stimulate workers. Some managers may occasionally threaten to take away privileges, to transfer workers to less desirable jobs, or to fire workers if they do not do as they are told. When workers share a common motive to hang onto their jobs, they will follow orders.

Managers who rely solely on fear to stimulate their workers will cause more problems than they will cure. Employees who live in fear of doing things wrong and being punished will be afraid to work or think on their own. They quickly will learn to do only what is necessary to get by. Fear-motivated workers will care for nothing but themselves. As soon as better jobs come along, these workers will jump at them.

A more modern and more acceptable practice of motivating employees is through systems of monetary incentives and rewards. Pay raises and benefits are always popular with employees. They are not, however, an organization's panacea. Here are some reasons why:

– Many workers feel they need more money. They expect more.

They do not see a pay raise as a reward for excellence, but only as a temporary satisfaction. Later, they will need and expect more.

– Pay raises given as an incentive often fail to bring about desired results. Again, many employees feel they already deserve the money. They are likely to give little thought to improving performance.

– In some instances, pay raises fail to satisfy employees' real needs. Employees in dangerous occupations may demand more money for the risks they take. But getting a substantial pay raise does not reduce the risks. Boring jobs, too, such as standing all day on an assembly line and performing the same task over and over again, cannot be made more satisfying through pay raises alone.

Industrial psychologists have classified the wants and needs of workers. Around these, organizations continue to experiment with ways to satisfy their workers and, at the same time, improve productivity and profitability. How organizations and employees think regarding pay schemes depends to a great extent upon the economic conditions at the time. In times of high prosperity, pay raises and benefits – as rewards, incentives, costs of living increases – rise in generous leaps. In times of recession – or worse yet, depression – organizations tighten their belts and resist spending. Employees may then be more interested in keeping or getting a job than in demanding more money. As motives change, so will the ways and means to motivate.

As a line manager, you will have little say or control over the use of monetary incentives and rewards. Nevertheless, you already have considerable power to motivate – to influence your employees' motives – by:

– applying the eight managerial functions with skill and balance
– keeping yourself and your work organized
– remembering your tasks and keeping your promises
– being observant and aware of all that goes on around you
– talking with and listening to your employees
– having earned the respect of your employees
– getting along with your boss
– orienting and training your workers thoroughly and equally
– delegating training roles and cross-training workers
– analyzing jobs as carefully as you appraise the employees
– using performance reviews constructively
– providing avenues of assistance for troubled employees.

Performing in these and other ways, you will do much to motivate your employees and give them reasons to work with you, on your terms.

Motivation

There might well be instances when you will need to motivate an employee in a specific manner. To do so, it will be important to understand the workings of the employee's motivation.

Motivation consists of an individual's motives. For simplicity, look at motivation in this manner: Motives – impulses – can be expressed in terms of desire and expectancy. Using these expressions, a simple equation provides an easy-to-remember definition.

$$\text{Desire x Expectancy} = \text{Motivation}$$

Desire is a wish, a need, or a want for something. Expectancy is what a person believes can be done, achieved, or attained. Motivation is sometimes referred to as force.

Although a person's motivation cannot be expressed as a scientific fact, the equation does give an indication of how motivation can be measured by estimating the values given to what a person wants and what a person expects.

How to Estimate an Employee's Motivation

To estimate an employee's level of motivation, follow these steps:

1. Carefully consider what the employee has done in the past, what is being done now, and what the employee says is desired and expected for the future.

2. Express the factors, desire and expectancy, as numbers. The numbers range from a high of 10 to a low of 1.

3. Numerically express your estimate of an employee's desire and expectancy toward the assignment you have in mind.

Think, now, of your most ambitious and confident employee. What number would best represent this worker's desire for the difficult job you have in mind? Perhaps you believe this worker's desire to be worthy of a 10. How would you rate this person's expectancy to succeed at the challenging job you offer? Another 10? Your candidate's motivation can now be expressed as:

$$\text{Desire (10) x Expectancy (10)} = \text{Motivation (100)}$$

Think of another employee whom you believe to have average motivation. This person goes along with the crowd. If others want the job and believe they can handle it, then this employee believe so, too. So you give desire and expectancy each a 5. This would appear to describe an average person, but notice how it comes out in the equation:

$$\text{Desire (5)} \times \text{Expectancy (5)} = \text{Motivation (25)}$$

Notice that an employee who has average desire and average expectancy falls far short of having average motivation.

Once in awhile, you might find an employee who has a rather strong desire to have a position of power and responsibility, but for some reason – lack of experience, lack of education, an inferiority complex – this person has little expectancy of being selected for promotion. You might express motivation as:

$$\text{Desire (8)} \times \text{Expectancy (2)} = \text{Motivation (16)}$$

Then there is the employee who is just the opposite; who shows all the qualities essential to a challenging job, including self confidence and the expectancy of successful accomplishment. But, for some personal reason, this capable worker has no desire to accept the job being offered:

$$\text{Desire (0)} \times \text{Expectancy (10)} = \text{Motivation (0)}$$

There is a possibility that something at work is bothering this person. Perhaps it has something to do with the way in which the organization operates, the other employees, or you. It is important to find out specifically the reason for this complete lack of desire.

Now that you have an idea of how to estimate a person's motivation, see how well you can apply the knowledge in practical experiences.

How to Bring About a Change in Motivation

Before you ask an employee to do something new or different – take on new work, learn to operate a new piece of equipment, accept a promotion or transfer – plan the steps that you will take:

1. From observations and direct conversation with the individual, have an accurate idea of the levels of desire and expectancy and the reasons why.

2. Give thought to this person's values. Which are of higher interest,

which are of lower importance. Consider the driving force. Is it to make money; to hold a responsible position of power; to solve work problems and make workable innovations; to be liked by people and to help others; or to work comfortably in an orderly environment where clear-cut rules govern individual behavior? Here, you are trying to find a person's "hot button."

3. Give the employee a complete briefing. Explain the project that must be done and the position you want filled. State the reasons why you have chosen this employee for the assignment.

4. Get the employee to talk, to ask questions, to express personal thoughts. If you observe any noticeable differences in desire and expectancy from your original estimates, gently probe for reasons. Be cautious. The true explanation may be different from the one being told to you.

5. Revise your estimates of the employee's desire and expectations, as necessary. Determine which of these you might want to work on to influence a change, and by how much.

Your next step is an attempt to bring about a desired change. Here are a few general openings. As you think of other possibilities, add them to the list:
– Whether you like the assignment or not, I guarantee you that, when it is finished, the experience will have been worthwhile to you.
– Have you ever tried something you thought you wouldn't like, then discovered that you really enjoyed it?
– Please do it as a favor to me.
– Don't worry, you'll be thoroughly prepared before you start.
– Don't worry, you'll have all the support you need as you go along.
– This is an opportunity to become what you have always wanted to be.
– Here's a chance to have those things you have wanted.
– Now you'll be able to do those things you have wanted to do.
– Sorry, but this is the way it has to be. You're it. Before you say anything more, give it a try. Then we'll talk.
– Let me show you what you'll be involved with. I think you'll like it.
– Here's an offer you're going to like.
– Talk it over with your spouse. I think you'll both be happy with this opportunity.

The opener you chose will depend on the employee's desire or expectancy you want to influence. To increase a person's desire, you might choose words that inspire, challenge, arouse curiosity, arouse interest, or remind the person of needs and wants that can be satisfied. To increase a person's expectancy, you might choose words that assure, protect, encourage, improve confidence, or flatter.

The three examples that follow illustrate how managers can influence a change in an employee's motivation.

A manager needed a machine shop supervisor. The most experienced mechanic was offered the job. The mechanic refused the job because of "all the paper work."

The manager was patient. At a later time, the manager asked the mechanic to step into the office and assist with ordering new tools and parts for the shop. Another time, the mechanic was asked to step into the office, "just for a few minutes," and share some views on setting up tighter inventory controls. Then there was an occasion to ask the mechanic for help in organizing some cross-training programmes, so that the less experienced mechanics could take on some of the more difficult repairs.

One day, the manager went out of town. The mechanic was left to look after things.

When the manager returned to the office, the mechanic had something to say. "I'll take the job as supervisor. If I'm going to do all the work around here, I might as well get paid for it. Besides, it's sort of interesting."

An executive was not happy with the lack of sales efforts. The sales people just sat around waiting for prospective customers to walk in or telephone.

The executive had heard that an office manager, a single parent, wanted to buy a house, but was £500 short of a down payment. The office manager was asked to go out and sell 40 new contracts in the next thirty days, without benefit of office leads or drop-ins. And, of course, the office manager must continue to keep up on all regular duties.

The office manager, who had never had a day of sales training or sales experience, emphatically described a lack of expectancy and desire for the assignment. The executive knew, however, that the need to buy a house and move away from parents was the *hot button*.

"I'll make you a bet," the executive said. "If you can self-solicit 40 new contracts in thirty days, on your own time, I'll give you £500. If you don't make it, you pay me a pound."

The office manager's desire came up considerably. As the office manager trudged from door to door, before and after normal working hours, lessons were learned, experience was gained, and expectancy rose to a cautious 10.

The bet was won by the office manager. The executive had the entire sales department in attendance during the pay off. The executive had not only motivated an office manager to reach beyond a pre-set desire and expectancy, but he had motivated an entire sales department, as well.

A service manager heard that employees were complaining about the dull, weekly training meetings. They frequently arrived late for the meetings, or gave excuses for not attending at all. The manager asked one of the service personnel for a favor – to conduct a portion of the next training programme.

The announcement of the meeting and who would be conducting the training was posted. All the other service people came to hear how their friend would perform. There were a few hecklers who teased the speaker. They were the ones selected to participate in the training meetings to follow.

In time, teasing was replaced with better speaker preparation. Employees took pride in what they learned as they prepared for their assignments. They developed increasing confidence in their abilities to speak and instruct. There were no further problems in attendance or tardiness.

To be a successful motivator (or manipulator), keep these sensible rules in mind:

1. Follow the preliminary steps in preparation for your attempts to influence changes in an employee's expressed motivation.

2. Earn the employee's trust.

3. Look for the employee's *hot button* – the key want or need that can likely be used as a counter to an initial resistance.

4. Never motivate an employee for solely selfish interests – neither your own, nor those of the organization.

When an Employee's Words Are Not Backed with Deeds

A manager may occasionally have an employee who expresses a

sincere desire and confident expectancy regarding an upcoming assignment, yet may not act like a motivated person.

Complications can be far reaching when a manager provides assistance in preparation for an advancement to an employee, and the person
offers excuses for not attending special meetings and training sessions and
fails to study the materials provided:

– A manager can be left without a qualified replacement in time for
the fast-approaching job opening.

– Employees who do not move along in jobs that serve as career
stepping stones prevent others from moving up.

– A manager might be asked to explain to superiors why employees
are not being made ready for advancement.

– An organization may be forced to promote workers into positions
for which they are not prepared.

– Some managers may become discouraged and quit trying to motivate employees. They come to think that employees only want titles and
more money, without the work that goes along with the promotions.

Control and Test an Employee's Motivation

1. Know the candidate's qualifications well. Should an ambitious,
confident employee lack specific qualities which are essential to the job
being sought, but which cannot be developed through further effort –
intelligence, for instance – it might be a wise course to help your employee
seek a more attainable goal.

2. Have a prepared programme of development: training outlines,
assigned study materials, quizzes and final examination.

3. Determine where and when training sessions are to be conducted.

4. If applicable, select the trainers you will need for the programme.

5. Consider the feasibility of selecting more than one candidate for
the immediate advancement. Competition might stimulate greater individual motivation.

6. Give individual orientations to the candidates, in private, since
private, individual meetings are more personal and effective. Review the
job description of the position being offered and explain the training
programme that has been developed.

Be firm in explaining that there are to be no late arrivals, no absences, no excuses; that there is a deadline for the completion of all assignments and the training programme in general. Be no less firm in explaining that the candidate must satisfy the requirements for all phases of development. Further, the candidate must be prepared to demonstrate knowledge and abilities to any and all persons involved in the selection process.

Make it understood that a candidate's failure to comply with the terms will be cause for instant disqualification. Also, an employee might no longer be considered for advancement.

At this point, get the candidate to again express a desire to attain the advancement and the expectancy to measure up to the challenges.

You are the one who must determine the terms you expect an employee to agree to and the degree of discipline in your programme. You will be the author of your plan. Keep in mind the plan's purpose – to prepare an eligible but not yet qualified employee for advancement, or to eliminate the employee from consideration.

When you are investing time and effort for an employee's benefit, don't put up with a person's unwillingness to pay the price of success.

Conformity is each individual's choice.

27
HOW TO DEAL WITH PROBLEM EMPLOYEES

Consider what you and the organization provide for the employees. You provide them with training; the means by which their opinions, complaints, and ideas can be made known; and the means by which they can be informed of what is happening within the organization. You give them the guidelines by which to work: policies, rules, and goals. You set reasonable standards of personal performance, and you inform employees as to how well they are doing. The organization rewards its workers with fair compensation.

Most workers are happy, or at least satisfied, with their jobs. Most are productive. There are few wrongdoers, and most wrongdoings are isolated instances. When employees repeatedly violate the organization's rules, or fail to meet known standards, they become problems you don't need.

Managers take pleasure in working with employees who understand the rules and stay within the organization's boundaries of conduct. When employees submit to rules and authority, they are said to be disciplined.

Disciplined employees don't just happen. Somewhere, at sometime, people must be taught to obey. For many, obedience lessons must continue throughout a lifetime.

Children are taught to obey through systems of rewards and punishments. Punishments are penalties applied to injure, hurt, or repay another person for a wrongdoing. But workers should not be treated like children.

Workers have a freedom of choice: they can take whatever actions they choose, but they must accept the consequences. When workers don't like the resulting consequences, they can choose to leave. When an employee has been told, for instance, that repeatedly sleeping on the job will result in termination of employment, and the employee chooses to continue sleeping when there is a job to do, this person's termination is not a punishment. The worker has chosen to be fired.

Why Workers Disobey

Problem employees will disobey the rules or fall short of known standards for any of the following reasons:

– They quit trying to meet established standards because they cannot meet them, or because they are not motivated to meet them.

– They forget. Their violations of the rules are not intentional, but are simply moments of forgetfulness.

– They purposely break the rules and standards. They do not agree with them, so they ignore them.

– They are testing their managers. This frequently occurs when there is a new manager. Some employees want to see what misdeeds they can get away with.

– They don't believe that the managers really care what workers do.

– They have excuses. There are employees who don't think that rules and standards should apply when workers have good excuses to ignore or bend them.

When problem employees are asked why they left their previous jobs, they often reply, "Personality conflict." This is a catch-all phrase that means, "My boss didn't like the way I conducted myself, and I didn't like the way the boss responded."

Dealing with Small and Serious Incidents

Although failings in work performance are dealt with during performance evaluation interviews, the immediate breakdown or error in performance may be written as an incident. Generally, most incidents are written for breakdowns in discipline resulting in unacceptable conduct.

The process of maintaining discipline is a relatively simple one. It progresses from dealing with small incidents of misconduct to more serious incidents. Repetition is a factor to consider. The repetition of small incidents might eventually be considered a serious problem. Another incident might be so serious as to demand an immediate termination of employment.

React to disobedience quickly.

Managers who fail to react promptly to employees' disobedience will likely bring new and bigger problems down upon themselves, such as:

– Unpunished rule breakers become encouraged to move on to even bigger misadventures.

– Other employees may believe that they, too, can take liberties.

– Employees lose respect for managers who condone misdeeds and substandard performances.

– Bosses of managers who can't take charge usually begin looking for stronger managers who can.

Give small incidents the attention they deserve.

No break from accepted conduct or performance should pass without being dealt with. By merely mentioning an incident, you are dealing with it. Employees must continually be made to know that you notice the things they do, even the little things. Furthermore, you show that you care. A few words spoken when small incidents arise are usually sufficient to restore and maintain order.

– A worker arrives at work one-half hour late. The manager glances at the clock and asks, "What happened?"

– An employee is swearing loudly. The manager quietly says, "Knock it off. We don't talk that way in this office."

How to deal with serious incidents.

In most organizations, fighting and stealing are considered to be serious incidents. A series of small incidents – continually using profane language, continually breaking things, continually arriving late for work – may also be considered serious.

When you are faced with a serious incident of misconduct, follow logical steps:

1. Gather all known facts.

Don't jump to hasty conclusions. After a fight, each participant will claim that the other person started it. An accusation that a person has stolen something will mean nothing without evidence. Check out the workers' stories, excuses, and all shreds of evidence.

– A salaried employee explained to the boss, "My grandfather died. I need a few days off to help the family." By checking with supervisors in other departments, where the employee had worked before, the manager learned that the employee's grandfather had died four times during the past year and a half.

– According to a telephone message, one of the employees was home, very ill. The manager decided to visit the sick worker. Recovery was miraculous. The employee had gone fishing.

In some instances, you may need to check records or listen to the testimony of witnesses.

2. Look for the underlying cause.

It is important to know who started a fight, but it may be more important to know why the fight started. The worker who threw the first punch may have had justification – a provocation may have gone beyond a point of retreat; a thrown punch may have been in self defense. The worker who has been sleeping on the job may have been caring for a sick spouse, night after night. Learning of an underlying cause is not meant to prevent you from taking corrective action, but rather it is to help you to take a wise and proper action.

3. Talk with the wrongdoer.

Hear what this employee has to say. Put the employee at ease. Give your assurance that by telling the truth the employee will have nothing to fear. Your only objective is to correct the wrongdoing and prevent its reoccurrence. Attempt to discern what is fact and what is fiction. Probe deeply into your employee's explanation. Ask questions, then question the answers.

4. Write an incident report.

When you feel certain that an incident is truly a serious matter, write an incident report. An incident report is a written statement of an employee's misconduct or performance breakdown. It includes all the known facts and becomes a permanent record in an employee's file. Sound judgement is required to determine when an incident is considered sufficiently serious to justify a report.

– A needy employee, from a large poor family, steals food from the restaurant where you are employed as a manager. Should an incident report be written?

– Should an incident report be written when an office worker is seen taking pencils and paper home to the children?

– What about a mechanic who takes a few small parts from the garage to fix the mechanic's own ailing truck?

– When is arriving late for work a serious matter? One employee arrives ten minutes late every morning; another employee comes in an hour late, once in awhile.

To determine whether an incident report is appropriate to the situation, give thought to the harm that has been done.

– Does the incident interrupt the flow of work?

– Does the incident cost the organization money?

– Does an employee continually repeat acts of misconduct with the belief that anything is permissible, as long as you do nothing more than give an occasional reminder to stop?

– Will the morale of the disciplined workers be harmed if you allow another employee to break a rule that everyone is supposed to obey?

– Is the incident sufficiently serious as to threaten your position as a manager if you fail to report it to your superior?

– Is the incident of such an illegal nature that it should be reported to the police?

An incident of misconduct must justify the permanent mark that will be placed upon an employee's work record. Thus, it is essential that you think clearly. Never write an incident report when you are angry, despondent, or in any way stressed.

Organizations that have an incident report programme will generally have forms for reporting the incidents. If your organization has no such programme or forms, you can still write an accurate incident report with the aid of a simple outline.

INCIDENT REPORT

Date: _____

Employee's Name: _____

Job Title: _____

Work Location: _____

1. Accurately describe the incident, misconduct, or performance error.

2. Describe the supportive evidence (records, witnesses). Do not refer to witnesses by name without their permission. Keep confidential information in a private file.

3. Describe the corrective action that the employee must take.

4. Describe the consequences that the employee must accept should the person fail to comply with the organization's rules and authority.

5. State exactly the employee's promise of compliance. Include a future date for the review of the employee's conduct and performance.

Employee's signature: _____ Date: _____

Manager's signature: _____ Date: _____

You should keep a copy of the report in your file, the personnel – or human resources – department must have a copy, and your immediate boss should either have a copy or at least see a copy, as it is routed on up to the personnel department.

The employee's acceptance of the report's factual accuracy is proven by the worker's signature.

Discipline with a Sense of Balance

Continue to bear in mind the purposes of an incident report:

– To impress upon an employee the seriousness of a misdeed.

– To inform an employee of the corrective actions that are to be taken.

– To inform an employee of the consequences that can be expected should the employee fail to comply.

– To gain an employee's agreement that the actions and the consequences are fair.

– To help the employee meet all the organization's standards of conduct and performance.

These purposes can be further served by your common sense.

1. Do not make rules as you go along.

It is not fair for a manager to suddenly surprise a worker with an announcement that there will be a one week suspension, without pay, because of a misconduct. This is not an expected consequence; it is a punishment.

2. Apply the organization's rules fairly to all employees.

You must know the rules before making a judgement or taking an action. Once an action is taken, a precedent is set. Similar situations, later on, must then be treated in the same manner as before.

A company policy may state that an employee who is off work for more than three days, due to illness, must return with a doctor's statement, or the employee's pay for the time off will be withheld. A manager who allows one employee to violate the rule will find it impossible to enforce it later. Other workers will be encouraged to report in sick, stay away from work for a week, return without a doctor's statement, and expect to be paid for their unauthorized *sick time*. If the manager then penalizes these workers, they will feel unfairly treated.

3. An incident report can be written without bringing harm to an employee's work record.

Your objective is to maintain discipline within your work group.

You need not discredit an employee in the process, if you have good reason and if the incident was a minor one.

– A young worker was caught sleeping on the job. The manager learned that the employee was engaged to be married and was seeing the intended spouse every night. The manager was sympathetic, but a rule had been violated. The incident could not be excused. Other employees were waiting to see what the manager would do. The report was written. The consequence was stated: Termination of employment would receive serious consideration if the employee was, again, caught sleeping at work. The worker promised to get more sleep at home during the work week.

The other workers quickly learned of the manager's written incident report – a black mark on the young employee's work record. But the manager did not route the report on up to the personnel department. The incident was filed in the manager's desk.

A month after the employee's wedding, when it was evident that there had been no more sleeping on the job, the manager destroyed the incident report. The worker's work record remained unblemished. All the employee's continued to believe that their boss was a stickler for adherence to the rules.

Employment law is, however, an area fraught with dangers for the new manager. Whenever in doubt about the best course of action, it is always wise to consult the personnel department.

Some employees do not easily learn the lessons of discipline. Some will continue to misbehave.

Repeated Incidents Signify a Troublemaker's Choice

Incidents, even minor ones, become more serious as they are repeated. A second incident must be treated accordingly. The offender must be impressed with the seriousness of this situation.

One way to make a strong impression is to arrange to have your boss meet with you and the errant employee. Let the boss and the worker do most of the talking. Don't interrupt. Speak only when you are asked to do so.

Your boss will ask the worker to explain the reason for this repeated incident of misconduct. After the employee's explanation, the boss will get straight to the point. "What do you want to do about it? Do you want to stay and work according to the rules and standards, or do you want to leave the organization?"

The employee can be expected to promise, once again, that there will be no more incidents of misconduct.

Some managers will impress a problem employee, further, by giving *sweat time*. A manager may say, "Before you answer whether you wish to stay at your job or leave it, I want you to spend the remainder of the day at home. You will be paid for the full day. Think over your decision. The three of us will meet in my office tomorrow morning at nine o'clock."

When a worker is sent home from work early in the day, family members and friends will ask questions. They will want to know why. Their concerns will do much to impress the employee with the seriousness of the decision that must be made. The employee will have time to think, to worry, to *sweat*.

For a given offense, an organization may allow no more then three incident reports. Thus, at the conclusion of a second encounter, a problem worker will be told that there will be no more meetings. One more incident of this kind will indicate the worker's acceptance of the inevitable consequence – dismissal.

There are times when there will be no warnings, no second chances. Once again, however, great care must be taken before considering the dismissal of an employee. No manager wants to deal with the problem of an "unfair dismissal".

How to Tell an Employee Goodbye

Most managers dread having to dismiss workers from their jobs. It can be an emotionally distressing experience. Understandably, a manager may postpone the task indefinitely, or it may be forgotten altogether.

Experience will not make the task of dismissing an employee any easier, but it should improve one's confidence. A manager who has never before dismissed an employee, or who has done so only rarely, will find these following thoughts to be helpful:

– Do not, in a fit of anger, suddenly fire a worker. Explosive anger might provoke an unexpected incident – one, perhaps, that is more than you could handle.

– When the thought of an employee's dismissal first occurs to you, ask yourself these questions: Am I at fault for this employee's failure? Have I given sufficient training? Have I taken every possible step to counsel and direct this person? Have I given adequate supervision?

– Check your legal position *before* you act. Discuss the problem with your personnel department.

– Plan ahead. Choose the proper time and place to dismiss the problem employee – a time that will least interrupt your work and the work flow of your unit; at a place that is private and free of interruptions.

– If you were to ask a surgeon for advice as to how a malignant tumor should be removed, the doctor might reply, "Cut quickly, cut deep, and close quickly." You, too, have a cancerous situation to eliminate. Don't prolong the agony of the occasion. Get on with it. "I'm sorry that things have not worked out well for either of us. As of now, your services will no longer be needed."

– Some managers begin a notice of dismissal with, "I'm sorry that I must ask for your resignation." If an employee refuses to give it, a manager will continue, "Then there is only one alternative. I must dismiss you."

– Should you have a tendency to feel sorry for a departing worker, concentrate on the reasons for the person's dismissal.

– Some organizations have a policy of giving employees advance notice of a dismissal. The employee is expected to work until the date of separation. With your organization's permission, you may find it advisable to pay the worker for the remaining days of employment and allow the employee to leave immediately. There are good reasons for doing this. An employee, knowing that the dismissal is no secret, may be greatly embarrassed or angry. The employee's continued presence could lead to more harm than good. A terminated troublesome worker who is allowed to stay on the job might be tempted to steal items from the organization. A dismissed employee will be appreciative if allowed to use the remaining paid time to seek other employment.

– Most dismissed workers, when notified, experience a sense of relief. Most have lacked the courage to quit. Now the decision is not theirs to make. For these workers, there will be no more of the organizations restriction and no more of your criticisms.

– Before the final paycheck is given to a dismissed employee, be certain that all issued properties including keys have been recovered.

– Be pleasant and polite to the departing worker. There should be no reason for a dismissed worker to leave feeling hurt, bitter, or angry. This dismissal was not your decision. The employee had a choice.

– To avoid any traumatic aftermath of an employee's dismissal, advance planning is important. Have you given thought as to how the vacated position is to be covered until a replacement can be recruited, hired, and trained? Have other workers been cross-trained for this position? It is important that you have a workable plan.

– Some people may question the wisdom of your action in firing an employee. You may be challenged by some of your other workers who might have been friends of the dismissed employee. Outside of the organization, the terminated employee's friends and relatives might call to challenge your action. To all people, except your superiors, say as little as possible. If you are pushed to give an explanation, just say that all such inquiries must be directed to the personnel department. Avoid making any statements that could possibly fuel legal complications. When higher authorities within the organization ask for a report on the dismissal, have your facts documented and on file.

Again, remember that workers who have been fired from one job will surely find employment elsewhere. As a rule, they will be much happier in their new situations. In nearly every instance, the dismissal of a worker will be to everyone's advantage.

What to Do When You Can't Get Rid of a Problem Employee

A manager was heard to say, "I can't fire anyone, so how can I maintain discipline?"

Another manager said, "I dismissed a worker one day, but my boss sent this same, uncooperative, nonproductive foul-ball back to the job the next day."

Why do some managers feel that they have no power to rid their work groups of problem employees? One executive offered this explanation: "Of course, managers can have unsatisfactory workers removed. However, all too frequently, managers do not provide sufficient justification. They do not support their reasons with factual information. They do not properly document the instances of misbehavior or performance breakdowns. Managers must learn of these things."

What the executive said is true, but some managers still believe there is more to be said:

– "I followed the organization's procedure, but my request to have an employee discharged was refused."

– "I supported my charges with facts; they were well documented. I went through proper channels. Then, somewhere along the line, the employee's file was *misplaced*. I looked in my office files. The copies I had prepared were gone. In the personnel office, the original copies were also missing."

– "Someone higher up used influence to have a relative hired. The relative was assigned to my work unit. There was trouble from the beginning. Rules and work standards meant nothing to this person. My boss would not let me get rid of this person who was destroying the morale within my group. I think my boss was intimidated by someone higher up the ladder."

When you feel it necessary to rid your work group of an undisciplined, poor performer, yet you feel powerless to do so, the following suggestions may prove helpful.

1. Carefully document each misdeed immediately after it happens. Write down the facts. Do not vaguely state that a worker never does as told; that a worker is always fighting; that you think a worker is stealing; that a worker cannot learn to do anything correctly. Be specific.

2. Document equally well all the instances of help you have given to the problem employee – training, cross-training, counseling.

3. Learn the answers to the following questions: What exactly is the organization's procedure for the dismissal of a troublesome employee? Who makes the final decision? What information will convince the decision maker that a problem employee should be dismissed? How should the material be prepared? To whom should the request and the documented evidence be submitted? How soon can a reply be expected?

4. Keep additional copies of all documented evidence in your personal file. If you believe that items might be removed from your office files, keep vital copies at home. If your personal records are requested, make copies before letting them go.

5. When the organization fails to act promptly and favorably upon your request to have a worker's employment terminated, do not allow yourself to become angry. To make loud, angry arguments will only weaken your case. Continue to record the problem employee's misdeeds. The ever-increasing mass of evidence cannot be ignored forever.

Also Say Goodbye to Those Who Are Not Needed

There are managers who mistakenly share one or more the following beliefs:

– They best serve the economy by providing as many jobs as possible.

– The more employees they have, the quicker and easier the work will get done.

– They feel more pride, more important, and more powerful when they manage a large, although over-staffed, work group.

Successful managers have proven the opposite of these beliefs to be true.

Every organization has projects yet to be started. The excuse for their delay is generally lack of money, so when managers eliminate nonessential employees, money is saved. The savings can be invested in expansion, new jobs will be created, and the organization will prosper and the growth cycle can continue.

There is an old saying that goes, "Idle time makes for idle hands." There is little motivation to do a task when there is no sense of urgency. When a worker looks around and sees others who have little or nothing to do, who cares?

The office workers are gathered around one desk chatting. Across the room the telephone rings. No one hurries to answer it. No one even moves. The chatting continues. The phone stops ringing.

Workers are happiest when they are busy at their own assigned tasks, and when they can see that other workers are busy as well. Time passes quickly for employees who are busy. And busy employees stay at their work stations. Little things get done – such as answering a telephone.

Managers can take pride only when results are attained. Well-managed, well-trained, highly efficient, tight-knit groups of workers will produce the results. Through accomplishments, managers will know the feeling of power. Workers, as well as managers, will feel pride from knowing that standards and goals have been met.

Look carefully within your own work unit. Do you have any undisciplined or unproductive workers? If you do, take no pity on them. They have none for you. Plan to rid yourself of those who do not serve your purposes, which are the purposes of the organization. Perhaps you need not hire replacements. Analyze each job. Review the employees' training records. Have all the workers on your team been cross-trained for other positions? Examine the performance evaluations.

Trim the fat from your payroll. If you have people who can fill these vacated positions, hold off on hiring replacements. Write new job descriptions as needed. Motivate your remaining crew of known producers to pull together and keep work flowing. Motivate your employees to develop self discipline, self motivation, and pride in what they do. You will likely learn that more can be accomplished, with less stress, when you have busy, efficient, effective employees.

Don't let anyone slip you square pegs
when you have round holes to fill.

28

HOW TO WORK THE HIRING PROCESS FOR ALL IT'S WORTH

Managers and their employees will likely spend more waking hours together at work than they will spend at home with their families. Thus, the joining together of managers and their employees under one roof for a common purpose is an important *marriage.*

A work organization and a family have similarities. In each, the people involved experience divisions of responsibility, joys of accomplishment, mutual respect and admiration, disagreement and bickering. And certainly a divorce that results in a broken family can hardly be more painful and ugly than an unfortunate, unhappy termination of an employee or a manager from gainful employment.

Too frequently, it seems, a manager must pull together skills and energies to provide extra training for workers who were thought to be experienced; to counsel workers who have personal problems; to pamper sensitive or insensitive personalities; to discover an habitual thief; or to discipline the undisciplined. A manager under such stresses may wonder if such problems could have been suspected and prevented.

Success or Failure Begins Here

Hiring the right person for the right job will do more to prevent work problems than any other single activity, but the subject of hiring is best learned after managers have had time to understand the jobs they supervise, the essential qualifications workers must possess, the training required, and the behavioral problems that occasionally arise. Also, managers must have had time to appraise themselves – to measure their abilities and to function as leaders.

Hiring functions are alike, processes differ.
The hiring functions consist of:
– recruiting
– screening
– interviewing
– testing (when appropriate)
– checking References
– selecting
– processing
– orienting.

The methods by which various organizations and managers apply these steps differ greatly. A person in charge of a small organization may do all the hiring. A manager in a medium size organization may be allowed to hire people, but a higher authority may have the final word. In some large organizations, specialists may have the responsibility for carrying out most of the hiring functions.

Hiring situations differ, too. A situation may require the hiring process to be simplified, with functions performed simultaneously, or even omitted.

– In a large organization, an employee from one department may be transferred to fill a vacancy in another department.

– A building contractor calls the union hall to send out skilled workers.

Whatever the manner of hiring, whatever situations arise, whatever your rank in the organization, you are accountable for the consequent actions of whomever is hired into your work unit. Therefore, you must be assured that the most capable and reliable person is hired for each specific job.

Before the Hiring Process Begins, Be Prepared

1. Learn how the hiring process works in your organization.

What exactly does the organization process consist of? How is each step performed? Who are the people involved in the hiring process? What specifically is the role you are expected to play?

2. Review the laws and policies that apply to the hiring process.

Governments throughout the world have laws to prevent discrimination for reasons of race, religion, sex, or age. Where such laws prevail, the color of a person's skin or a religious belief cannot be held against a job applicant; a woman must receive the same consideration for employment as does a man; an older person cannot be considered unqualified for reason of age alone. When a manager consciously or unwittingly violates an anti-discrimination law, the organization can be in for serious legal trouble. Check with your personnel or human resource department. Learn what interviewing questions can and cannot be asked.

Your organization may fall under a law that requires it to advertise all job openings publicly. In such an instance, a job must be advertised as open to all qualified applicants, even when the organization has planned to promote someone from within to fill the vacant position.

Some organizations give preference to the hiring of men and women who have had military service. Some give preference to people who are physically handicapped. Some organizations forbid the hiring of people who are related to workers presently employed there. Other organizations allow relatives to be hired, but, in some instances, the related employees may not be permitted to work together in the same department. Still other organizations may actually encourage the hiring of employee relatives. Why the differences? Employment rules are founded upon experiences. For each organization, the rules are sound. Ask the people in Human Resources why the rules in your organization exist. It's good to know when you talk with present and prospective employees. The main point is to avoid the pitfalls.

3. Review your understanding of the job to be filled.

A job description is the cornerstone of the hiring process. When a job opening occurs in your work area, pull the job description from your file and study it.

Keep in mind that a job has a personality of its own, and applicants have distinct personalities of their own. Aside from the job's functional requirements, it is essential that you consider the behavioral requirements as well. There may be many applicants who can do a specific job, but you will want to hire one who will enjoy doing it. In each of the following demanding job conditions, think of personal traits that would indicate an applicant's suitability.

– The employee must work alone. There will be no one else with whom to talk.

– The worker will be continuously surrounded with noise and apparent confusion.

– The employee must stand at a fixed work station for eight hours a day.

– An occupation is known to be a dangerous one. The work could be a threat to health and life unless the employee remains alert continuously.

– The worker must pay close attention to a variety of details. Concentration must be maintained for many hours at a time.

- The employee must sit at one place throughout working hours.
- The employee must continually be courteous, friendly, and helpful to the general public, regardless of personal feelings.
- The job is routine, repetitious, and physically demanding. It requires little thinking.
- On a daily basis, the worker will be under extreme pressure to complete urgently required tasks, within seemingly unreasonable deadlines.

Think carefully of what applicants may not understand or know of until after being hired. Things that remain unknown or misunderstood can cause needless frustrations, even anger. For instance, a job may require an employee to be available for emergency duty at odd hours. The job description may read:

> The job incumbent will be required to perform occasional duties during other than normal working hours. Compensatory time will be granted in lieu of overtime pay.

Some job applicants cannot be expected to understand the true meaning of the word *occasional*, but a manager would know. For instance, a line manager would know that there have been an average of three emergency night calls a week for the past six months.

An applicant may not understand the meaning of *compensatory time*. A worker may put in a full day's work, only to be called out that night to slog through a rain soaked forest to repair a downed power line. This worker may be understandably disappointed to learn that there will be no overtime pay for the extra work, only time off to compensate for it.

A manager may forget to ask if an applicant can be readily reached at night or on weekends, and if the prospective employee has dependable transportation. An emergency is no time for a manager to learn that the telephone number on the application form is really that of the employee's relative who lives some distance away. Or that the employee who rides the bus to work can't work nights because the bus doesn't run that route at night. An applicant should have a complete understanding of the job being sought. It is a manager's responsibility to make certain that an applicant understands and accepts all the conditions of the job.

How to Improve Your Hiring Skills

Only infrequently does a job opening come as a surprise to a manager. As an alert manager, you will likely be aware of these possibilities:
- An employee who is about to be promoted or transferred.

— An employee who is about to quit.
— An employee who is about to be fired.

When you even suspect that one of these situations may occur, it is time to act.

With a thorough understanding of the job to be filled, your organization's hiring policies and processes, and any laws that can affect these, you are ready to accept your role in the hiring process. Here, again, are the seven functions that compose the hiring process. Remember, some of these functions may be omitted, some may be performed simultaneously, and some may be tortuously stretched out.

1. Recruiting

Either in your own files or in the personnel office files, there are likely to be large numbers of applications from job seekers. Those applicants who meet specific job requirements can be drawn upon to fill suddenly vacated positions quickly.

Do not judge a person's availability by the date on the application. In other words, if an application was submitted six months ago, you should not throw it away on the assumption that the person is now happily employed elsewhere. A person may prefer to work for your organization even though presently employed somewhere else.

Few line managers, particularly in large organizations, are responsible for recruiting job applicants. Whether this step is your responsibility or not, you should always be alert for good, prospective employees. You may have applicants on file who meet minimum job requirements, but by doing a bit of recruiting you may find people with superior qualifications. Certainly, a trained master mechanic is better than a self-taught *knuckle buster*. An office employee who types 110 words per minute will get out much more work than one who only comes up to the minimum standard of 55 words per minute.

Talk with your better employees – the ones whom you trust for their sound judgements and loyalties to the organization. Ask if they know of people who can measure up to your high standards and who will take pride in what they do. Good employees will feel a sense of responsibility when recommending prospective employees. They will either recommend a person who will be successful, or they will suggest no one. The recommendation of a marginal employee should be treated cautiously. Let everyone understand that your intention, at this point, is to get a large number of applicants from which to choose. You are making no promises to anyone. When there is a job opening you must hire the most qualified person, or you must recommend your choice to the person in your organization who actually does the hiring.

Headhunting is not generally thought of as a nice word, but it is a common practice in recruiting exceptional employees. As you go about your way outside of your organization, be aware of other people at their jobs. If you think a person might be an ideal employee in your organization, strike up a conversation. Ask of the person's background and ambitions. Let this individual know who you are and how you feel about your organization. Invite this person to contact you at your place of work if a job change is being considered. When the prospect accepts your invitation, arrange for an interview with the person responsible for hiring.

2. Screening

Screening would seem to be a simple task. Actually, there is more to it than just sifting out the applicants who don't qualify. In large organizations, screening is done by people in the personnel department. There are several advantages in sparing you of this duty:

– When someone else does the screening, you don't have to deal with a stream of job seekers interrupting your work.

– Applicants need not jump from manager to manager filling out an application form for each one.

– In a central location, the files of all applicants provide a single reference source of available manpower.

– Ideally, the people who do the screening will know of all job openings throughout the entire organization. As an example, if a welder applies for a job in a machine shop, and there is no opening there, a knowledgeable screener may know that another welder is needed at the dry dock.

There are, however, some possible weaknesses in a centralized screening system:

– A person in the personnel department is not likely to have the same knowledge and feel for a job that you have.

– A personnel specialist may accurately screen out all those persons who do not qualify for a certain position, but may fail to note an applicant's other outstanding qualifications.

– Overly qualified is a label frequently used to turn away exceptional applicants whose previous successes and incomes have been markedly higher than what can be expected at the job now being sought.

Fortunately, most screening specialists, when impressed with an applicant for a job they do not fully understand, will communicate with managers who do understand. A screener who is impressed with the knowledge and experiences of a person who appears overly qualified, or a generalist – one who cannot be slotted as a specialist – may send a resume to one or more department heads with a notation, "Would this person be of interest to you?" It is not uncommon for an organization to make room for a valued applicant, even though no job opening exists at the moment. An organization will gamble that, at some future time, this talented person will be called upon to fill a yet unknown position. Understand that an organization can only afford to make such a gamble on a person when times are prosperous.

If you work in an organization where the screening of applicants is done by specialists in personnel, keep in mind that they are challenged by the task of pleasing a variety of managers who are engaged in diverse forms of work. There are some things you can do to make their jobs easier and, at the same time, bring about better results for you. Get to know the people who screen job applicants.

– Review with them the functional and the behavioral requirements of the jobs in your department. Let them know what you are looking for in a prospective employee.

– Ask how they feel about your personal recruiting efforts and the recommendations of applicants you favor. Some human resources people can be somewhat possessive of their roles in the hiring process. Make no demands. Ask questions about how the hiring process works. Most people enjoy talking about themselves and the work they do. A bit of tact will do much to develop a cooperative spirit.

– Explain that when none of the applicants sent to you is satisfactory, you will ask the personnel specialists to search further. Explain, too, that you will again be willing to talk with them about the particular qualities of worker you are looking for.

The hiring process is not unlike a budding romance. The screening step is nothing more than an introduction when interest is first aroused. The courtship begins with the interview.

3. Interviewing

All qualified job applicants should be granted an interview. Screening and interviewing may occur simultaneously: A job seeker fills out an application form, the boss compares the applicant's qualifications against those essential to the job and asks questions as the application is being studied.

In a small organization, a boss may give one interview and make a quick decision. In a larger organization, for important positions, there can be a series of interviews. Personnel specialists may interview applicants who meet minimum requirements so as to narrow the number of those to be recommended for further consideration. The most qualified applicants will then be interviewed by the appropriate line manager. In most instances, the applicant chosen by the line manager will be introduced to the line manager's superior. This is sometimes a matter of courtesy, sometimes an opportunity to gain another opinion of the applicant, and sometimes it is the boss who will have the final say.

In all organizations, large and small, however the hiring process is conducted, line managers should always have an opportunity to interview qualified job applicants and have a say in the final selection.

Before advertising for job applicants, give some thought to what you may be letting yourself in for.

– How long should an interview be? Let the job description be your guide. You may need only 15 to 30 minutes to interview a laborer or an entry level office clerk. Several hours could be needed to interview a person seeking a technical position. Also, allow some time between interviews so you can jot down some notes and refresh yourself.

– Should applicants be asked to arrive at the same time, to sit and wait, each in turn, for an interview? Would you prefer to give individual appointments at specified times? When you anticipate lengthy interviews, it is best to schedule interviews at fixed times. When interviews are to be brief, you might choose to have applicants arrive within a time limit you have allowed for interviews.

– Give thought to the number of applicants you might expect. If there are to be 10, 20, or 50 job seekers, how will you ever get around to interviewing them all? Where will you put them? In large organizations, line managers need not contend with this sort of problem. The personnel department will control the number of applicants that a manager is to interview. Do let the personnel office know when you will be available for holding interviews.

– Never allow job seekers to come to you whenever they wish and expect an immediate interview.

– Before beginning your interviews, your desk should be cleared of all other work. The people around you should be notified that there are to be no interruptions.

– Be prepared to write notes of each interview. Writing notes during an interview may cause an applicant to become nervous. This is not desirable. Notes, however, are desirable. After a string of interviews, without notes to jog your memory, you might easily forget which of your thoughts and opinions go with the various names and faces. Even the names and faces may be difficult to match without the aid of notes. Do not write your views and opinions on the application form. Job applications become permanent records. You have no control over who will see the application files. Unwise comments written at the time of an interview could lead to embarrassing explanations or even legal complications.

As you begin an interview, try to get an overall picture of the applicant. If the interview was scheduled for an appointed hour, notice whether the applicant arrived on time. Take note of the applicant's appearance. For most positions, an applicant need not be well dressed but should appear scrubbed, neat, and in clean clothes. A job-seeker who claims to be a diesel mechanic will have hands that, though washed, show the deep, dark lines and tough calluses of that trade. A person who seeks a job serving the public should smile easily and frequently. When you first meet an applicant, try to visualize that person working at the job you have in mind. Watch how each individual walks, sits, talks, and listens.

Make the applicant comfortable and at ease. Your goal is to get the person to talk. Some people are basically shy and not very talkative. Some are nervous and afraid of saying something wrong. Your first comments or questions may be solely for the purpose of getting the applicant to talk. You may see something on the application form or resumé that will prompt you to initiate a conversation, whether it be on sports, hobbies, school, work, or any other subject. Getting over the applicant's initial uneasiness will do much to make the interview flow smoothly.

An easy way to get into an interview is with the use of the application form. Study it carefully. Use it as an outline for your interview. As you read the entries, ask any questions as they occur to you. Make mental notes of each answer. Once in awhile, job seekers will omit a few facts. They may be failing to tell the whole truth, and hoping that you won't notice. Under direct questioning, these people are not likely to lie. They know that you suspect an untruth. They know that most organizations check the information given on an application form. They know, too, that when new employees are found to have lied, they are fired. So bore in with your questions. Here are a few concerns to be aware of as you study each employment application:

– Are all the spaces filled in? If not, why? Did the applicant forget? Would this person always be so inattentive and forgetful? Is the applicant concealing information by omitting it? What might it mean if a telephone number is missing? Is being available by telephone an important issue?

– Are there any breaks or interruptions in the applicant's work history? Why would a period of time be unaccounted for? Was the applicant omitting a job where a job reference might be unflattering? Was the applicant simply unemployed during this time?

– Has there been a recent illness or injury that might hinder the person's work performance? Would it be advisable to ask for a doctor's release before employing this person?

– The applicant's address may indicate a long distance to and from work.

Transport costs and the time needed for travel to and from work can make some candidates less than ideal.

Do not be satisfied until you are certain that the information asked for on the application form is complete and correct.

Ask questions that pertain to the applicant's knowledge, skills, and experiences. A manager who knows and has done the work will ask specific questions and will not be misled by vague answers.

If you have had little or no experience with a certain line of work, it may be advisable to have one of your experienced employees present during the interview. A knowledgeable worker can ask more penetrating questions that will reveal the applicant's true qualifications. Later, after the interview, the employee can offer a summation of what was learned during the interview.

Explore the human factors – those of the job and those of the applicant. These factors should be the basis for some of your questions. It is important to learn, before the point of selection, how an applicant will probably react to the work environment, to various work situations, and to other personalities within the work group. Explain the job, with all of its details, pressures, and demands. Ask the job seeker if there are any questions. Watch to see if the applicant appears less enthusiastic about the job, or more so. If the applicant begins by asking about money, holidays, and how much work is really involved, you should be forewarned that this person is probably more interested in having a job than in doing a job. An applicant who initially appears interested in the work itself will most certainly impress you.

When you are satisfied with the answers to your questions, and if you feel that the applicant may be a good prospect for the job, continue with an explanation of the organization's history and structure. Now is the time to explain the wages, holidays, and other benefits. During this portion of the interview, you are buying and selling. You are attempting to buy – with attractive wages, benefits, opportunities, and other job satisfactions – the most qualified person you can find. At the same time, you are selling the applicant on the fact that your organization is a good place to work.

Be polite, courteous, and respectful toward every applicant you interview. Every job seeker should leave your office hoping more than ever to be selected for the job. One manager was too ignorant to learn this lesson:

The head of an organization learned of a highly trained and experienced computer programmer who turned down an excellent job offer because of the manager who conducted the interview. In the applicant's words, "The manager was belligerent, rude, and insensitive, and had the personality of a shark. I wouldn't work for such a person no matter how much money I was paid.''

In closing the interview, thank the applicant for the interest shown for the job and for the organization. Tell the applicant that the final selection will be made after all the applicants have been interviewed and evaluated. If possible, give the job seeker some idea as to when the decision will be made. Some managers and organizations take too much time in reaching a decision. During this interim, there is a risk that the better applicants may find other jobs. However, if the selection date is made known, a potential candidate for employment will be inclined to wait for the results.

4. Testing

There are organizations that give tests to measure intelligence, behaviors, values, honesty, aptitudes, skills, and even drugs. The results of these tests are intended to help an organization to make better selection decisions. The information also helps line managers to know more about a newly hired employee.

Even without the services of professional testing, you can still conduct certain tests that are practical for your purposes. You may ask applicants for an office job to take a simple typing test or a test in operating a calculator. By asking a few questions, a shop manager should be able to test an applicant's knowledge of mechanics. Given a few tools, the applicant should be able to demonstrate needed skills.

5. Checking References

The central hiring office of a large organization will attend to the matter of checking references. Personal references are of little value since job applicants will only give the names of people who are sure to give favorable references. Many organizations have dropped personal references from their application forms.

Job references are of far greater importance. Places of previous employment tend to offer little information, other than to confirm the jobs held, and the dates of employment. A question that should be asked of all previous employers is: ''If you had an appropriate job opening, would you consider rehiring this former employee?'' A yes answer is a good recommendation. The reason for giving a no answer would probably not be explained, but the warning would be clear.

No matter who performs this task, the personnel office or you, applicant references must be checked. Check the applicant's driving record as well – also seek proof of citizenship, or a work permit.

Learn everything you can about the person you are asking to join your organization.

6. Selecting

When the recruiting, screening, interviewing, and testing have been expertly performed, selecting the best of the candidates would appear to be an easy task. In many instances, however, there could be several considerations to be argued.

Some jobs require multiple talents. For example, an office receptionist may also need to know how to type and use a ten key calculator; a heavy equipment operator may need to know how to make repairs in the field. These instances are where the selection becomes difficult. Should the organization hire the person who is superior as a personable greeter and message taker, or should a person who is a better typist, but who is lacking somewhat in personality, be hired? The same is true for the job opening for an equipment operator/mechanic. One applicant may be a better operator, the other, a better mechanic. How would you decide?

To resolve such conflicts, the selection maker must first set an order of task priorities. In each instance, this person must decide which job tasks have the greater importance. Give thought to the tasks that can be most easily and readily taught on the job. It might be relatively simple to train a good equipment operator in basic field mechanics. It may be nearly impossible to change someone's personality.

With bits of wisdom and common sense, these kinds of selection problems can be resolved. The selection step is made easier when aggressive recruiting brings in one or more applicants who have multiple talents and skills.

7. Processing and Orienting

Paper processing is the responsibility of the personnel department. In many organizations, managers are asked to see that the essential work forms for new employees are filled out properly. These forms and records are then forwarded to the personnel office.

Some organizations make a big production out of orienting its new employees, with handout materials, films, and speeches by top executives. Even then, managers must not assume that new employees know all that they should. Regardless of whether your organization is big or small, question new employees about what they know, and also what they don't know. Consider the true orientation of new employees to be your personal responsibility. Explain the organization's rules, policies, and all the other matters that pertain to work.

A well-hired employee will prove to be a valuable asset. A poorly hired employee can bring untold problems to a manager and needless expense to an organization. The hiring process will seem, at times, to be time consuming, tiring, and frequently frustrating. Have faith that your sincere, knowledgeable, and skillful efforts shall be rewarded.

From life experiences we must learn.
For life's hard lessons unlearned leave us fossilized and impotent in
a desert of ignorance.

29

HOW TO ASSESS YOUR SUCCESS AS A MANAGER

As a manager, you will be faced continually with challenges. These challenges will take the form of tests in three important areas:

The test of effective management.
The test of continual change.
The test of emotional stress.

The difficulty factors of these tests will be proportionate to the demands of your job.

As you complete the various parts of each test, you will be able to assess your own progress. You will be graded by your bosses, other superiors, and those ever-watchful employees. Some scores will be reflected by performance evaluations, paychecks, and by appointments to new challenges, responsibilities, and positions. Employees will grade you for leadership. If you pass their tests, your employees will follow you; if you fail, they won't.

Periodically, score your own performance and grade yourself on your self satisfaction, pride in your work, and feelings of accomplishment. The accuracy of your personal grading system will depend on a willingness to be truthful to yourself.

This book's closing offers only a basic introduction to what can be expected, along with some suggestions as to how you can become better prepared to deal successfully with whatever is to test your managerial knowledge and skills.

The Test of Effective Management

From the beginning, you will be tested by one or more of the following experiences:

– The occasional loneliness as your employees stand apart waiting, watching, sometimes complaining, or demanding.

– The various problems: shortages and breakdowns; incomplete, inaccurate, or falsified reports; lost or stolen items; absent or lazy workers; the countless questions you must answer; the explanations you must give; and the seemingly endless periods of waiting for answers, directions, authorizations, and requested supplies.

– The disinterested workers, indifferent managers, blundering bosses, interfering leaders, hidden corruption, favoritism of the privileged; and, in some instances, a clamoring public.

These and similar problems are familiar to managers the world over. They bring out questions that must be answered, solutions that must be offered, decisions that must be reached, and actions that must be taken.

Those of you who have passed a majority of these test problems are, at the moment, considered to be efficient and effective. For the remainder of you who now struggle with such problems, or have not experienced any of them, this is your first test.

How to prepare for the test problems.

An efficient, effective manager is one who produces desired results with a minimum of waste and effort. You have already learned the practical fundamentals, the systems, and the techniques. All you now need to do is practice them.

The greatest difficulty in practicing is in remembering what and when something is to be practiced. The habit of remembering depends upon the habit of practicing. In other words, develop a practice habit, first.

Habits are not too difficult to form. Here are two practical ways by which you can develop the habit of practicing the uses of basic management systems and techniques:

1. Review the basic systems and suggested techniques that you have studied. Choose those that in some way can apply to your work. Design these to serve your own managerial needs. These systems and suggestions will then become yours. You will be far more motivated by your own ideas and creations than by someone else's. You will exercise your systems and methods because you need them to accomplish what you do. In other words, what you need to master, you will remember to practice; what you practice, you will remember.

2. Form a clique of a few well-known and trusted managers. Trust is an important factor. You would not want to spill out your problems and feelings to another manager who may be inclined to tell others.

In the beginning, you may be content to have only one or two colleagues in your clique. These trusted managers may serve your purpose. It would serve little purpose, however, for you to share a problem with these few should they have no more of an idea of a solution than you do. The advantage of having more associates is that you will have a wider cross section of management having broader and deeper depths of experiences. Somewhere within a clique of worthwhile people are those who will have answers, suggestions, and, perhaps, workable solutions to serve your problems.

When others are added to your group, impress upon them that they, too, are to keep confidential what is said and heard in private. Unless your clique is quite small, seldom will all managers meet together. On some occasions, you may reach an associate by phone and say, "Can you meet with me sometime today? I have a problem that is bothering me. I think you can help me straighten it out."

Here are some benefits you will realize as a member of a clique where managers share experiences:

– It is therapeutic to be able to pour out pent-up frustrations to trusted, understanding people. Family members may listen, but they cannot be expected to understand. Employees seldom listen to the problems of bosses, and probably wouldn't understand them, anyway. Then there are those feelings you just don't want to share with your boss, but which you are confident your close colleagues will listen to; they will understand and be supportive.

– When you become emotionally enmeshed with a problem of management, you will learn that you are not alone. Most other managers have experienced the same or similar problems. Surprisingly, this will make you feel better.

– When another manager's problem is unfamiliar to you, something can be learned from it. Someone else's solved problem can, perhaps, prevent the same problem from happening to you.

– To hear of another manager's problem may make your problem appear smaller by comparison.

– Other managers may offer new ways of looking at a problem and new ideas for solving them.

The shared, tested, and proven experiences of other managers will shape your own basic concepts of management. Their systems and methods, that you might possibly adopt as your own, will be worth remembering.

The Test of Continuous Change

Time does not stand still, nor does anything else. Our political, economical, and social needs are ever changing. New discoveries flood our pools of knowledge. From these, new technologies are spawned.

For those who move along the path of a new advancement, new questions must be answered, new problems must be solved, alternative solutions must eventually boil down to final decisions. It is inevitable that those ambitious dreams of men and women – an idea still incubating in the mind of tomorrow's inventor – will bring about changes for untold numbers of people.

There are also the everyday human changes in age, health, attitudes, and a complex assortment of other elements. These changes inevitably produce still other changes. A single change is like a pebble dropped into a pond. The expanding concentric ripples diminish somewhat as they change the surface of the water, but they will in time embrace the entire pond. As an example, advanced age might lead to a decline in health, which could bring about a change in a person's values and attitudes.

New advancements bring about new methods of production, services, marketing, accounting, administration, and management. Managers who are concerned with any phase of a new development will need to react quickly and effectively.

The deftness by which you contend with changes successfully is your second test.

When a change occurs, the key to a smooth transition is preparation. A successful manager does not wait to become prepared until after, or even during, a change.

Be prepared for any eventual change before it occurs.

It is important to know what is going on in the world around you and the new changes that are taking place. A change that has taken place elsewhere may soon be a change that can affect your career. Here are some examples of changes that are taking place rapidly:

– Improved computers are providing more data, faster. Managers can analyze specific information, make decisions, and take initial or corrective actions more quickly than before.

– Energy sources, other than those derived from crude oil and coal, are taking giant, technological steps. Wind generators are providing low cost electrical power to remote areas. Solar energy powers automobiles and heats swimming pools. Nuclear energy will become safer and cheaper to provide power for homes and industries.

– Electronic devices are being spewed out by new, start-up industries to serve a variety of human needs in hospitals, homes, offices, shops, and entertainment.

– Video and audio devices are bringing expert teachers and impressive demonstrations of new knowledge into classrooms and training centers throughout the world.

– Space exploration not only unravels the mysteries of the universe, and beyond, but translates scientific technologies into products that will provide new jobs, and benefits that will be of practical application in the daily lives of almost all people.

As a manager, you might be asked to teach and direct some new manner of advancement. When such a situation occurs, you can expect to receive specific instruction. But, so as to prepare yourself to accept a new and challenging assignment, and to understand a course of instruction, there are certain essential and basic blocks of knowledge and skills you should have to stand on.

Here are a few additional habits you will do well to develop:

– Measure your personal strengths and limitations in accordance with your field of work. If you are weak in a subject or skill that could benefit your career, seek ways to improve yourself.

– Prowl the bookstores, and public and school libraries. You will find books on every imaginable subject. There are books on how to improve your reading, writing, and speaking abilities; on every technical practice; and on every business method. The list of books that can serve your personal development is practically endless.

– Read the trade magazines that apply to your specific kind of work. There are magazines for managers, supervisors, engineers, mechanics, plumbers, accountants, sales people, school teachers, nurses, police officers, farmers, and many more.

To become aware of and to prepare for continual change, continual study must become a habit.

The Test of Emotional Stress

Examples have been given of problems that test managers' systems of management, and of changes that some managers perceive to be *sudden and unexpected*. Any one of these can produce emotional stress.

Generally, it is not one stress that can cause managers to fail at their jobs, or quit. It is more reasonable to suspect a series of mind-numbing stresses, much like repeated blows to the head.

Emotional stresses can reveal themselves in many forms. Some managers find that they hate going to work in the morning; they may become quieter, more withdrawn than usual; they may fail to pay attention to details or follow-up on work in progress; they may become angry over little things; they may have moods of depression that cannot be shaken. The accumulation of these feelings can result in an emotional state commonly referred to as *burn-out* – managers simply feel that they have had more than they can take; they have had enough. Burn-out first destroys the effectiveness of managers who lose that delicate sense of emotional balance, and then goes on to affect the health.

The prevention of emotional stress is your third test.

The weapons that will eliminate many of the causes of emotional stress include your carefully practiced systems and techniques of effective management, your awareness of pending changes, and your preparations for their eventuality. Nevertheless, your ability to cope emotionally with changes must be equal or superior to your systems of management.

Effective management and preparations for the future will reduce most stresses. Yet, despite these prudent measures, stresses will leak through the preventive screen. Stress may build from the little, unnoticed things and the small, unexpected changes that were impossible to foresee. The accumulation of ceaseless, re-occurring, small, formless pressures can madden some managers as surely as the ancient method of Chinese water torture. The final line of defense, then, is the control of personal emotions.

Much has been written on dealing with stress. All sorts of advice has been given: take up a new hobby, seek new friends, get more exercise, and so on. There is nothing wrong with any of these. Each can be helpful. But the eventual control of stress must come from within, from the manner by which you think. In 1937, J. K. Morly wrote, "The size of a man can be measured by the size of the things that make him angry."

Now, think of yourself. You are a manager; you do make the decisions.

– Decide to maintain a sense of humor. Tasteful humor has never made a difficult situation worse. On the contrary, humor generally relieves tensions. Still, when upright people are involved, especially those who outrank you, prudence would dictate that you let the light, humorous thoughts of your real inner world whirl around in your mind without spilling out through your mouth.

– Decide that you will maintain your enthusiasm. Let your enthusiasm be spurred by small kicks of success.

– Decide on the thoughts that you will keep. You cannot hold more than one thought in your mind at any given moment. When you choose to think of being happy, you cannot have thoughts of unhappiness. When you decide to have a positive outlook, you cannot have a negative one.

– Decide that there is no one, anywhere, who can break your spirit.

– Decide that each day will be a good day.

It may be a good idea to write your decisions daily, on your calendar or task list. In this way you will remember to practice what you decide.

Understand that your decisions will be tested. How much faith will you have in them?

– A pencil breaks as you hurriedly sketch a new floor plan. Will you angrily hurl the inanimate pencil across the room, or will you quietly reach for another one?

– Someone steals your money? Will you become sick from the loss, or will you concentrate on ways to improve the protection of what is yours?

– You lose some priceless, sentimental mementos of happy, bygone days. Will you cry in despair, or will you be grateful for your vivid memories, locking these in your heart where they cannot be stolen?

– Someone becomes angry, loud, and abusive. Will you respond in kind, or will you remain calm and attempt to get to the bottom of the other person's anger?

– Someone close to you is depressed. Will you allow this person's feelings to spoil your day, or will you continue with your usual, cheerful, optimistic, and positive outlook?

Each day, as frequently as necessary, make a personal decision that no person, no circumstance, can make you feel less than what you want to feel.

Every man who rises above the common level has received two educations: The first from his teachers; the second, more personal and important, from himself.

Memoirs of Edward Gibbon, 1795

INDEX

About The Author

Armed with a university degree in business and technology, Donald Wellman began his climb up the managerial ladder from the bottom rung, gaining first-hand experience in levels of line, staff, and executive management. Wellman is well known for his successes in developing, owning, and managing a variety of small businesses, and for the expertise he has shared with others in many areas of business management.

At age 55, Wellman traded business challenges for worldly adventures. He and his wife, Marilyn, sold everything except their loaded backpacks and set out for the South Seas.

On the Samoan island of Tutuila, at the request of the government, Wellman conducted workshops for supervisors and managers in both the private and public sectors. On the island of Savaii, the Wellmans teamed up to design and implement an industrial safety programme, and trained logging and sawmill supervisors on how to make the programme a success.

After five years of backpacking around the world, observing and researching businesses and industries, Wellman settled in Arizona where he serves as a college instructor, a consultant-trainer, and a writer on subjects of line supervision and management. He is also an active member of the American Society for Training and Development.